Red

The story of Ginger McCain and his Legendary Horse

IVOR HERBERT

With a new introduction by the author

Aurum

To all horses of courage however humble
in admiration and gratitude

First published in this new edition
2005 by Aurum Press Ltd
25 Bedford Avenue, London WC1B 3AT

A catalogue record for this book is available from the British Library.

ISBN 1 84513 059 6

1 3 5 7 9 10 8 6 4 2
2005 2007 2009 2008 2006

Printed by Bookmarque, Croydon, Surrey

Contents

Introduction

AMBERLEIGH WRITES NEW CHAPTER IN MR NATIONAL'S AMAZING TALE was the headline in the *Racing Post*, and this is how it described the closing stages of the 2004 Grand National.

> Yards from the spot where Red Rum is buried near the Aintree winning post, Amberleigh House, a 12-year-old whose best chance was seemingly behind him, evoked the spirit of his illustrious predecessor. Amberleigh House's prospects did not look good from the early stages, when he found himself anchored towards the back of the field by the events that unfolded in front of him. Held up by a succession of fallers, he was barely in sight for a large part of the race as Hedgehunter launched a bold bid to make virtually all. Turning into the home straight for the final time the race looked to be between Hedgehunter, Clan Royal and Lord Atterbury. But tiredness was becoming evident coming to the last, and Hedgehunter crashed to the ground. Clan Royal, his jockey Liam Cooper without his whip over the last four fences, wandered off course to the left, forcing Cooper to drag him back to negotiate the elbow. Amberleigh House was finishing the strongest and was roared home to a three-length triumph...

Amberleigh House was trained by Ginger McCain, who had saddled the winning horse again at the age of 73, twenty-seven years since Red Rum had won his historic third National.

The great Red Rum, by now the most famous horse since Black Beauty, certainly led an amazing life. It was stuffed with luck. It crackled with coincidence. But the trainer who made him, just as the horse made the trainer, is quite as extraordinary a character. Ginger McCain's life, too, emerged from years of struggle and setbacks and sorrows to great fame. His long search for 'The One Good Horse' which he used – often vainly - to describe to his tolerant and loyal wife Beryl, would have made most struggling trainers pack it in. He was devoid of advantages, save for the great wide beach.

He started from nowhere. Just as his beloved Rummy – he often called him 'Red' or 'The Horse' – had the most unlikely, unhelpful start any great steeplechaser could have: running as a two-year-old on the flat in a selling race. But this was at Aintree, of course, where they then ran the flat racing that Ginger despises, with some 'sellers' for precocious animals of the lowest grade. Exactly what great staying steeplechasers – bar the one – never are.

Ginger McCain was Aintree-fixated. He has a truly weird obsession with the Grand National. He feels about the race as a good father feels about a loved child. 'You can have your Gold Cup days at Ascot with all those upnosed people. You can have your Cheltenhams with all those county types and tweeds. This is the people's place and this is a people's race. Mustn't be tampered with... Leave the old fences as they always were...' He has snorted and grumbled and roared over the years. He raged like old King Lear when his Amberleigh failed to 'make the cut' for that earlier National.

The great good fortune which brought Ginger and Rummy into glorious partnership, and the fierce fixation with Aintree and the Grand National, was also held by the hugely rich elderly gentleman, Noel Le Mare who, sitting in Ginger's taxi in Birkdale, was finally cajoled and driven not only to his grand home, on the other side of the tracks, but also into buying Red Rum. Neither Ginger nor Noel Le Mare had any inherited reason to be National-fixated. The Le Mare father had been a missionary in India and his mother a schoolteacher. They were almost penniless. Le Mare and three young men just after the Great war, formed a tiny company which grew into the huge Norwest Construction, with projects all round Europe. In 1906, as an apprentice fitter he'd been told to bugger off and see what had won the National. It was Ascetic Silver. Le Mare was hooked that day.

Ginger McCain and Beryl and some secondhand cars and some second – or even third-class – horses lived on the opposite side, the 'wrong' side of the railway line in Birkdale. Bar his army stint – Ginger was born on 21 September 1930 so was caught for National Service – and a few horse-linked jaunts into the Cheshire countryside, he never left Birkdale till his final move to his squire's house on the Marquess of Cholmondeley's sweeping Cheshire estate at Malpas in December 1990. 'Yes, some of Birkdale's smart enough,' he declares. 'It's also had the muckiest slums ever!' Ginger has always been prone to lively hyperbole. It colours his chat and our lives, and I've known the splendid old fighter since I first stayed with him and Beryl between the old cars and old horses in Birkdale after Red Rum had won his second National.

Ginger was conceived in Birkdale and born there, less than half a mile from his old stables. There, seemed the opposite of a dream racing stable. Possibly just a small urban livery yard. But not for the most famous Grand National winner ever.

Ginger's fourth Grand National winner, Amberleigh House in 2004 (matching the great Fred Rimell's record), was trained not on those broad Southport sands that cured Red Rum of his ominous pedalostitis – he was lame the very first day after Ginger had paid what was then the highest price of his life. Amberleigh House is at Bank House, Cholmondeley, 'trained the modern way,' as Beryl McCain neatly puts it. 'Interval training, you know. Up an all-weather strip.' Did they miss the beach? 'Yes, in this wet weather. The ground gets heavy here. The horses' heels get sore. Never got those on the beach, in the sea. But that was a long old walk – hour and a quarter – to get to the beach. And through all that traffic...'

Beryl has had to look at the bright side all through the dark years. When she wanted furniture for their first home, Ginger wanted horses. That's where the money went. They have had ferocious rows. Once Ginger roared that he was leaving. Beryl waved at him in his car. 'Going home to Mummy?' she taunted him. And in fact he did; for a night. He calls her 'Woman!' But they are firmly interlocked, ever since she 'had a crush on him at school.' They were married, needless to say, on Grand National day, went racing, of course, then honeymooned in Newmarket, not the romantic selection of most people.

Ginger's father Bill worked 40 years in the local department store, Marshall and Snelgrove, dispatching parcels. In the war he served in the RAF. Ginger's mother, sadly, did as so many wartime women did: worked in a munitions factory. Their absences made Ginger free to roam, and he often cut school. He kept dogs, a whippet or a lurcher – 'The Waterloo Cup was down the road.' Coursing and racing dogs and pigeons gave the boy an early joy of racing creatures.

And in wartime Britain, horses and ponies were trotting up and down every street. The local dairy had 40 horses, the laundry 24. Ginger loved the sight and sound of them. They entered his blood. He pestered his grandfather for a pony, even built a shed for one. It never came. It was the first of the hundreds of equine setbacks in McCain's life that made his final triumphs so glorious by comparison.

He began riding when a family friend started a little riding school. He had the knack. And then he was allowed to ride out with racehorses for the first time at Frank Speakman's stables, near Tarporley in sought-after Cheshire, where he is now spreading himself over 200 acres. Finally he got a job with Speakman and walked out of the wallet factory where his father had placed him. 'I picked up the racing side of things.' He was bitten. But he was far too big.

Then, he says, 'I got into a bit of trouble with a girl and came home and got a job working for the local taxi firm.' This was the happy lead that drew him to Noel Le Mare and on to Red Rum's unequalled triumphs. As Rummy was the 'One Good Horse' he had spent 30 years seeking, so McCain became for cynical racing people 'A One Horse Trainer.' It was a cruel jibe, though in one of Rummy's years, he was the only winner from the little stable up till that National.

Few people would have guessed that nine years after Rummy's death at the age of 30, the tall, beaky, laughing, now-grizzled Ginger would win another National with Amberleigh House. But in April 2004 Ginger proved he's got the National knack. And no fluke, either.

Ginger is now rising 75, but full of that energy and those hopes that kept him kicking on. In January 2005, with a heavy cold and one runner, he was driving his lorry down to Leicester – 'dreary place' – and back in one very long day. When he got back, 'You'll go straight to bed,' said Beryl. He did, roaring defiance, covered with loving dogs.

He thinks with reason that 'Amberleigh' is, like Rummy, a real National horse, even though at 13 he is statistically 'too old'. He's run seven times at Aintree in the National, Topham and Becher Chases, clocking up two victories, two seconds and a third. He's jumped 150 of the big Aintree fences.

The new stables are going well. 'Thirty-odd,' says Beryl proudly. 'The most we've ever had. And for the first time we've had winners in double figures by Christmas.'

'We were struggling for years and years,' says Ginger. 'No one round here sent us horses. I lost five of John Halewood's horses once!' Halewood is Amberleigh House's owner. 'But I'm very grateful to him for backing me.' Ginger recounts with all the old relish that made him a shrewd used-car dealer the twisting series of good deals he's made or nearly made with horses of all sorts. He's still busy buying, selling, breeding. 'I've got too many, o'course. Ought to cut down. But I love it. How many horses d'you think

I've got here?'

I hazard 35, thinking of those in training.

'We've 38 here being paid for,' he corrects me. 'But I own fifty-odd odd horses meself,' trumpets the grand old man of Aintree. 'My own, including ten yearlings, ten brood mares on my 200 acres.' It sounds as if, after Red Rum Ltd, dear Ginger has got at least £250,000 locked up in horses. 'When I think of the dear old Queen Mum, buying yearling stores and brood mares when she was a hundred, I think, why not?' And he gives his customary roar of deep laughter. He delights in life.

Ivor Herbert
Bradenham
January 2005

ACKNOWLEDGEMENTS

The research for the original book and for subsequent editions would have been impossible without the full co-operation of Red Rum's many connections, past and present, who gave me so freely of their time, recollections, notes, albums and photographs. I am grateful to them all. I acknowledge, too, my use of the *Sporting Life, Raceform* and *Chaseform Notebook*, and thank, as usual, BBC Television for providing transcripts of their superlative Grand National commentaries.

I.H.

1. 'The One Good Horse . . . '

The horse worked between the blowing sand dunes and the grey sea tide. Ahead of the beat of his feet the dunlins scampered for safety and the gulls rose in a white cloud shrieking. The wind brought a steely wall of rain racing towards the horse across the broad beach. The red danger flags were blown out stiff as scarlet boards, cracking in the wind like thunder.

The horse was bent over his bit like a bow. His head was tucked into his left and his mouth was open showing his parrot-teeth in a snarl. The horse, as was his habit, led with his near-fore leg and, now that he was really galloping, the leg flicked outwards whistling through the air, the hoof thumping the ground, like a boxer again and again left-hooking. It was an action which would have gained him no rosette in the show ring, but which in a race, after a distance when the pressure was on, showed clearly to those who knew him that the great horse had really begun to fly.

His front hooves hammered the sand, so that the shock – when at such instant one small foot supported half a ton propelled over it and forward – was so great that you might think the feet would never stand it. Yet these were the feet which had in his mid-career been so crippled with a bone disease that he had only had a fifty-fifty chance of recovery.

His mane blew backwards and so did his lad's thick hair. The lad's body was short and broad, and it bobbed and bobbed above the horse's back, braced against arms and legs like ram-rods.

The horse was the joy of this lad's life and that life had

had its troubles of every sort. Once, in another place, the horse had been the particular love of a stable girl, and his forced parting from her had smashed her interest in racing and, in a small way, had broken her heart.

On this lad's face now, racing across the sand, ecstasy and anxiety mixed and flickered, for the horse was triumphantly well – and thus nearly running away with him. The conflict in the lad's face reflected the still unresolved temptations of his life.

The trainer stood very tall by the side of his old truck. Behind it were coupled the harrows with which he had just combed a two-mile-long strip of wrinkled sand, just wide enough for two horses to work upsides. An old tweed cap, greasy-peaked, was perched atop of his very large head. Bursting out around it, the hair which had given him the nickname 'Ginger' flickered grizzled in the wind. His eyes, screwed up against sea-spray and the sting of sand, watched nothing but his horse. On his face burned the glow of exultation.

For this was the horse for which he had been waiting down all those dark years when he and his wife had camped in small rooms with a few sticks of furniture, and money was so short that he was down to borrowing a fiver to pay for a horse to run. Through all those years, driving a taxi, dreaming of finding one day, somehow, for someone 'The One Good Horse' which would make his name, the trainer had spent money he did not have on horses which were cheap and old and lame and bad. He bought experience most dearly, but he stored it up against the day when the one good horse would come.

The trainer, so far from being born with a silver spoon or golden mangers, had been reared in a back street far from the open world of thoroughbred racehorses and rich friends and introductions into stables. He had no background of horses whatsoever. He had no relation in even the lowest echelon of the racing industry. He was, in addition, the wrong build for the game.

He had glimpsed hope winking fitfully at the end of a shadowy tunnel of setbacks and disasters. He had lost faith sometimes. He had thought the distant light beckoning him on might turn out to be only the winking eye of a harlot. But he, like the horse who now rushed past him like a conquering express into the lashing wall of rain, had struggled on against the odds. For the horse had received in his life much unjust punishment. He had been subjected to sufficient pain from whip and bone disease to make him, had he been human, turn crook or layabout.

The rain passed across the sea. The horse came back walking in the frothy rim of the tide. There, in the shallows a few years earlier, horses and carts had been drawing nets for shrimps and codling: horses with torn tendons and twisted joints had become remarkably sound again. . . .

The horse played with his bit and splashed his now sound hooves against the sea's surface like a child larking. The horse knew that his work was done, for he was, as his trainer said, 'a true professional'. He was relaxed now. His arrogance had melted into a jaunty content.

He sprang up, plunged down, the steep sand hills behind the Royal Birkdale Golf Course and made his way home, feet clipping the tarmac, leading the little string along the tree-lined avenues of Southport's smarter suburb. Here, where Victorian magnates had erected their red residences in ornate gardens with extensive coach-houses, mothers from flats and newly developed little homes, bustled their children off to school. Because the horse was famous now throughout the land commuters slowed to let him pass. Eyes followed his progress with awe from cars shuttling into Liverpool, where he had struggled for humble victory in his very first race, and later, achieved his glories.

In one commodious mansion in a tranquil street the horse's octogenarian owner lay abed. Slightly later rising was the sprightly old gentleman's only concession to the rigorous length of his life. It had begun in poverty in the last century. During it he had created great constructional works across the world and a fortune which he had now settled on his children. For him, as for his trainer, victory at Liverpool, *the* racecourse of the country, in the Grand National, *the* great race of the whole year, had been a dream born in adolescence. The owner always remembered his mother running a school and teaching the children to sing each day, 'If at first you don't succeed, try, try, try again'.

So it had been with him, with his trainer and with the horse who now turned towards the railway tracks and the poorer part of Birkdale. He waited at the level-crossing while a Liverpool train clattered past. The gates opened. He crossed and was in his humble street again. On his left lay, in a long and rather dingy row, a sweet shop and tobacconist, a pet centre, a Chinese fish-and-chip shop, a butcher, a small wholesale grocer. . . . On his right behind the bus shelter, behind the row of parked secondhand cars belonging to his trainer and partner, lay the alley leading into his cosy stable-yard, overlooked by the backs of houses and embracing one solitary tree.

The trainer's wife looked up and out from her modern kitchen into the yard to watch the horse walk in. All those years when weeks were hard and months a struggle, and she had been worried sometimes close to breaking point, her husband had said – and she had not fully understood him – 'All we need is one good horse'. Now she comprehended for what he had striven. The horse had come.

The horse was Red Rum.

2. 'Strange to think we had a 'National winner at all. . . .'

Like most great steeplechasers Red Rum was conceived and born in Ireland. But his triumphs are not so much an accident of his breeding; they are a denial of it. For he was bred to be nothing more than a sprinter on the flat. He was planned to be inexpensive, of no consequence, and precocious enough to run quickly in the spring of his two-year-old season (before, in fact, his second birthday), with the chance of an owner winning something over a short distance without having to keep him too long. His prospects by blood were as far removed from winning a Grand National as are possible within all the muddled realm of racing.

The distinction of breeding our first postwar double Grand National winner, however unintentionally, belongs to Martyn J. McEnery. He is the owner and manager of the Rossenarra stud, near Kells in County Kilkenny, a quiet-spoken, pensive man, bespectacled, young-looking and born in December 1930. He received no financial reward for Red Rum's triumphs, either directly (for there are, as yet, no breeders' prizes for the winners of our great steeplechases), nor indirectly: he sold Red Rum's dam the year after he sold her son, and he had already sold Red Rum's two elder sisters. When Red Rum galloped to glory McEnery had no relations left at home whose values, by their son's or brother's triumphs, would have trebled overnight.

McEnery is still drily amused and slightly bemused by the fact that he bred by accident a horse who has now joined that élite band of steeplechasing's immortals. 'Strange to think we had a Grand National winner here at all!' he says slowly. He speaks quietly, after deliberation and to the point, never luxuriating Irish-fashion in the pleasure of six words when one suffices. He is the antithesis of what strangers to Ireland conceive to be a typical Irishman. Nor does he claim with the benefit of hindsight, as is so often the ludicrous case in racing, any credit for or prescience about the subsequent glories of Red Rum.

It would be the easiest thing in the world for Martyn McEnery to declare that he always suspected his colt would turn out to be 'a grand lepper', that he had bred him with that thought half in mind, that he smelt steeplechasing in his yearling action. Many other connections of great horses have, when history has safely rolled past, jumped on the band-waggon and blown their own trumpets. Martyn J. McEnery has never done any such thing.

There rests, for all that, in pride of place on a coffee-table in the centre of his combined living-room and study a cigar-box adorned by a golden horseshoe. This is the 1973 award presented by Goff's Bloodstock Sales to the vendor of that horse sold through them which, in the opinion of the Irish Racing Writers' Association, has done most to promote Irish horses internationally.

The award presented to Martyn McEnery at a reception in Dublin's Shelbourne Hotel on 28 May 1974, was for Red Rum's first record-breaking 'National victory in the previous year. He was selected from nine other nominees all of whom had passed through Goff's on their paths to 1973 fame, including such notables as Captain Christy, Bula and Killiney.

During Red Rum's racing career in three most dissimilar training stables a number of very different people were to remark independently on the horse's 'professionalism'. They were to detect under his exceptional exuberance that seriousness of purpose, that pursuit of an end, which marks successful human beings. Few winning people are totally grave. They, like Red Rum, are happy to play about, to vent energy and to relax, so long as nothing for any length of time diverts their important course. Early environment moulds human and equine characters; it is significant that Martyn McEnery's Rossenarra stud was no charming, amateurish farm with an old Georgian house and rough fields split Irish-wise by tousellled banks and tumbled walls and cheerful decrepit bedsteads. It was a newly established, efficient and professional undertaking, and Red Rum lived there for the first sixteen months of his life.

The McEnery family are very much Kilkenny people. They used to live several miles further south on the Carrick road at Rossenarra near Kilmoganny. The present stud, which now bears the name of the old McEnery property, was bought by Martyn's father Jack in 1941. In the war's darkest days no one knew who might win and what the victors would do with property even in neutral Ireland. Even so its price now seems incredible. For Jack McEnery paid under £10 per acre; a sum of about £2300 for 240 good acres. It was what they call in Ireland the 'out farm' and there was no house on it.

When Jack McEnery died the family's Kilmoganny property had to be sold to pay his death duties. The Government's Land Commission acquired most of the farm for re-distribution and the novelist Richard Condon (author of *The Manchurian Candidate*) now lives in the old McEnery house. By 1961 an ultra-modern house of Swedish design had been completed – red brick with a mass of external woodwork – on the 'out farm' near Kells, and in 1963, when Martyn was rising thirty-three, he moved the stud there and settled down to establish himself as a commercial breeder of flat-race horses. Any connection with steeplechasing seemed buried for ever. . . .

The land is excellent; the countryside flat and featureless. The soil has the desirably high limestone content, but except for those trees bordering the road and two survivors near the house, McEnery extirpated every tree. Now there are neatly railed paddocks divided by a central access passage. The stable-yards are new, practical and plain. Concrete abounds. 'It is,' notes Neville Ring, the Irish racing writer, 'very much a *commercial* establishment.'

Martyn McEnery had hardly moved into his new establishment when he had to make the decision which would produce the horse Red Rum. He had been the owner since 1960 of a bay mare called Mared, a name strangely similar to that of the future owner of her famous son, Noel Le Mare. It was compounded from her sire's name, Magic Red, a sprinter who won a few races over five and six furlongs during the war.

She was foaled in 1958. Her mother was Quinta by the useful jumping sire Anwar, and her grandmother Batika was a daughter of the world-famous Blenheim. Mared and her mother Quinta were both bred by Mr S. J. Parr at his Athboy stud in Co. Meath, Quinta was totally undistinguished. Mared, to be blunt, was crazy.

At the end of her two-year-old season in which she had run for her breeder's wife, Mared was hastily disposed of. She was put up for sale at Goff's and bought by Martyn McEnery for what must have seemed the suspiciously low figure of 240 guineas. Trained by John Oxx at The Curragh she had finished second in her first race when, quite unfancied in the Balrath Plate at Dublin's smart Phoenix Park in June, she had been beaten only half a length by the odds-on Another Phoenix. She had flattered to deceive: in none of her four subsequent races that summer did she even get into the money.

Her mother Quinta was placed on the flat three times as a three-year-old in 1956, but had subsequently disappointed the Parrs. She had produced a full brother to Mared in 1959, called Via Con Deo who won on the flat as a four-year-old in 1963 and was later placed hurdling in 1965. But in 1960, when Mared was running for the Parrs as a two-year-old, her mother Quinta was proved barren. The Parrs decided to sell her as well, and she died two years later after slipping twins. The Parrs were happy to cull Mared. She showed them a considerable loss when the cost of her creation, production and training were set against the 240 guineas (less sale commission and expenses) which they received from Martyn McEnery.

3. 'She's mad . . . Take her home!'

But McEnery's policy then was buying fillies out of training to race himself the following season. He liked Magic Red's speedy pedigree. The horse was by Link Boy and his grandmother was a famous brood-mare, Black Ray, who would turn out to be the ancestress of the illustrious Mill Reef.

There was also much to like about Mared's maternal grandmother Batika. Unlike her disappointing daughter Quinta she had also produced Mared's 'aunt' Spring Offensive (by Legend of France) who had proved a rattling good race mare in top-class staying flat races and then produced a series of offspring of the highest class. One of them, Fabergé II, ran second in the 2000 Guineas and became the sire of the great Rheingold, winner of the Prix de l'Arc de Triomphe.

Some of these highlights lay far ahead when Martyn McEnery took cheap Mared home from the sales at Ballsbridge. But there were sufficient glinting strands in her breeding for him to weave a few small dreams during the winter of 1960–61. He resolved to send her into training not too far away near Carrick-on-Suir with 'Phonsie' O'Brien, brother of the all-conquering Vincent O'Brien.

Both the new trainer and the new owner of Mared received a nasty shock when Phonsie O'Brien discovered the full horrors of Mared. He did not mince his words.

He told the unhappy McEnery that Mared couldn't be held, that she was mad, that she did nothing but steam up and sweat all the time and that she was 'mad hot'.

'Take her away, take her home', said Phonsie O'Brien, and Martyn McEnery seemed lumbered with a lunatic filly and an apparently hopeless case.

He was cast down, but not defeated. He possesses an equable, methodical character. He approached his neighbour Mick Butler and enlisted his help with the problem creature. Butler, now training himself in a small way, patiently took Mared in hand. Weeks passed, and eventually he persuaded the filly to settle down sufficiently for another attempt to be made to train her.

It is one thing to allow an over-excited racehorse to relax on its own, rambling round fields, though a rider with busy heels, harsh hands and an electric backside cannot even contrive that. It is a very different matter when the animal must start to do sufficient fast work to get fit enough to run. The first gallop, sometimes even the first explosive excursion onto any grass which looks like a gallop, can knock down in minutes the steadiness built up over months.

McEnery had only started training himself in the previous year, and had won his first race, suitably enough at Gowran Park.

Mared was now a well-grown filly of 16.1 hands but not, in McEnery's view, well made. McEnery bluntly remembers her as 'Very straight in front, terribly like Red Rum! I always considered', says McEnery, 'that Red Rum was too straight in front and too light around his middle. . . .' It is refreshing to hear from the breeder of a future wonder-horse, an unusual, honest opinion unvarnished by the gloss of hindsight.

McEnery vividly recalls the horrors of taking Mared racing. 'In her stable, she was a rich bay in colour. But before a race she would turn black with sweat and white with froth *everywhere*.'

In her first two races for McEnery she ran, as they had feared, far too freely. She proved almost impossible to hold. Then McEnery sent her off to Galway on 2 August 1961, to run in the seven furlong Mervue Maiden Stakes. He engaged Jackie Power to ride, the jockey who had been on her in her first and only promising race at the start of her previous year. The Mervue Maiden Stakes was of small consequence and worth £202. Mared's conduct before the race was crazy. She became so laced in a froth of sweat that 'we had to throw a bucket of water over her,' says McEnery, 'and then try to dry her off again *before* she even came into the paddock!'

In spite of this ominous overture Martyn backed her at 10–1. This time Jackie Power persuaded her to settle down for the first time in her career. Instead of racing off like a mad cat, she consented to remain with the field until they reached the bottom of the hill at Galway about a furlong and a half from home. At that instant Power let the mad mare loose and '*swoosh*', as McEnery recalls, she flew like an arrow through the opposition and went clear to win by two lengths. 'I had,' says McEnery quietly, 'a little "touch" on her.'

Too often plaudits acclaim only the connections of big race winners. The temperamental problems of the wild filly Mared required more patience, more handling, more sympathy than many a placid and honest contender in a Classic. It was a small triumph on the part of Martyn McEnery and his helpers to have won any race with the creature at all. It is extraordinary that her son was not equally mad, instead of turning out, after years of punishing races, to be the epitome of burning equine courage.

Mared ran but twice more and got placed third round the swooping seaside track of tiny Tramore. Her astonishing racing career was over. Comparing her now with her famous son, Martyn McEnery shakes his bespectacled head in continuing amazement. 'It is just *unbelievable*', he declares, 'that Red Rum could go on racing for so long without showing any signs of that temperament of his mother's.'

He resolved, however, to breed from her. There was a stallion literally on Mared's doorstep. Neron, fourteen years old when Mared was first covered, stood at £98 a service at the Rossenarra stud itself. So she visited him two years in succession, accepting his attentions without too many tantrums and producing in 1963 and 1964 bay fillies, named Neared and Quintula. Both turned out for McEnery even more unrewarding than their mother had proved on the racecourse. Both went to the sales making the pathetic sums of 110 guineas and 190 guineas respectively. Neared, who never raced 'owing to injury', as her owner Mr Christy Mooney reported to Donald McCain, was offered to Red Rum's trainer in 1974 by Mr Mooney, who lives near Portarlington, in County Offaly. She had been covered by Even Say. Quintula was exported as a yearling to Germany in 1965. There may still exist somewhere out there another half-sister to the greatest post-war Grand National winner by, what is more, a horse who proved an excellent sire of jumpers.

It is the misfortune of owners of jumping sires, and the great difficulty of jumping breeders, that most good jumping sires are dead before they have established their prowess. With a steeplechaser reaching his prime at nine years old, the decision to send his dam to be covered by his sire must have been made eleven years earlier. Since few stallions start serving mares before they are four they will therefore be fifteen years old before the first of their sons reaches his steeplechasing prime. Neron died in 1966, the year after Red Rum was born. . . .

Perhaps Red Rum's two elder half-sisters were ugly. Certainly the reputation of their crazy mother will have run before them at the sales. But the dreadful prices poor Martyn McEnery received for them were no more than their carcass value to a butcher.

For the following year he made a change of mate.

Magic Red mares were doing quite well at stud (by the end of 1966 their progeny had won seventy-three races worth £31 675). McEnery resolved to breed for pure speed from Mared. He chose the grey stallion Quorum, who then was standing at Paddy Clarke's Balreask stud close to Dublin Airport. The stud, one of Ireland's oldest (it was founded in 1847), was a large one of 400 acres, usually stood three stallions and lay in that part of the country made famous by Arkle. Very close to Balreask were bred or reared not only Arkle, but the superlative 'chasers Golden Miller, Gregalach and, as if those were not coincidences enough, the only other dual Grand National winner of the century, Reynoldstown. The black horse, the previous double victor round Aintree in 1935 and 1936, was foaled in those parts in 1927, nearly forty years before Red Rum.

These considerations did not concern Martyn McEnery when he contacted Paddy Clarke at the Balreask Stud to book in his disappointing Mared to Quorum. He was influenced mainly by a family friendship. His father Jack had enjoyed many friendly dealings with Paddy Clarke and his father before him. Martyn had, as he says, 'only just started on my own'. Furthermore horses by Quorum had proved financially rewarding to the McEnery family. 'Every Quorum we'd sold before had made in the region of 1500 guineas – respectable enough in those days', says McEnery mildly.

Studying the top line of Quorum's pedigree suggested that he would produce sparkling sprinting speed. He traced back through the sprinters Vilmorin, Gold Bridge and Golden Boss. It was only way back that you came via The Boss to Orby who won the Derby of 1907.

But Quorum had shown on the racecourse that he was slightly more than a sprinter himself. He nearly won the 2000 Guineas, being second to the great Crepello, and he won the Sussex Stakes at Goodwood over a mile. He won

£7306 in stakes over distances from five furlongs up to a mile, including the Jersey Stakes at Royal Ascot.

The extraordinary puzzle of the source of Red Rum's immense stamina has naturally cast the breeding pundits into disarray. When you worship the gods of the stud book and make your living like a Delphic priestess by interpreting the oracles of misty blood-lines, it is painful to find yourself presented with a nonsense. It is worth noting perhaps that, if you peer in deeply enough, you can disinter a little stamina from the recess of Red Rum's sprinting pedigree. His father's mother's grandsire was the real old stayer Noble Star. But Noble Star was merely one of Red Rum's sixteen great-great-grandparents. If you go that far back among anyone's ancestry you can prove the source of anything you want.

Mared was dispatched north to the Balreask Stud in the spring of 1964 for her visit to Quorum. She was successfully covered and returned in foal and with a bill for £251 12s., of which £198 was for Quorum's services and the balance (a fortnight's worth by 1974 levels) for her keep. Eleven months elapsed, her time duly came and on the evening of 3 May 1965, at 6 p.m. the foal who was to be named Red Rum was born at Rossenarra. 'Mared was the same foaling as she was racing,' Martyn McEnery drily recalls – 'All smoke and steam!'

A bay colt of average size was born in good shape. For the commercial breeder a colt is nearly always more valuable than a filly. There immediately follows an anxious inspection: are the tiny creature's limbs perfectly fashioned or malformed? Does it seem healthy? Will it take milk from the dam? A score of things can be wrong with, or happen to, the newly born foal. But all looked well and went well with temperamental Mared's first son in those first few hours.

McEnery was '*delighted* to get a Quorum colt, I thought my fortune was made. . . . But I was to get another rude awakening.'

4. 'Where the gypsies pulled in to rest their caravans'

The young man who cared for Red Rum as a foal was Roddy O'Byrne from Kilmacthomas in the neighbouring county of Waterford. He was nineteen at the time and learning the business of running a stud by living with the McEnerys who were family friends.

Roddy O'Byrne, born in December 1946, went to school at Rockwell in Co. Tipperary. When he left he had itchy feet: he wanted to go off to Australia 'to do something on my own for myself. I had it in mind to learn to run stud farms in Australia.'

The plan never came about. But 'I still wanted to prove myself'. Thus he arrived with the McEnerys on the Rossenarra Stud.

Neither of the two senior members of the McEnery staff have any particular recollections of Mared's foal by Quorum. The stud groom, James Duncan, a tall quiet man in his late thirties when Red Rum was born, had already been eight years with the family. In his time the McEnerys have sold over 150 horses through Goff's. To his mind, and to that of the 'herd', Dick Butler, who had worked for the family since 1941, there was nothing special about Red Rum's character in his baby days.

It is another strange coincidence in the Red Rum story that the first time stud groom James Duncan ever saw racing on television was that day at Liverpool when Red Rum (twenty-two months after his birth) and his filly companion from Rossenarra ran against one another in a humble two-year-old selling race.

The stud, now a large place with fifty boxes and standing two stallions, was then much smaller. McEnery in 1965 had only two colt foals: 'The Quorum' (foals are called on studs by their sire's name) and 'The Miralgo' which subsequently was sent to England to be sold. Both colts were weaned from their mothers in the autumn and then turned out together in a field called 'The Gypsy'. McEnery explains: 'We've always kept the colts in "The Gypsy Field" ever since we came here. Long ago it was probably "the commonage" where the gypsies pulled in to rest their caravans.' In one instance at least, the dark people brought the field good luck.

Roddy O'Byrne, while learning the workings of a commercial stud, did most of the feeding of the foals. He carries his small head slightly to one side and nods it for emphasis. 'I was *amazed* at the amount those foals could eat.' Red Rum was to keep an enormous appetite all through his training.

'Nuts weren't the thing in those days,' says McEnery, 'so Red Rum as a foal and a yearling was fed crushed Canadian oats.' The high protein feeding value of imported Canadian oats, their uniformity, dryness and clean bright colour from the prairie sunshine have made 'Canadians' (and 'Australians') keenly sought-after – in spite of their great expense – in nearly every high-class British racing stable and on most studs.

Roddy O'Byrne helped prepare the Rossenarra yearlings for Goff's September sales in Dublin. Two months before the sales Red Rum and his Miralgo companion were brought in from 'The Gypsy' and exercised daily with plenty of walking in hand. 'All I can say about Red Rum then,' says Roddy O'Byrne, 'is that he was a *grand* horse to handle, and with a lovely temperament.'

Knowing too well the neuroses of the mare and dreading their reproduction in her son, Martyn McEnery had been watching the colt's behaviour over the year with anxiety. It was the greatest relief to him that so far Red Rum had shown no signs of having inherited Mared's manic traits.

A party of six yearlings left Rossenarra for Dublin

accompanied by Roddy O'Byrne whose first experience of commercial yearling sales this would be. Red Rum's companions consisted of three fillies belonging to Martyn McEnery, including the bay nearly three months older than he by Golden Cloud out of June the Fourth whom he would meet again at Liverpool. There were also two more yearlings belonging to someone else which McEnery had been getting ready. So six youngsters were loaded into one lorry with a great deal of excitement and set off on the eighty-mile journey to Dublin. They were driven from Gowran by Matt Murphy, who later drove articulated refrigerated trucks to and from the Continent.

The living animals which he was that day taking to the capital were catalogued to come up rather too early on the middle morning of the sales, Tuesday, 20 September. The 'bay colt, (Third Produce) (Foaled 3 May) by Quorum (Grey, 1954) out of Mared (Bay, 1958)' had been selected as the first of the Rossenarra stud's draft as Lot 201. His box, No. 201, was waiting for him. In a three-day catalogue of 549 entries the last day's offerings had to wait for their boxes until the first day's lots had left them.

Human selection exaggerates the general lottery of sales. The auctioneers, having trained noses for truffles of value and the passing scent of current fashions, have only the breeding of sales' entrants to work on when they assemble their catalogue. They do not know until the sale starts several months later what shape the animals are in, or in what condition they will be presented. So they will be influenced by the importance of the vendor, and by whether he is an old-established client, or a new man with a lot of money who has recently purchased a large stud (and thus may be persuaded to sell here rather than at rival auctions). These types of vendors with good-sounding yearlings will be placed in better positions than the unheard-of owner with one ill-bred yearling who may never come again.

Egalitarianism does not exist in the world of racing. The slowest thoroughbred will always beat the fastest carthorse. Opportunities are grotesquely unequal. One foal will be underfed on wretched land, his needs ignored by poor, ignorant, feckless or idle people. Another will enjoy the best of food and attention from experts with time and money. The horse's early stud days are his formative childhood. His days in training are his career. Again, some will receive all things good and helpful; others will get the kicks and ha'pence. Red Rum was to have his share of both from a wide variety of men and women.

The first half of the epigram may be true: Men may 'be equal *under* the turf'. But they are absolutely unequal upon it. So by breeding, birth, upbringing and training are the horses they own, and train and ride. An occasional great horse like Arkle has it good all the way; another, like Red Rum, has survived parts of his life in spite of, not because of, the hands into which he fell.

5. 'I knew we were in for a disaster'

Luck starts very early in a yearling's life. The worst places to be drawn in most sales are the beginning or the end. Bloodstock buyers who are early birds know that most of the early lots are likely to be unpalatable worms. They wish also to test the market: to watch a dozen or so lots sold before they gauge how the economic and political events of the last few days have affected prices. By the end of the sales, buyers are surfeited. Their order-books have been filled. They are weary. Missing the last lots, they return early to homes or hotels to refresh themselves with restoring liquor and tales of horses long ago.

The auctioneers, knowing men's habits, put the apparently less attractive yearlings early and late in the day. A vicious spiral so begins: buyers believe that the auctioneers *know* that the early and late lots aren't much good....

Martyn McEnery's Rossenarra Stud in 1966 was only at the start of its transition from his father's old place dealing with half-breds to the important commercial undertaking it has now become. So its offerings came up very early on Tuesday: Red Rum was due only fourteen lots – about forty minutes – after the sales' ten o'clock start.

As Captain Michael Hall, that able and charming manager of Goff's for what he describes at 'twenty-five blissfully happy years', recalls, his office noted both attractive and unattractive features in Red Rum's entry. On the bonus side: his sire Quorum was enjoying a good year. Since he had started at stud in 1958 he had already sired the winners of £65 179 in eighty-eight and a half races.*

The maternal side of Red Rum's pedigree was less attractive in September 1966. In spite of their good statistical record the produce of Magic Red mares were now drifting out of favour. Michael Hall recalls 'they were not particularly popular, though there had once been a time when Magic Red colts – especially the greys – had been all the rage!'

Only eighteen months after Red Rum came up at the Ballsbridge sales a horse by Magic Red was to win the 1968 Grand National: Red Alligator ridden by one of Red Rum's future jockeys, Brian Fletcher. Freakish results attend the Grand National, but it did show that, against all the odds, Magic Red could produce a jumper. If Red Rum had been born two years later . . . if Red Alligator had won round Aintree two years earlier . . . with hind-

*The ½ race denoting in racing parlance a dead-heat, common enough before the advent of the race-finish camera.

sight everything is easy. But there were at least a handful of people around the sales of 1966, including the author, who well knew from their own experience that the offspring of Magic Red mares made very good staying steeplechasers. Maigret (whom I trained) was one such. Muir, his full-brother in Ireland, belonging to the Willis family was another. The former, winner of six long-distance steeplechases had already proved his stamina, his jumping ability, a touch of class and – as Red Rum was to do – his marked preference for firm, fast ground, before Red Rum came up for sale. Before Red Rum was even born Maigret had won two three-mile Irish point-to-points. But was anyone perspicacious enough to contemplate buying good-looking, cheap yearlings out of Magic Red mares to store away as future steeplechasers? They were not.

The rest of Red Rum's entry in the catalogue did not impress. There was 'not much black about it', as buyers say, meaning that there were few winning relations in the pedigree standing out in black bold-faced print. The Irish world knew about Mared's madness. She had so far bred no winner. Her two first offspring had been sold for peanuts.

Political and economic considerations that year depressed the sales. Michael Hall remembers, '1966 was a pretty disastrous year for breeders. There was a Labour Government. The credit squeeze was beginning to bite. There was the new Betting Tax. There was Capital Gains Tax. And it was a particularly bad year for the unfortunate Martyn McEnery. . . .'

The day dawned ominously. Nothing tempts out buyers like bees and adds warm fervour to their bidding fingers than a bright day. But the morning echoed the economic situation: it was grey and cold and raining. 'I was in a pessimistic mood from the start,' says McEnery.

The only possible buyer who took any real interest in Lot 201 was Pat Rohan the successful Yorkshire trainer, an Irishman by birth, son of a well-known dealer and fox-hunter in Co. Cork, and a few years younger than Martyn McEnery. He had left Ireland for Yorkshire ten years earlier to go as assistant trainer at Malton to Billy Dutton. He had taken over that good stable on Dutton's death and married his daughter. He liked sprinters. He knew McEnery. He spent some time looking at Red Rum and, McEnery remembers, 'expressed enough interest to make me more than hopeful'. When you are a seller you hang upon the murmurs, nods and becks of those who 'have your horses out'. Would they smile, wondered McEnery, when they saw how well his colt moved? Would they shake heads, purse lips if they believed that Red Rum's forelegs were too straight? Would they merely glance, grunt and pass on to someone else's offerings down the long line of boxes?

It was worse than all these things. Hardly another soul braved the wet to look at his colt at all. McEnery only recalls Tim Molony, that former great steeplechase jockey and small Leicestershire trainer, looking at Red Rum while Pat Rohan had him out in the rain. McEnery then hurried off to the auctioneer's office to place reserve prices on his horses.

It was while McEnery was away that an accident befell Red Rum. Its nature was going to be repeated later in his career, but its occurrence at the sales determined the trainer and the owner into whose hands he would first fall. In McEnery's absence Red Rum, while being led out of his box, slipped heavily. He hurt himself. Though not actually lame, he was walking a shade stiffly as he was being led around the preliminary parade ring, in full view of any other possible buyers. McEnery did not see the incident. Neither did he see his horse's stiffness. Heartened by Rohan's early interest, he was in the auctioneer's office putting a reserve of 800 guineas on Red Rum. He put exactly the same reserve on the Golden Cloud filly whose path was going to cross Red Rum's so closely six months later.

'Well, we got into the ring,' says McEnery, 'and I knew we were in for a disaster. There was no one there.' That was hyperbole, but in sales talk 'no one' means likely bidders. Sales rings are always occupied – particularly on cold wet mornings – by old men and women nattering together, keeping snug and intending to spend no more than a quid all day and that on tea or drink and sandwiches.

'There was Pat Rohan,' McEnery says, 'but he wasn't bidding *at all*! I couldn't think why. I couldn't understand it then. Though I know now of course.'

Rohan, unaware of the colt's accident, had been back to have another look at him walking round. He saw him walking 'that little bit stiffly', and he was put off. There is no point in 'buying trouble' in a horse. They develop enough later. It was early hours yet in the sale. There would be other colts just as attractive, better bred probably, who would walk out freely. He did not bid.

Bob Jeffares, a good man who sadly died well before his time in May 1973, was the auctioneer that day. McEnery hovered in the box behind him. The earlier lots had sold so badly and Rohan wasn't bidding and the price was stuck at a mere 400 guineas, half the minimum McEnery had decided upon half an hour earlier. At this flickering juncture in a sale the auctioneer, leaning back from the microphone which would otherwise amplify his doubts, will urgently ask the vendor – sometimes merely by an interrogatively raised eye-brow – whether he should now forget the reserve and accept the last bid. McEnery had a few seconds only to decide. Hesitation on the vendor's face will be instantly communicated to the last genuine bidder down there below. You must shake your head firmly, demonstrating you will not let your good horse go so far under his real value. Or you may sadly nod and shrug.

Utterly depressed McEnery made a quick decision. He murmured to Bob Jaffares, 'Let him go'. Red Rum's reserve was cancelled. The 400 guineas bid bought the horse. McEnery was surprised to see that it had come from Tim Molony.

6. 'I'll buy you a yearling'

For the first of four times in his astonishing career the horse Red Rum was thus sold in a public market and available to any passer-by. On the first two occasions anyone with the price of a second-hand 'banger' could have taken him home. Even on the third occasion when he had proved his ability by winning twice, he made no more than the price of a family car.

McEnery watched him being led out of the ring to his left as his next lot, a Dicta Drake filly, entered from the right and began her slow clockwise circuit. Worse was in store for her: she failed to reach her reserve. Miserably McEnery watched her led out unsold. Then followed his Golden Cloud filly out of June the Fourth. Coincidentally McEnery had placed upon her the identical reserve he had selected for Red Rum: 800 guineas. Coincidentally the price she reached in the bidding was exactly the 400 guineas fetched by Red Rum. Only in the world of fiction would it seem possible that these two animals born together, who had travelled together, then been sold together at the same place within minutes for the same price, would finish together, dead-heating whisker to whisker in the first race each was to contend six months later across the Irish sea at Liverpool.

As eleven o'clock approached in Dublin on 20 September 1966, the unhappy McEnery had raised a wretched

800 guineas on two of the three yearlings he had offered. His last chance, a Palestine filly also out of a Magic Red mare, slightly improved the situation by selling for 975 guineas. The Rossenarra consignment had raised 1775 guineas between them and McEnery had to take his Dicta Drake filly home. From this gross amount Goff's took 'the guineas', their five per cent. There were also all the travelling expenses. 'All in all,' McEnery sums up, 'a *very* disappointing sale and I was a very disappointed man that day.'

Roddy O'Byrne, who had cared for Red Rum for his first year, and brought him to the sales, only to see him sold for half his reserve, hated the whole day. 'I was *disgusted*,' he said eight years later, his small face flushing pink in recollected rage. He said to McEnery, 'This is scandalous! You should never have sold them!'

Martyn McEnery gave him quietly an example of the philosophy bloodstock breeders must hold. He explained that if you are breeding commercially you must sell, even at low prices, even if you were a loser on the deal, in the hope that your horses would win and that the following year buyers would therefore come back again and pay more. In McEnery's case this happened. Where he had sold for hundreds in 1966, in the years to come he was to sell for thousands.

But Michael Hall, after a quarter-century of selling horses, summed it up: 'Martyn McEnery's luck at that time was of the variety to put a less dedicated, less philosophical person out of horses for good!'

It is too easy for the casual observer of the racing scene to notice only the rare high price and to deduce that breeders are printing money. One really bad year may erase the profit of five. And the risks when your capital is tied up into feckless horseflesh capering about fields are twenty times higher than those endured by shareholders in public companies, even in falling markets. Keepers of horses must dismiss their dreads if they are to sleep at nights. It was, as Michael Hall commented afterwards, the worst September sales that Goff's had experienced in five years. The top price of the sale was made four hours after Red Rum was sold when the full brother to the Derby winner Larkspur made 13 000 guineas. Called Phoenix Bird he ran only five times and won just one race worth £465 15s. Red Rum costing 400 guineas had, by 1 January 1977, run in 101 races, won 2½ flat races worth £970 and won 23 races under National Hunt rules worth £73,230.80. Only L'Escargot by that date had topped Red Rum's record set for a jumper in any one season: £36,781.80 in 1973–4.

The buyer of McEnery's Golden Cloud filly for 400 guineas was that lively racing character Major 'Ginger' Dennistoun, a bushy-browed, darting-eyed terrier of a man, skilled in his trade, abrupt in speech and a shrewd and most successful gambler when the time arose.

The Major took his filly home to Letcombe Regis, near Wantage in Berkshire, named her Curlicue and gave her to his wife. He had it in mind that she would win early next season, perhaps first time out and that he might be able to land another nice gamble.

Tim Molony, the purchaser of Red Rum a few minutes earlier, had exactly the same intentions. But his were even more specific. A man with whom he had been long acquainted had instructed him to buy a yearling who would six months later win the five furlong Thursby Selling Plate, the first race at Liverpool on the Friday of the Grand National meeting. While Curlicue left Dublin for Letcombe Regis in Berkshire, Red Rum came over to the heart of England's best foxhunting country, to the little village of Wymondham, near Melton Mowbray.

Tim Molony, the first purchaser of Red Rum, had been training exactly six years when he first sat down in his small narrow study of The Manor at Wymondham to study Goff's September sales catalogue. His 47th birthday was coming up the week before the sales. He had been riding as an amateur in Ireland from 1936 until the war (he rode over a hundred point-to-point winners over banks and walls), had turned professional and gone to the very summit of that hazardous tree, riding over 900 winners in his nineteen-year-old career, and being champion jockey five times between 1948 and 1955. Tim and his brother Martin carried off most of National Hunt racing's greatest prizes and dominated the 'chasing scene for a dashing decade.

Though he has, like all retired jockeys, thickened in thighs and quarters and shoulders since his racing days, Tim Molony still possesses the profile of a Roman centurion, with blue eyes and claret-coloured cheeks. He has had his share of life's swings and roundabouts, surviving them with the equanimity which comes less easily to the English than to the Irish, inured historically to national misfortunes. He has one daughter by his first wife, and three sons by his second, the admirable and competent Stella to whom he was married in his riding heyday back in 1951. He has no enemies on the racing scene. He has charm and is a good companion, and to the callow author on his first quivering race on a proper course (at Market Rasen) the admired then Champion Jockey was helpful, heartening and highly amusing.

One of Tim Molony's remarkable achievements was to win four consecutive Champion Hurdles. Three of these, from 1952 to 1954, were on that supreme French-bred hurdler Sir Ken, owned by the man for whom Molony had just bought Red Rum. Sir Ken had been bought and trained by the redoubtable Willie Stephenson, one of only two trainers alive to have won that improbable double of the Derby and the Grand National. Sir Ken, one of the greatest hurdlers ever, won no less than twenty-four National Hunt races. Tim Molony rode him nineteen times, one after the other, without being beaten.

Sir Ken was one of many horses owned by Manchester businessman Maurice Kingsley who became, through his admiration of Tim Molony's skills, Red Rum's first owner. Kingsley, now an elderly man of some mystery, was engaged in the textile trade and involved both in mills and in the selling of cloth. Back in the early fifties he had been introduced to Willie Stephenson as a potential patron by the bandleader Maurice Winnick. The association proved bounteous. He had horses trained by Stephenson on those soaring gallops at Royston for several brilliantly successful seasons. In that exciting spell any horse owned by Kingsley and trained by Stephenson would be dreaded by the opposition. Willie Stephenson produced over a hundred winners for Kingsley, many the media of spectacular, even legendary gambles.

One other horse owned by Kingsley and trained by Stephenson became the connection by which Red Rum arrived with his second owner and trainer, that long-standing Yorkshire link-up of Mrs Lurlene Brotherton and the late Mr Bobby Renton. For it so happened in the autumn of 1958 that a three-year-old hurdler rejoicing in the name of Dagmar Gittell had, after a preliminary outing (finishing fifth at 100–8), landed a nice gamble next time out at Haydock for Messrs Kingsley and Stephenson, winning a selling hurdle race by six lengths at four to five on and being bought in for 1050 guineas. He won once more for the original combination and was then sold to Mrs Brotherton to go to Renton. For this new partnership Dagmar Gittell did great things, and because of this satisfactory purchase it happened ten years later that Maurice Kingsley approached Mrs Brotherton about Red Rum and murmured to her that he had for sale 'another "Dagmar" '.

Maurice Kingsley has patronized a number of trainers. At times he has been in racing with large strings; for stretches he has been out of it entirely. None of his particulars are revealed in any of the five editions of the *Directory of the Turf* (racing's comprehensive Who's Who) published between 1961 and 1976 and, alone of all the connections of Red Rum, he gave no answer to my enquiries. . . .

In racing circles Mr Kingsley has enjoyed for many years the reputation of relishing a gamble. The success of Dagmar Gittell was one of many well-backed victories.

Soon after Tim Molony had started training on the flat, Maurice Kingsley approached him one afternoon at Pontefract races and asked him if he would look out for a horse for him. Any small trainer is delighted to be approached by a possible patron. A few brazen fellows accost likely owners – 'I've just the horse in mind for you. . . . Wouldn't the missus like to see her colours carried . . . ? Time you 'ad an 'orse agin, we was lucky once, eh . . . ?' But most trainers with pride and sensibility prefer, like a lady, to receive the approach rather than to make it.

Tim Molony knew Maurice Kingsley very well. If he could do well for him one horse might multiply into several. . . .

Molony is an excellent judge of a horse. He originally bought for 1500 guineas Fred Winter's future great horse Pendil, and his brother Martin bought Bula for Winter in Dublin. Tim Molony had no sooner started training on the flat than he produced several two-year-old winners. These successes, following the two men's wonderful association with Sir Ken, drew Kingsley back to Tim Molony.

'Sure,' said Tim, delighted, 'I'll be going to Dublin sales in September. I'll buy you a yearling.'

'Right,' said Maurice Kingsley. 'Buy me one to win that two-year-old seller at Liverpool next March.' Molony's brief was short, speedy and specific.

Kingsley particularly liked winners at Liverpool because he had a box there. It was for him a very local meeting. He told Tim to 'spend around the four to five hundred mark', but said nothing at all about the shape, type or breeding of what he wanted. In this he showed business acumen and racing sense. If owners will say simply what they seek and what they can pay, like anyone entering a shop, they will get the best help from the trainer who is as anxious as they that the product will win. Some owners new to the game will say 'buy me a 'National winner for four hundred quid' and be surprised at the trainer's shock or mirth. But Kingsley with experience had accurately balanced his target with his outlay. With good picking, for that money the winner of a two-year-old selling race might well be bought.

Molony had Goff's catalogue, 'so I sat down and did a bit of researching and marked off those with a pencilled cross which I thought might be cheap enough'.

Molony knew his job exactly. There were yearlings in the catalogue bred well enough to win a classic let alone a humble seller. They could make a hundred times what Kingsley wished to pay; no point in wasting time on them.

Combing a catalogue of 500 names is tedious work, but practice makes speed. The knowledgeable eye racing over four yearlings on each double page can discard in a second those by sires too grand or too inclined to produce stayers. Molony flipped through the pages, checking the breeding, and marked down a dozen possibles for Mr Kingsley and, when he came to Lot 201, thought 'speed, pure and simple – *early* speed. Magic Red was a sprinter. Quorum was a sprinter . . .'

His deductions were perfectly sound. They would prove correct in the short run – and Molony had been instructed to plan for next March. That a horse by Quorum out of a Magic Red mare could develop into one of the greatest staying 'chasers did not occur to him. But then anything of supreme quality is a sort of freak.

Over in Dublin another expert Michael Hall had reached the same conclusion: 'One could see Red Rum maturing early and winning over five furlongs as a two-year-old, but certainly it isn't *anyone's* idea of the pedigree of a 'National winner! It looked as though a mile would be absolutely his limit.'

Molony, with his marked-up catalogue, went over to Dublin with orders all together for four yearlings including the 'Liverpool Seller' one for Maurice Kingsley. He walked down the wide grassy avenues of those Ballsbridge sales grounds, now lamentably sold for development. He looked carefully at all the yearlings he had marked, accompanied most of the time by his brother Martin. Four good eyes are better than two. As you bustle down a row of boxes noting and marking, it's the greatest help to have with you a knowledgeable friend who can murmur behind his catalogue (as you're examining a horses's head) 'Funny sort of little lump just inside in his hock . . .'

Two things immediately struck Tim Molony about Red Rum. First: 'Good front and smashing head.' Second: 'Very good mover.'

He did notice that the colt was 'rather gassy, quite gay'. The last word has a different meaning among horsey folk than it now possesses among the pretty pouting people. 'A bit gay' from a man selling you a horse means that it is as wild as hell.

This natural exuberance led to that first accident in Red Rum's career. But Tim Molony did not see him slip and fall. He had bustled away in the rain to look at others. The Quorum yearling filled his bill. He reckoned 'I should probably get him around the 500 mark. I would have gone two or three hundred more, but I couldn't have gone further.'

Fortunately for him, and for Kingsley and the rest of our story, Molony did not observe Red Rum's stiffness in the preliminary paddock. He was inside, waiting to bid for him in his customary position: 'Under the number board where they come in'.

To his surprise (pleasure mixed with doubt: had others spotted something he'd missed?) he saw no one else bidding for the horse. Only one small, stocky person, past champion jockey, present small Leicestershire trainer, was in there nodding. Outside the rain fell greyly. Inside the colt to be called Red Rum circled the neat ring, neighing occasionally in the strange enclosure of the small amphitheatre. 'Four hundred guineas,' said Bob Jeffares, looking round vainly for any other bidder, aided in his search by the clerk in the box below him and one of Goff's attractive secretaries by his side.

Tim Molonv under the number board looked cool, but feared the sudden manifestation of a new bidder. Those seconds when it's your last bid, and the auctioneer strives to get another, drag like minutes. . . . Slap went Bob Jeffares' gavel on his desk. He looked across and gave Tim a little nod. 'Sold Mr Tim Molony 400 guineas,' he anounced. 'Property of the same owner. . . .' The filly to be called Curlicue waited to come in and Major Ginger Dennistoun was waiting to bid for her.

7. 'Oh, he was gay all right'

'I was delighted with him,' says Tim Molony, 'no recriminations.' He meant there was none of that chilled unease which can mark the conclusion of a deal: will the animal, so desirable when its possession was only a possibility, seems as satisfactory when it is finally yours? There are parallels in other walks of life. . . .

Dick Morgan of Waterford and Dublin, a leading horse transporter, sent Red Rum across the sea from Dublin to Holyhead and thence on by road across Wales to Molony's neat little tree-centred yard behind the main street of Wymondham. The village lies at a meeting of five roads and lanes within the triangle made by Melton Mowbray, Grantham and Oakham. It is a sporting part of Leicestershire. A few miles north is the famous Garthorpe point-to-point course. A few miles south was run in 1974 the celebrated Melton Hunt Club cross-country ride. Molony's Manor is cosy rather than spacious, convenient rather than grand. Its stables occupy a corner of the main street and the lane from the north. The house abuts the south-eastern edge of the yard and its study looks out onto it. Red Rum's box was the one furthest away in the north-west corner. Various impedimenta of the Molony children, bikes and push-carts, adorn the other entrance to the house. The yard, full of trees, is dark.

On his return Tim telephoned Maurice Kingsley and told him he'd bought him a horse. This is always a fraught moment for a trainer. An owner, so expansive when he asked you to 'look out for something', may by now have got cold feet, a red bank balance, a big deal brewing, or merely a moaning wife or rapacious mistress. He may renegue, roundly denying any such commitment made in a racecourse bar. 'Told you to buy me a horse? Never! Said you might *look*. . . .' Or: 'Bought me a bay yearling colt! I told you I wanted an old grey mare.' You may be left to pay for the horse, or, if you are without funds (and few small trainers boast big bank balances) you must find some other patron to take over the discard double-quick before the bill comes from the sales.

A predicament of this sort over Red Rum was going to face Tim Molony eighteen months later. But, at the moment, all was well. Mr Kingsley expressed himself 'quite pleased' and said he'd come and see him.

By the time, several months later, that Maurice Kingsley arrived at Wymondham, Red Rum was no longer a colt, but a gelding. There had been no doubts about the decision to castrate him. By no stretch of even a breeding pundit's imagination could it be said that his blood carried classic potential. It was remotely possible that he might turn out a high-class sprint handicapper, but so it is every year with several thousand yearlings and there is barely room for a score of these at stud. He was, furthermore, obstreperous. He was saucy. 'Oh, he was gay all right!' Stella Molony remembers. Best then to have him 'cut' without delay. A colt who is overfresh may do himself damage.

Tim Molony's decision to geld Red Rum denied our hero those particular brief pleasures of the flesh, prevented him from breeding, but concentrated his mind wonderfully and enabled him to become a superlative staying steeplechaser. The operation was swiftly done by Molony's vet from Melton Mowbray, Claude Farmer, and at the right time; in a yearling's autumn. You may geld horses later, even up to four-years-old, but the results are unsatisfactory: the horses become neither one thing nor the other, still interested but now inept and thus, like damaged men, disappointed, disagreeable and bloody-minded.

The deed performed with a local anaesthetic is totally painless. So long as the small cut heals normally there are no complications. The yearling is out in the fields again immediately, or, as in Red Rum's case, back to being broken.

'Right from the start,' says Tim Molony, 'I put a breaking bit in his mouth, and then a cavesson over the bridle and we started lungeing him. I don't do a lot of lungeing with yearlings once they know what they're doing.' Nothing is more monotonous for horse and man than jogging round and round in a circle at the end of a lungeing rein. After a week a roller and side reins were put on Red Rum's back. 'He protested and bucked,' Tim remembers, grinning, 'but not too much.' Then they put a saddle on and started 'driving' him.

At this point in Red Rum's career he had a stroke of luck without which he might never have made a steeplechaser of consequence. He had fallen into the hands of a trainer Tim Molony, who was a great horseman, and a lad Jock Mayes, who took time and trouble to break the yearling properly. He might have been bought by the trainer of an understaffed, third-class yard, who cared little about breaking himself and who entrusted the most important stage of a horse's education to moronic baboons with hands as brutal as butchers', with thumping tempers and roaring voices. In such hellish places horses are 'broken' in days and ridden away, ignorant and fearful and with mouths untutored and ruined. From then on they will neither steer properly, nor turn nor check when required. Lack of steering, lack of brakes, lack of balance, deportment and control may not matter too much for rubbishy little flatrace horses, but they wil render a future steeplechaser almost useless. . . .

Tim Molony, like most good horsemen, is a great believer in driving young horses in long reins. He runs the reins back through the stirrup-irons on the saddle. Many of us keep the irons from swinging about by linking them with binder twine under the horse's girth. Like this Red Rum was driven round the paddock, then down the lanes. The benefits of the system are that the horse learns to accept the feel of the saddle, the slight pressure of the stirrup irons and the feel of the long reins along his sides and quarters as he turns. More important than any of these things, he develops the boldness to go forward *alone*, which is counter to a thoroughbred's basic caution and gregariousness. You are yards behind him with the end of the long rein in each hand. He must pass by, with no one to lead him by the head, the terrifying straw bale, the ominous dust-bin, the parked car in which lies panting a gigantic monster.

Red Rum was good with traffic 'until he'd got some more food in him and he was a bit fresh. Then he decided he didn't like the traffic at all.'

When the moment came to back Red Rum, Jock Mayes, then Molony's head lad, led the yearling onto the concrete with a breaking bridle with side-reins, and an ordinary saddle with a breast-plate. Some people first get up on a young horse inside his box. He is in familiar surroundings and there is deep straw around, in case the horse goes mad.

Others, like Tim Molony, believe in getting the horse out into the open where there is more room to manoeuvre should the horse start acting the bucking bronco. Molony always fitted a breast-plate to prevent the saddle slipping backwards 'in case he went right up. The girth wouldn't be too tight,' Mayes explains.

Over the breaking bridle was the cavesson and on it the lungeing rein – 'so's not to hurt his mouth'. Tim Molony held him very short indeed. 'The Guv'nor keeps a *very* tight hold of his head with his left hand, while he just *puts* me up, his right hand under my left knee, so I'm just *layin'* over his back, see? He keeps hold of me leg and pulls the horse round in a *tight* circle. I have one hand on the mane, and one hand behind the saddle, and I'm coaxin' the horse on and talkin' to him all the time.'

Tim Molony and Jock Mayes did this four days running with Red Rum, their average time, till they got to the next stage. This was for Mayes to swing his right leg over the saddle, so that he was at last sitting in it, rather than merely lying across it. This is the Rubicon. Up to that point you may, if the horse starts to panic, slip back a few feet on to the ground without loss of face or blood. Once you are sitting right up there on a young animal who now feels for the first time another creature bestriding him, with strange limbs hanging down either flank, explosions can erupt. Trepidations are mutually transmitted. You may feel the horse quiver under you, note his ears flicker – that first portent of alarm – see his eyes roll back, feel him start to stir beneath you, poised to leap like a lunatic into the air, lose his feet, have you off, come crashing down, break his knees. . . .

'But we've never had anything go berserk,' says Jock Mayes. 'Why? Well we've got a good man in the Guv'nor on their heads!'

Initially he kept his feet straight down out of the stirrup irons while Molony led Red Rum round in a circle. After a few days circling the yard, Molony led the bay yearling out and down a private concrete lane away from all traffic. The trouble with traffic, which lasted for years, was to start almost immediately.

8. 'We both laid down on a bank'

The uninitiated, who suppose all racehorses are trained on regulated, multi-shared, galloping grounds, like the vast expanses of Lambourn and Newmarket, would be astonished to see the thousands who do their daily work, particularly with jumpers, up little grass strips on the headlands of farmers' fields.

But to prepare a more delicate, less developed yearling to win first time out in the spring of his two-year-old season usually requires excellent gallops and enough 'trial cattle' to test the young horse. It is particularly to Tim Molony's credit (for as a former jumping jockey his interests could be expected to lie with chasers) that, training on farmland (and now down an old railway track) and with a small stable, he has bulls-eyed a quiverful of two-year-old winners, fired off first time out.

As soon as Red Rum started going out for exercise with the rest of the Molony string he showed he was 'A character'. Stella Molony says grinning, 'Nearly every day he was getting into scrapes because he was so fresh and above himself. He dropped the lads many times. It was always a sort of joke: "Will he get another notch on his gun this morning?" '

'For the lads,' says Stella, 'it was frightening but fun, because everyone really loved the horse.' She did not ride him much herself, 'because he was so dangerous! He had to have a lot of work to settle him, to prevent him hurting himself when he was messing about.' As a precaution against him falling in the road after bucking, Red Rum always wore knee-boots.

It was long disputed whether Red Rum had actually dropped Jock Mayes or not. 'Well, there's a story,' Jock remembers ruefully, 'that we both laid down on a bank by the roadside, when this lorry came tearing towards us so fast. The lads said "You've either been dropped, or you pulled Red Rum down!" But there was nowhere else for us to go,' says Jock, 'so the horse got down on the bank on his side! And I did sorta slip off him, I s'pose. He got up when the lorry was gone.'

From then on in Leicestershire and later in Yorkshire Red Rum was angry about traffic. But it is typical of his character that he resents traffic rather than fears it. A few arrogant horses are like this. While timid horses cower into hedgerows the really bold horse occasionally aims a kick at a passing car, like an aristocrat of long ago booting a churlish peasant from his path.

'He'd eyes so sharp,' says Jock Mayes, 'he'd see a tractor half a mile away up the lane and he'd whip round.'

The winter was open and mild. In December the yearling was cantering upsides with the others. Jock Mayes rode him eighty-five per cent of the time: 'The only time you could relax on him was when he was workin'. *Then* he was the most relaxed horse. He didn't really pull till he was a three-year-old. When he first started to canter, he was a very, *very* smooth-actioned horse. And quick.' His wind as a youngster was always very clear.

Tim Molony was very pleased with him. 'He was enthusiastic. He *wanted* to go.' Just before New Year's Day when Red Rum, though not yet twenty months old, became, by racing's rules, a two-year-old, Maurice Kingsley came down to name him. He did it instantly, standing by his loose-box at the end of the line. 'Ma-*Red*,' he said in his elderly Lancashire voice, 'Quor-*Rum*. So it must be Red

Rum.' Molony applied for the name. It was available. He registered it. The horse was no longer 'The Quorum Yearling', or 'the bay gelding'. He had his own official name and had become one of ten thousand registered identities on the racing scene. And now he could be entered in races.

Everyone in the yard knew that he had been bought to win 'the seller at Liverpool'. Jock Mayes grins, 'He'd been bought for this purpose! The owner had *specified* it!'

There was tremendous confidence. Even in December he was showing much better promise than Molony's other two-year-olds, and very early in the New Year he began to gallop upsides. Now he really excelled.

When they wanted a change of scene for faster work Molony would take four or five horses over by box to Skillington, the place belonging to that Corinthian pillar of Leicestershire foxhunting, Mrs 'Urkie' Newton. Between New Year's Day and his first race, Red Rum went over to Skillington three or four times to gallop four furlongs. He galloped in company with older horses who, Molony knew, 'could go a bit, and often with a good jumper who'd take them along well, because he was so much fitter'.

But Red Rum's programme, perfectly designed to prepare an early two-year-old winner, contradicted in every respect the proper preparation for a potential steeplechaser. These expensive beasts remain unbroken till they are at least three years old, developing and growing usually on good Irish grass. They may have a quiet run or two as four-year-olds, start serious racing at five and, on the same slow progress, reach a 'chaser's peak at nine. 'You'll ruin a decent staying 'chaser by doing *anything* with him before he's four,' has been the precept – proved year after year in practice. Until Red Rum! Until this extraordinary horse, no 'chaser of real eminence has started as he did. So far from growing for three years quietly on grass, Red Rum was broken and ridden and cantering as a *yearling*.

Even the short careers of flat-race horses which usually end at three are thought to be harmed by racing a potentially good three-year-old too much or too early in his two-year-old season. Strain on the undeveloped frame damages next year's development. Furthermore, precociousness (as with people) often diminishes adult ability. A sharp early two-year-old is often (like the young scholarship lad) burnt out by his next stage. In a horse's case he may be no good even at three. Yet here was Red Rum already breaking the basic rules of racing. He was broken at least two years too early. He was raced at least two years too soon.

Red Rum's last pre-race gallop at Skillington took place during Cheltenham week. Tim Molony was so serious about his programme and so hopeful of its outcome, that he drove back specially from the scene of his riding triumphs and the merry company of a thousand racing friends to watch his two-year-old complete his preparation. He was delighted. So were the stables. 'He was *far* better than the others,' says Jock Mayes, who intended to have his maximum bet.

Molony reported his satisfaction to Maurice Kingsley and engaged Paul Cook to ride him. Since those days Molony has generally used George Cadwaladr or 'Taffy' Thomas, but then he would shop around and chop and change according to jockeys' availability. Mayes took Red Rum up to Liverpool. 'He boxed up okay and was a good traveller. He just sweated up round his neck, just got a bit warm – took nothin' out of himself. I imagine he just wanted to get on with the job!'

It was Friday, 7 April and the English flat race season had been open less than a fortnight. There had been little rain. The ground had been hard at Doncaster: it was still firm beyond the Pennines at Liverpool.

A horse called Blue Spider, who had already a run at Baldoyle (the Irish season starts earlier than ours), opened favourite. But there was heavy backing from two different quarters for the two unraced youngsters who had made their way to Dublin from the Rossenarra Stud six months earlier and were now meeting for the first time since then.

It would be nice to know that they recognized each other and that some of the shrill whinneying in the saddling-boxes and paddock was due to their cries of recognition and 'How *are* you?' It is unlikely. Horses remember places most of all, then special people who have tended them. They set up very quickly strong bonds with paddock companions, bellow at parting and then, because they are both fickle and dependent, swiftly forge new links with a new friend. Common ponies are a great deal more constant than thoroughbreds.

The Golden Cloud filly which Major Ginger Dennistoun had named Curlicue (it means a fantastic curl) had been putting in some pretty fantastic work on the Major's Berkshire gallops. He reckoned her good enough to win. Word had leaked out already: she opened second favourite at 4–1 and was backed down to 7–2.

But Red Rum's home prowess from remoter Leicestershire was no secret either. In the big training areas of Berkshire, Yorkshire and Newmarket everyone knows there's a fast two-year-old as soon as it's done its first bit of work. His lad's natural pride sees to that, and even the most cautious trainer will murmur to his rivals over an evening whisky, 'I've one who *does* go a *little* bit . . .' and droop an eyelid.

When stable lads were indentured slaves, they were literally locked up in their quarters in remote training areas while a big coup was being plotted and brought off.

There is a friendly pub in what was then Red Rum's little village of Wymondham. Mr Maurice Kingsley had many busines associates in nearby Manchester. He had the reputation of being a gambler. Molony had the reputation of being able to bring off first-time two-year-old winners. . . . Red Rum, who'd never seen a racecourse or been tried on public gallops opened third favourite at 6–1 till pressure of further wagers brought him into 5's. Money for the Irish horse and money for each of the two young Rossenarra graduates kept the price of each attractive. Tim Molony told Maurice Kingsley in his private box that he could have a good bet on Red Rum. 'And the Boss did!'

9. 'He was catching the filly so fast . . .'

When horses have never run before only gossip about home form suggests, till stable money confirms, that they can go a bit. The Molony and the Dennistoun camps looked askance at the money punting on each other's horses. Perhaps, thought Tim, this attractive filly of Ginger's is a real flyer and faster than ours by far. He did think, however, that she looked a little backward. Major Dennistoun knew how Maurice Kingsley loved to gamble. He remembered those famous coups when Willie Stephenson trained for Kingsley. Perhaps Tim's got a really good one in Red Rum, the Major wondered. He reckoned it must have been very well galloped to be so well backed on its first appearance. The situation is that of poker. When there is no public form, hands are unseen. You hold 3's. Has the opposition, the way it's betting, got 4's?

It would have carried the extraordinary coincidences of Red Rum's and Curlicue's sales and reunion too far, if they had been drawn side by side at the start of their first race. But Red Rum was best drawn, nine of nine runners; Curlicue in the middle, drawn four. Paddock critics noted Red Rum as being workmanlike, but a bit leggy. They were off at two minutes past two.

'The horse *started* all right,' says Tim Molony, 'but he was a bit slow into his stride. Paul definitely gave the little horse too much to do. I was a bit worried, and I wasn't very pleased with him.' Tim Molony had had a tenner on him. So had Jock Mayes. 'My largest bet is a tenner, and that went on. And I'm sure the rest of the yard backed him, too.'

Curlicue was very quickly away and into the lead. The small Irish filly, the favourite Blue Spider, cruised along at her side, comfortably on the bit. Behind them Red Rum was running very greenly in circumstances quite new to him. Young horses, however well tutored at home, are always slightly astonished by the real thing first time out. They look about them like children in some alarm. As their attention wanders they drift off a true course. Only with racing experience, as with soldiers in action, comes steadiness, concentration, complete control and instant obedience.

Red Rum had been bewildered by being suddenly asked to gallop flat out. Now at halfway Paul Cook had to sit down and start to ride him strongly. He began to improve. About 300 yards from the winning post Blue Spider led. A few strides further and she started to weaken. A furlong out Curlicue led again. At that point Red Rum suddenly found his racing legs, started to accelerate, came after the flying filly hoof over hoof – and caught her in the very last stride of the race. They crossed the winning line nose to nose. Red Rum had forced a dead-heat. He had achieved exactly one half of the objective set by Maurice Kingsley for an unknown horse the previous summer.

Tim Molony thought that, ridden differently, he would have won outright. 'He was catching the filly so fast he was ahead of her a stride past the past.'

Red Rum, had, however, been hard ridden by an experienced jockey for most of his first race, driven along under strong pressure from halfway, and really pressed with whips flying in the last furlong. He had enjoyed no quiet introduction to the utterly strange business of racing. He had endured a hard race. It was to be one of many during his strange career. For most horses it would have been one of far too many, because as with people so with horses: repeated pressures and pain result in anxiety or resentment. The punished horse, knowing that sticks smite in the forefront of the battle, learns to hang back. Timidly or sullenly they drop out. They become useless.

It has astonished everyone in racing not just that Red Rum survived his hard races, but that he did so being the son of a neurotic mare. Somehow the fire in her made his will as strong as steel.

Red Rum's first contest, and strangely on the course where he was to return to world fame, had taken a mere 64.6 seconds, a fraction slower than average. The prize money was split, Mrs Denistoun and Mr Kingsley each being enriched by £133 of 1967 money. Wagers just paid off on the odds to a half stake (the other half stake being lost in the dead heat). On the Tote to the then obtaining 4s. stake Red Rum paid out the first winning dividend of his career: 11s. 6d. to win, and 5s. 10d. place (Curlicue paid slightly better) and those clairvoyants who had achieved the forecast received £5 19s. 6d.

Both winners under the race conditions now had to be offered for sale. A convention exists among racing's brotherhood that it is bad form to bid for winners of selling races. These contests, the lowest form of racing, were originally designed as a rewarding method of disposing of stable rubbish. They have altered over the years. The temptation to run better-class, non-disposable horses in them; and to gamble on them became very strong. While it is illegal under the Rules of Racing actively to dissuade someone from bidding for your nice winner, it soon became the custom for possible bidding trainers to enquire *sotto voce* of their winning colleague, 'D'you want to keep it?' If the answer was a nod, no sporting trainer would dream of bidding at the auction.

The convention about not bidding is naturally unknown to strolling players or passing pork-butchers who, hearing 'The winner will now be offered for sale . . .' are tempted to unfurl a roll of 'readies' and bid.

The race had been watched with delight on television by their former stud groom. Martyn McEnery was 'charmed' when he heard the result. It was in two ways an excellent verdict for the Rossenarra Stud. In the first fortnight of the season two of its progeny were now listed officially as winners.

Curlicue was first to be offered for sale. There was no bid for her. Then Jock Mayes had to lead Red Rum around. For the second time in his first two years the future great 'chaser was publicly on offer – and with dramatic irony, on the site of the Grand National. One of those who had cursorily noted him and liked him was a tall ginger-haired man, a humble permit trainer in a very small way indeed from nearby Southport, one Donald McCain. For McCain, then rising thirty-six and a taxi driver and used car dealer, Liverpool was already his favourite course. He had got engaged on Grand National day 1959, and gone racing. He had got married two years later on Grand National day and gone racing. Ahead in his life he would be going racing on Grand National day to the greatest of all possible tunes – all due to this workmanlike little bay gelding for whom the auctioneer was now soliciting bids.

Donald McCain was a casual bystander on Aintree racecourse, loving its atmosphere, unknown to almost everyone in the racing game there, dreaming dreams of winners he might train, whose eye had been taken by the horse who had just dead-heated for the Thursby Selling Plate. But what good was a two-year-flat racer to a man without proper stables in a backstreet of Birkdale who was struggling along part-time with the odd cheap old 'chaser? McCain did not bother to watch the auction. His path through life, and that of Red Rum did not so much cross that April day in 1967: they lightly brushed and parted, for a while.

10. 'I've got another "Dagmar" for you, dear'

Tim Molony positioned himself so that he could catch the auctioneer's eye lest anyone bid for his colt. Kingsley, delighted with his winner and enriched by his wager gave Molony no ceiling for a buying-in price. 'He was,' says Tim, 'determined to have his horse back.'

Someone, no one yet knows who, did unsportingly bid for Red Rum. But his depth of pocket did not match his perspicacity. The man ran Molony up to 300 guineas at which pittance of a price our hero was knocked down for the second time in his short life and was safely bought in.

Another trainer, however, this time a prime veteran of his profession, who had then been training for the forty-seven years since the Great War ended, had also observed Red Rum. For the late Bobby Renton who in April 1967, had already passed his seventy-ninth birthday (he was born on 31 January 1888), Aintree was (as for young McCain) his favourite racecourse.

But whereas McCain was a racing nobody, barely begun on his remarkable career, the famous Mr Renton had already trained the winners of every single steeple-chase round Aintree, including the Grand National with Freebooter for his special owner Mrs Brotherton. He had trained in his long career for some of the grandest and richest owners in the game. But in 1967 and still at his home, Oxclose, near Ripon in Yorkshire, he was training solely for Mrs Brotherton, and searching for another Grand National winner for her.

He knew Maurice Kingsley because of the successful deal they had both enjoyed over Dagmar Gittell nearly eight years earlier. So Bobby Renton approached Kingsley. In Tim Molony's words: 'Bobby went up to the boss after the race and asked him if he wanted to sell Red Rum. Bobby wanted to buy him then and there.' Mr Kingsley demurred. Later perhaps, but not then. Tim Molony had assured him that the horse was 'much better than a plater'. In that case, he would certainly win again that season as a two-year-old.

Perhaps then, and certainly at least once more before the following spring shrewd old Mr Renton persisted in his pursuit of Red Rum.

Certainly Maurice Kingsley approached Mrs Brotherton at Doncaster at the spring meeting of the following year. She remembers him saying, 'I've got another "Dagmar" for you, dear. But not quite yet. I want another punt.'

With no thought for Red Rum's long-term future as a 'chaser, he was run very often as a two-year-old. In retrospect and with a number of horses subsequently through his hands (though none of such fame) Tim Molony had the feeling, perhaps significantly, that he'd given Red Rum 'only about four races'. In fact he ran eight times from his early April start to his last appearance, wearing blinkers, again hard ridden, in the Nanpantan Nursery Handicap at Leicester on 25 September. The exertions of such a season on his young frame should have ensured that he was quite played out before he ever came to run in a steeplechase. But his connections naturally enough had no such concerns. Their minds were on more immediate, less improbable prospects. 'The Boss was very inclined to bet!' says Tim Molony wryly, 'and once you've won a seller, it's very difficult to win another....'

Red Rum, this time ridden by Joe Sime, did not appear to be much fancied when he next ran, not in a seller, but in an ordinary two-year-old race at Beverley at the end of April. As was to become his lot he was, however, briskly ridden along from halfway.

In the seven weeks before he appeared in a similar race one late evening at Teesside Park he had strengthened and improved. He was admired in the paddock. Racing's professional critics, like the sharp-eyed spotters for *Raceform*, put their praise in print. In a tiny way he had become a name to be noted. Approbation from the formbook compilers pleases any trainer: their acclaim is bestowed no more lightly than the Guide Michelin's stars. In their sense Red Rum now looked a good horse – *in his class*. And this, so far, remained the bottom league. Unfancied, ridden again by a different jockey, Larkin, he never really got into the race after (as at Aintree) rather a slow start.

But his seven weeks' break had come at an important time. Most horses begin to 'do' as flowers grow when spring unfurls into summer. They are, despite their artificial existence, still creatures of nature. Two-year-olds are at a particularly vital stage; and Red Rum throve. He was already indicating two factors at that early age which would dominate his long career: he enjoyed firm fast ground and he preferred the warmth and dryness of the summertime to the wet chill of winter.

To the general public he seemed again unfancied when he ran next in a much smarter race at Newcastle on a still evening on 30 June. He started, in this much hotter company, an apparently rank outsider at 33–1. But Molony had prepared the ground well. 'The Boss had him well-backed each way!'

In the paddock before the race Red Rum showed for the first time another enduring trait of character: when he was really well, he became extremely saucy. If he'd been a schoolboy he would have rushed around cheerfully punching people and bellowing 'Yarroo!' As an overfresh young horse, he swung his quarters, hunched his back to kick, swished his tail, crested his neck and champed on his bit. Horses in such form are a tiring 'lead-up' for their tugged and sweating lads. In the racing jargon used by *Raceform Notebook* Red Rum was 'on the best of terms with himself in the paddock'. He also had his fourth jockey in four races, George Cadwaladr. He ran a much improved race in this class to be third to the very useful winner, Mount Athos. So far, very good. He had landed two satisfactory, if not spectacular gambles. He was developing the right way.

After Newcastle Red Rum was qualified to run in two-year-old nursery handicaps and Tim Molony kept a sharp eye on his entries in the Racing Calendar, watching for when he was well-handicapped on a suitable track. He had won over five furlongs at Liverpool and been placed over six furlongs at Newcastle. Now Tim took a chance, against the odds of his breeding, that he would stay further as a two-year-old. The horse had worked well enough at home and run well enough behind Mount Athos to hint that he might stay another furlong. Two hundred and twenty yards may not sound much, but seven furlongs is forty per cent further than the five furlongs over which he had won.

If he did so, it would be the first sign of the prodigious stamina lurking inside his growing frame. The race finally selected was the Pinley Nursery Handicap at Warwick on 28 August. This time there was yet another new jockey on the horse: D. W. Morris. Red Rum had been given the fair weight of 7 st. 11 lb. but was drawn worst of all, number fourteen of fourteen runners. He opened at 7–1, was backed down to 6–1, went into the lead about 200 yards from the winning post, looked like getting caught by Parliamo, but battled on with another of those displays of courage which were going to be the hallmarks of his life. He fought on, head down, neck extended, under very hard driving, to win by a neck.

Over in Ireland Martyn McEnery shared in the victory. Another winner bred at Rossenarra helped his name. He had also backed the horse, thanks to a meeting with Tim Molony earlier that summer. It is the custom in Ireland on a private sale, and occasionally over one at public auction, for the buyer to receive back from the seller a 'luck penny'. This may be several hundred pounds on a horse costing several thousand. It is partly buying commission, partly really to bring luck, and partly so that the vendor may truthfully brag of having sold a horse for £5000 whereas, after he's paid out his 'luck penny' he receives net, say only £4250 – which doesn't sound so good among the neighbours. At the time of the sale of Red Rum at Ballsbridge there had been no 'luck penny' for Tim Molony. The price McEnery had got had been too abysmal, and McEnery was as he says, 'In too foul a humour'.

Nonetheless, Molony kept him in touch with Red Rum's pleasing progress and suggested that he might well win at Warwick. Everyone was happy, and it might well have been at this point in Red Rum's career that shrewd old Bobby Renton made his second approach to Maurice Kingsley to ask him to sell him the horse, 'Now that he's won, Mr Kingsley. . . .'

Mr Kingsley was constant in his procrastination, but the jockeys on Red Rum kept on changing. At York the following week he carried Sexton in a good nursery plus a 10 lb. penalty for winning at Warwick. He finished eighth of eighteen. A fortnight later and it was the mighty Lester Piggott who bestrode him at Pontefract. This time Red Rum not only had the 'long fellow' on his back, whose power in a finish is so acute that many two-year-olds wince in recollection, but the race was another furlong longer : one mile. He stayed on at his own pace to be third.

But in less than a week he was turned out to run again for the eighth time in six months. Pontefract and Piggott had occurred on 20 September. He had barely settled down at Wymondham before he was down the road to

Leicester for another mile nursery on 25 September. Perhaps the great Lester, whose astute judgements of horses briefly grunted out have helped trainers the world over, suggested to Molony after Pontefract that Red Rum 'needs blinkers'. No one can recall whose idea it originally was, but for Leicester's Nanpantan Nursery our battling hero appeared disfigured in blinkers, 'the rogue's badge'.

Even without Red Rum it would be wrong to say that every horse wearing blinkers is a rogue. In America they wear them all colours most of the time, like girls' hats at Royal Ascot. In Britain a few horses wear them 'to aid concentration', and 'to keep their mind on the job'. Discarding such euphemisms, most horses wear them because they are either nervous or idle, lazy or duck-hearted, reluctant, rebellious or downright 'dogs' and 'thieves'.

The supposition that Red Rum after seven races and two wins as a two-year-old could be any one of these things seems not only ludicrous but rather unpleasant. But we are now the riders in the stands. We know what lay ahead. Tim Molony at Wymondham in the late September of 1967 could have had no notion of the horse's amazing future. He believed – and he was not the last who would so believe – that Red Rum's racing performance might be improved by blinkers. And on the damn things went. He did, however, for the first time, in eight runs, not have a new jockey: D. W. Morris was back on board. Two furlongs out Red Rum was being as hard ridden as Morris knew how. Yet again severe pressure was put on the youngster. And he was carrying third top weight. He struggled grimly along on the far rails (he had been drawn unhelpfully sixteen out of seventeen runners) down and then up the undulating straight mile course. Three others quickened away from him in the last furlong. He finished fourth, beaten six lengths by the winner, a classy filly called Coonbeam, trained by future top champion trainer in Peter Walwyn and ridden by Scobie Breasley. Red Rum had been taking on something: the winner broke the course record.

Red Rum, mercifully, was retired for the season. It had been an inordinately busy one. While he had been battling on from April to September those of his age group designed for steeplechasing were enjoying a leisurely, growing summer at grass.

While their days followed the prescribed pattern for producing 'chasers, developing like beefy bullocks on good land, Red Rum's had been not only energetic but pressurized. He had been subjected to hard races. While his future rivals roamed free, he had been in his box from September to September. But there was no uniformity about the distances he ran over, the type of track or the jockeys who had ridden him. In his first six months of racing Red Rum ran from five furlongs to one mile, from Warwick in the midlands up to Newcastle on the border, and endured, stoically, the different methods of seven highly constrasting jockeys in eight rides.

11. 'And that's when the trouble started'

His small successes alone would not have endeared him to the yard. Lads like winners for pecuniary motives. There are presents for the lad who does the winner, for the head lad, and everyone else has a share in the pool. Winners inflate the *esprit* of a yard. *This* fiver was earned by *that* horse – and thank you.

Red Rum had won one and a half small races. But he came quickly to be loved because he was already that unusual thing: a personality. He was a hazardous ride, and therefore a challenge. But whenever he bucked or sprang about all the lads knew that he did it from *joie de vivre* and not out of meanness. Some loathsome horses will plot to fling you off, lurking sullenly beneath you like a pike, lulling you into idle insecurity – only to leap, twist, drop their shoulders, explode their quarters, decant you, and sneak off sneering.

Red Rum, through all the tough surf of his life, has always managed to stay on top of the waves. Meanness, however hard his punishments, has never flickered below.

His special popularity was marked by his being the only horse in Wymondham to receive Christmas presents that year. One, presented by the lads, was a rubber Noddy which was 'stuck in the top of his box. It took him half a day to assassinate it,' Jock Mayes chuckles. 'He quite enjoyed it!' Alas, poor Enid. . . .

But Red Rum's two wins were not sufficient to impress his breeder. Martyn McEnery took a practical view and made a colossal mistake. He decided to get rid of Red Rum's mother. Once again he makes no excuses, is not wise after the event and does not wring his hands over might-have-beens. He says bluntly, 'Mared's stock was making very little money. And it had become essential for Goff's sales to have mares which produce stock that made a lot!'

What was more, the year after Mared produced Red Rum she was barren, unfortunately to Democratic who might well have produced something good out of her. In 1967, the year Red Rum started to race and to win she foaled a bay colt by Typhoon. This was sold cheaply for export to Italy. McEnery had her covered by Our Babu and sent her in foal to him to Goff's November Sales. On this, her second visit to Ballsbridge and only fourteen months after her future famous son had been sold there, she made 600 guineas to the bid of Matt Galavan of Camolin, in McEnery's neighbouring county of Wexford.

Galavan had bought well. Mared rewarded him next spring with a handsome bay colt to be named Our Richard. He won a good flat race worth £603 as a three-year-old and in the autumn of that year, 1971, and trained by Ernie Weymes he was favourite to win a £1000 hurdle race at Ayr first time out. He finished second. Subsequently, to use the delicate euphemism which usually implies a horse has delicate legs, he has proved 'Difficult to Train'. He ran only once in the season 1972–73 and twice during 1973–74. This big, good-looking hard-pulling gelding was sold for 3500 guineas to Anthony Gillam at Doncaster in August 1974, as part of Mrs Brotherton's final clearance of her jumping interests.

Since Our Richard's birth and in the hands of Mr Matt Galavan, Mared began, for a thoroughbred, an unusually long monogamous relationship with a horse lumbered with the name of Fray Bentos. She was certainly fertile. She produced by him a foal every year from 1969 to 1973 – four fillies to date and one colt (foaled in 1971). The latter was entered in Goff's one-day sale in the R D S showgrounds on 27 August 1974, as an unbroken three-year-old, and much-heralded beforehand. However, in a gloomy day's sale (the market had started to slide in the summer of 1974) Mr Galavan's half-brother to Red Rum (like the majority of entrants) failed to sell. There is no shortage therefore of Red Rum's relations, though it is doubtful whether purchasers will knock each other over in a frenzied rush to buy the progeny of Fray Bentos. At stud since 1966 he had sired only one winner by November 1973, and none in that year at all. He had one winner on the flat and one better winner jumping in 1976. His name alone, suggestive of canned meat, is a deterrent in the world of horses hopefully bred to avoid that fate.

Back at Wymondham in the winter of 1967–68 all went happily with Mared's eldest son Red Rum. The lads were full of optimism about the approaching flat season. 'We hadn't *begun* to tap his potential,' declares Jock Mayes, still seething six years later over what was about to happen to his favourite.

'He was', says Mayes, 'a great doer.' Molony feeds mostly Spillers' nuts. Red Rum got three feeds daily: 'one before first lot, fed by my head man at 6.30. Then one at lunchtime and one at night. He ate everythin' we give him. Only left once, so far as I can remember, and that was when we tried to give him a physic powder. He smelt it right away in his feed. And he left it! We didn't try it again after that. He knew what was best for him.'

Red Rum enjoyed every sort of titbit: 'Everythin' and anythin',' says Jock Mayes, 'sugar, peppermints, carrots....'

New Year came and the horse became a three-year-old. Although there was no firm plan for Red Rum to go hurdling – there was a race or two more to be won on the flat – he had already started jumping at home. This, like his careful breaking, stood him in the greatest stead for the future. It is another thing for which the credit is due to Tim Molony. Abnormally early as yearlings, he pops his horses over two-foot jumps in his circular cinder track with three jumps in the circuit. It is the best of all natural starts.

Red Rum had no ailments of any sort during his stay at Wymondham which was about to end so abruptly. 'He was always', says Tim Molony, 'a very sound horse.'

His winter and early spring programme followed that of the previous year. As a three-year-old he was pulling rather more strongly. To match his development he needed proportionately extra work. There was no doubt at all at Wymondham: Red Rum had noticeably improved through the winter. This year he was again being prepared for a first-time-out gamble, but his target came even earlier than that of 1967. The plan was that he should win Doncaster's Waterdale Selling Handicap restricted to three-year-olds and run over seven furlongs on the third day (27 March) of the new season.

When the weights came out Molony saw that Red Rum was set to carry 9 st. 2 lb. very close to the top of the handicap. By now he knew very well that his horse preferred firm fast ground. When the season opened on Monday the Doncaster turf was yielding, but three days of wind had dried it out *au point* for Red Rum for the first race of Lincoln day. Molony had got the horse as fit as if he were running for his life as well as for Mr Maurice Kingsley's money. He had engaged yet another new jockey: this time the famous Geoff Lewis had the ride.

Everyone at Doncaster seemed to 'know' that Red Rum, though carrying topweight, was a 'certainty' to win this race. It looked like another Kingsley gamble. In a field of twenty he immediately opened favourite at 9–2 and was backed down to 11–4. It was a different kettle of fish to the Liverpool coup of the previous year. This time the next favourite was right out at 8–1. This was the colt Duo, who in Red Rum's last race as a two-year-old, had made up a lot of late ground at Leicester to finish two and a half lengths behind him. Then Red Rum had carried 4 lb. more than Duo. Now at Doncaster he had to give him 6 lb. The two fought out a desperate finish. Red Rum showed in front a quarter of a mile from home, but Duo, racing down the midle of the course against Red Rum's better position on the rails, was closing on him all the way. They were neck and neck for each striving stride of the last two hundred yards and Red Rum, hammering on great-heartedly, reached the post just in front by a head.

It had been a frightening last thirty seconds for his backers. And now, for the third time in eighteen months, Red Rum was once again up for sale at public auction. There was a big crowd around for Lincoln day. Jumping leapt large in everyone's mind: the Grand National loomed only three days ahead. The first day at Doncaster had included two National Hunt races. Wasn't a well-made three-year-old gelding just the sort to win a little three-year-old hurdle race come back end, t'other side of summer? This Red Rum might even win again on t'flat. . . There were jumping people about. Mr Maurice Kingsley, over from Manchester, had come up to Mrs Lurlene Brotherton, down from nearby Kirkham Abbey, (where all her winning racing-plates hang in the hall) to murmur 'I've another "Dagmar" for you, dear. I just want one more punt.' And so he had. 'Yes,' agreed Mrs Brotherton comfortably, six years later.

The auction began. 'And that . . .' said Tim Molony sadly, six years later in Wymondham where Red Rum no longer was, 'And that's when the trouble started.'

12. 'I was *disgusted* that he went without me knowin''

Once again, as after the previous year's seller at Liverpool it was Jock Mayes' nasty task to lead Red Rum around for sale. That rare thrill of looking after a winner, of seeing your horse out there victorious, is soon expunged after a seller by the awful dread again of losing him. Unless, as Mayes and all the stable fervently hoped, he could be once more bought in.

Another of the dramatic ironies which festoon Red Rum's story, are the two towns where he has been for sale in England. First, Liverpool, now Doncaster; and it would be at Doncaster again four years later in the sales ring beyond the Great North Road that another stable would see their favourite horse offered for sale against their will.

Mayes led the horse around the packed circle of people

in front of Doncaster's grand weighing-room. 'I could see the guv'nor biddin' all right, but I couldna see who was the opposition. I *thought* t'was the same man that had run us up previous for the horse, but I couldna be sure. I knew the guv'nor would bid as high as possible, for this was a good horse, but when the biddin' got up towards 1000 guineas, then I began to get really worried.'

Red Rum walked around. The auctioneer sang out his praises and the rising bids, for he was working for the race-course on commission. Mayes had one hand on the horse's reins and his eyes on Molony's face. At such critical points in a horse's life, of which the horse himself is ignorant, the man with him, accepting the horse's dumb trust, can feel a traitor. Each time as Mayes waited for Molony to nod to the auctioneer for another bid, he thought the horse might well be lost. Each time he saw Molony nod, relief soothed him. But only momentarily. Someone out there in that moon ring of circling faces was this time really bidding for their horse. Who the hell was it? How long could the Guv'nor go on buying back the horse with Mr Kingsley's money? What had they arranged between them?

The bidding had risen to 1000 guineas in advances of ten guineas. As the thousand was bid and passed, an extra buzz flurried through the crowd. Such levels for a seller were unusual. The bids rose now in fifty-guinea jumps. 'Eleven hundred . . . and fifty? Thank you. Eleven hundred and fifty . . . Twelve? Twelve I'm bid. . . .'

At about this point Jock Mayes received the frightening impression that Mr Maurice Kingsley no longer intended to buy his horse in: 'I sorta understood it, durin' the biddin',' Jock recalls, his face still puzzling over what was then a mystery.

'At 1400 guineas . . .' the auctioneer called, '1400 guineas for this useful winner. . . .' His eye returned to the unknown bidder who had run Molony up all the way. 'Last chance. . . .?' The auctioneer's eyebrows were raised . . . 'At 1400 guineas once . . . twice . . . for the last time then . . .' Slap, down came his gavel, '1400 guineas'. A momentary pause while Red Rum's lads still doubted, then – 'Bought in.'

Two words of quick relief for Jock Mayes. He led the horse happily away through the crowd back to his box, to be washed down. Well, he was still safe in the yard, though it had cost a lot to get him back. No one then knew, of course, how cheap those 1400 guineas would prove in the end, or what a grotesque insult it would seem that such a horse could ever have been run and risked in sordid 'sellers'.

Mr Maurice Kingsley, however, thought that 1400 guineas was too expensive. He declared to his trainer, 'I'm not having him.'

In practice the trainer usually bids on behalf of the owner. That is generally understood. Now faced with Kingsley's refusal, the unhappy Tim was in a quandary. Molony had done the bidding; Molony would carry the can.

'All right,' Molony heard himself say, both pained and angered, 'I'll have him myself.'

He remembered years afterwards the instant flutter of doubt. 'I didn't know *how* I was going to pay for him! Then I thought, "It'll be all right, I'll find somebody to take him on." I *knew* I'd find somebody.' So he probably would have. In which case could Red Rum's fate possibly have led through a different chain of hands to those unlikely conquests in the National?

In the meantime Red Rum went home to Wymondham the property, not yet confirmed nor paid for, of Tim Molony, who'd ridden the winners of almost every big race bar the Grand National. He would find those 1400 guineas for Red Rum, the selling plater, or another owner to pay for him. 'Then the next day,' Molony reflects sardonically, 'Maurice rang me up and said he'd have him.'

In the twenty-four hours of his brief ownership, Molony had already made plans for his horse's next race. He had been so pleased with his performance at Doncaster that it was his firm intention to take Red Rum to Liverpool the very next Saturday, Grand National day, to run him in a good mile handicap, the £600 Earl of Sefton's Stakes. Two flat races in four days is strenuous; and this was the first instance of Red Rum's exceptional resilience to rapid racing. So when Mr Kingsley rang to say he'd have his horse back after all, Molony said sharply, 'Right. But I'm still going to take him to Liverpool for the Lord Sefton Stakes on Saturday.' Mr Kingsley expressed some surprise. Molony was adamant. 'And I still think he'll win.'

'With his penalty?' queried Mr Kingsley.

'Even with his 10 lb. penalty,' said a resolute Molony.

So, for what would be his final flat race Red Rum made a second visit to Liverpool, his very special course. It was, furthermore, Grand National Day. And the winner of the great steeplechase off bottom weight was Red Alligator at 100–7 ridden by a then little-known jockey from Co. Durham, Brian Fletcher, whose path by a series of accidents would cross Red Rum's four years later; and to their mutual advantage. Watching, of course, as was his wont was Donald McCain from Southport, the permit trainer, still waiting for his 'One Good Horse'. And watching, too, was the ancient maestro Bobby Renton who had now arranged to have the horse he so much wanted.

Tim Molony had for the second time persuaded mighty Lester Piggott to ride Red Rum. This great jockey picks his rides with such acumen that his choice is accepted by the masses as divine selection, and is backed accordingly. Piggott was plainly impressed by Red Rum's chances. Whatever the driving dynamo may have said about blinkers the year before, there were none on Red Rum on 30 March 1968, when he stepped out onto Aintree two races after Red Alligator had won the 'National. Nor did

Red Rum show any alarm and despondency at being once again in Piggott's iron grip.

In spite of Red Rum's severe 10 lb. penalty for his Doncaster win which brought him – a selling plater – up to second top weight in a reasonable handicap, he was again made favourite and started at 11–4. But only one other horse in the field of twenty-one had enjoyed the enormous benefit of a previous race that season. This was the 20–1 outsider Alan's Pet who, with the claiming Eccleston on top, carried 7 st. 8 lb. to Red Rum's 8 st. 12 lb.

Red Rum, beneath the pushing, driving, flourishing, coercing frame of lengthy Lester Piggott, endured yet another vigorous set-to. He raced up with the leaders all the way and in the last furlong he and Alan's Pet fought it out to the post. They passed it, as he had a year before, nostril to flaring nostril. Up in the frame above a sea of applause (for he *was* the favourite and Lester's mount and he *had* shown guts) shot Red Rum's number as the winner. Piggott, too, believed he had just won as he rode back to the unsaddling enclosure.

Then the loudspeaker quacked: 'Correction!' Down came Red Rum's number. Up in its place went Alan's Pet's. The judge had changed his mind and reversed the placings. Tim Molony commented in the summer of '74: 'I still say the horse wasn't beaten at Liverpool!'

Red Rum without that 10 lb. penalty would have comfortably won the Sefton Stakes. It seemed a splendid augury for a profitable summer. The horse had proved what Tim Molony had always felt: that he was a good deal better than a plater. Now, too, Molony was planning ahead to the fun they would have when he could send the little horse jumping the following season. Such a balanced, gutsy horse . . . he could jump already . . . hardy too as well as handy, an ideal sort. . . .

The telephone rang at Wymondham. It was Mr Bobby Renton. He said to Tim like a bolt from the blue, 'I've bought Red Rum.'

Six years later Molony said how he felt: 'Heartbroken'. He wasn't told what Renton had paid for him. 'I think it would be £2000 . . . Bobby Renton came down, sat on him, rode him around the paddock and asked me questions about him, what he ate, that sort of thing. And then he took him away.'

Were the yard upset to hear Red Rum had been sold?

Jock Mayes remembers glumly. 'I was *disgusted* that he went without me knowin'. It just *transpired* that the owner had sold him.'

The loss of a winning horse hurt. The loss of a popular character pained everyone. But what particularly rankled was that the deed was done with so little said.

13. 'I don't want you to break your neck'

Red Rum's new owner and trainer, Mrs Lurlene Brotherton and Mr Bobby Renton had enjoyed a remarkable and famous association since 1945 which endured not only until Renton gave up training in 1973, but up to the day of his death in September 1975 aged eighty-seven.

Six summers after they bought the horse which they hoped might win them, at last, another Grand National to follow their Freebooter's victory of 1950, they were sitting facing one another in the small low sitting-room at Oxclose.

Yorkshire opinion suggests that Mrs Brotherton must have paid around £3000 for Red Rum. Tim Molony had supposed £2700.

Bobby Renton said '£1200' with complete assurance.

'Mrs Brotherton paid Kingsley £1200.' He pronounced the first syllable of her name to chime with *broth*, rather than with *brother*. Significantly, the octogenarian expert referred to her as 'Mrs Brotherton' throughout.

'Bobby paid Maurice Kingsley £1200,' confirmed Mrs Brotherton, known to her friends as 'Muffie'. She nodded her firm chin sharply.

£1200 seemed improbably little for Maurice Kingsley to take for a horse he had himself first rejected and then bought back for 1400 guineas. It seems a loss. But he makes no comment and Red Rum's next owner and trainer were sure that is what was paid.

Bobby Renton lived at Oxclose for over fifty years, and did all his great training from it. It stands on a very steep bank like a little cliff above the canal, beyond which lies Ripon racecourse clearly within sight and shout. Newby Hall was pointed out by Renton with pride lying in woodland further to the right. The canal is crossed by hump-backed red-brick bridges. Over these all Renton's horses would go to work on the racecourse, to jump the two schooling fences which were placed precariously close to the further bank, or to gallop 'Going between the Gates', as it was called.

No gallop exists as they would know it in Newmarket or Lambourn, but Oxclose had yielded hundreds of winners in the fifty-two years Mr Robert Renton trained there. The horses worked on open pastures: 'The Hilly Fields', then further beyond, 'The Highside'. They cantered about on 'The Riverside Fields', or over 'Harry's Land' (tenanted once by a farmer called Harry Kilmington). Ripon is over 200 miles north of London and Oxclose seems away in the wilds.

During Red Rum's four years at Oxclose he would have three completely contrasting trainers: old Bobby Renton with as much experience of jumpers as anyone alive; the young, quite inexperienced but very professional jockey, slim Tommy Stack, who was making his way up from nothing; and tall, thin Anthony Gillam, son of one Yorkshire industrialist, and maternal grandson of another.

He would have two constants over those years: the head lad in the little yard, old soldier Charlie Wright; and Sandra, his loving stable girl.

Talking of Red Rum Mr Renton's eyes glowed mischievously like a goblin's. He was always morally as well as physically fearless. Decades ago at old Bogside, where the Scottish 'National used to be run, he had hauled a most important titled lady – then an owner of his – scarlet-faced before the local stewards to report her for, and to make her officially recant, something she had said about him.

'Did I get the horse *vetted?*' he repeated about the Red Rum deal, as if he had misheard me.

Mrs Brotherton explained, 'Bobby always examines all his horses himself.'

This, by any standard of equine experience is extraordinary. I know of no other trainer who does not do every deal 'subject to veterinary examination' and then fully instructs his own vet to probe every aspect of the horse. The vet will examine and report on heart and lungs and eyes, as well as all external lumps and bumps.

So for a trainer, however elderly and experienced, to buy a horse, particularly for a special patron, without the benefit of any professional veterinary advice, demonstrates Renton's singular self-confidence. In Red Rum's case, there was unlikely to be much wrong with a three-year-old gelding who had survived eight races as a two-year-old, and then come out to run two cracking good hard races within four days. Not the preparation one would desire in a future jumper, but at least it suggested the horse was not only as sound as a bell but as tough as old boots.

Renton said, 'I went to see Red Rum at Tim's. I looked him over myself. He was a beautifully *coupled* horse.' He nodded his head over the recollection. He looked very small sitting hunched right in the sofa against the dark wall, wearing an old tweed coat, cavalry twill trousers and black shoes. The fire made the room very hot on the sun-filled May afternoon, but Mr Renton wore a thick knitted waistcoat. He clasped his hands so tightly together over his knees – bent as if he were still riding – that his fingers became small white sausages. He had ridden heroically in hurdle races when he was over seventy.

Once he had trained for the gold and diamond millionaire Mr Jim Joel. 'He said to me in this very room,' Renton recalled, ' "Go and buy the best horse in Britain for yourself to ride. And I'll pay. For I don't want you to break your neck".'

At the pinnacle of his career there were thirty horses in Renton's Oxclose stables. When Red Rum arrived there were only eight, all Mrs Brotherton's. Renton had bought and produced some triumphant horses down the years: Freebooter, for years every good judge's beau idéal of the 'Aintree type', Flagrant Mac (who won a Scottish 'National, as Red Rum was to do in someone else's care), Oakcliffe, Mischievous Mac, Merrycourt, Little Yid, Cushenden, Tudor Line (who was 'done' at Oxclose by a stable boy called Jimmy Fitzgerald, now a successful trainer), Cruachan, Mr Jim Joel's Glorious Twelfth and Caesar's Helm, Siracusa, Ernest, Old Mull, Chatelet, Dagmar Gittell. . . .

A great host of the winners had been Mrs Brotherton's. When she bought Red Rum in 1968 she had been trying for eighteen years to find a horse to win her and Renton another Grand National. Liverpool was Renton's target, and hers, and time was running out like sand down an hour-glass.

'I liked Red Rum when I first saw him,' said Mrs Brotherton in May 1974. Her one-time hope had just won his second Grand National and, uniquely, also the Scottish Grand National for someone else. 'He was such a taking horse, a lovely horse, but I did think he might be a bit small.' She had sold the horse – to the astonishment of the racing world – seven months too early.

Mrs Muffie Brotherton, clad in a pale blue skirt to match her eyes sat alertly in the armchair in front of the window in the shadowy room at Oxclose. Talking in a direct manner, but giving away dexterously little, she clasped her hands behind her head. She possesses the authority of all mature country-based ladies cushioned by ample funds. One could see young persons quaking before her, or being exceedingly grateful to her for her kindnesses. You would recognize, too, firm basis for her reputation of having been such an attractive girl. She has pink cheeks above the pointed chin and her brows arch sharply over quick eyes. When I enquired of Mr Renton why he had finally stopped training, she sprang into the question like a protective leopardess: 'He was eighty-three. Why *shouldn't* he stop? Why did *you* stop yourself?' she flashed.

'If Bobby had given up earlier,' Mrs Brotherton avowed, 'I'd have sold my horses earlier. I couldn't stand those terrible winter motor journeys, frost and fog and cold. And I said "I'll sell them".' A stern blue look defied me to doubt her: 'And I don't regret it at all.'

But no one, not the most charitable saintly person who ever graced the racing scene, can possibly sell a horse one August and see him win the Grand National next March without regrets. Was it that she lost faith in Red Rum too soon? Or that she lost patience with the quickly changing young trainers who followed Renton at Oxclose? Or that she simply wanted 'out'? Or had she, like many ladies acting on intuition, *afterwards* found a motive to excuse an awful mistake?

14. 'His isn't a story. It's a fairy tale!'

Someone in the south had said to me that Mrs Brotherton was akin to that forceful character and other famous woman owner of 'chasers, the late Miss Dorothy Paget. Bar their great strings, desire for victory, and a common inclination to gamble, nothing seems further from the truth. The legendary Miss Paget loathed almost all men and kept a weird establishment of female help-mates. She changed trainers and jockeys like a weekly wash. The hospitable and gracious Mrs Brotherton has two children, and stayed loyal to one jumping trainer for thirty years.

Mrs Brotherton started racing with Mr Renton as soon as the war ended in 1945. 'My first horse was Royal Ensign. Tim Molony rode him.' Molony rode many Renton horses in those days, and still marvels at the uncanny skill of the trainer. 'Quite soon I had twelve horses, sometimes more, each season,' said Mrs Brotherton, warming her hands over past glories.

When they were looking for Freebooter, 'I hired a little plane, practically tied together with string – and Bobby and I flew to Ireland. We went to Dan Moore's place and Bobby rode Freebooter. Then we went off to see Klaxton.' This was a slashing 'chaser who subsequently won three successive Grand Military Gold Cups for his owner-rider David Gibson, the first in Freebooter's 'National year. Renton and Mrs Brotherton had certainly narrowed their choice to two top-class horses.

'My husband,' explained Mrs Brotherton, 'had said to me "You can spend x thousand pounds – either on one horse or several." Bobby wasn't sure between Klaxton and Freebooter. So we went back to Dan Moore's for Bobby to have a second ride. And he liked him best. But Dan Moore said, "He takes a terrible hold. He'll be no good at Aintree. . . ." But there you are.' Mrs Brotherton looked proudly and affectionately across the room at her shrewd trainer.

Her late husband, Charles Brotherton, was one of Yorkshire's most generous philanthropists. He died in 1949 after some years of failing health and partial paralysis in his right arm and leg. He reputedly gave away (he was modest and sought no glory) more than one million pounds to charities during his life, and left almost another million when he died.

His widow still lives at Kirkham Abbey north-east of York, about thirty miles across country east of where all her great jumpers were trained by Bobby Renton. I had heard Kirkham was a beautiful place. Muffie Brotherton smiled, 'I love it, and it's very comfortable and the setting's nice, but it's early Vic – not beautiful.'

Renton said, 'You'd have had a good lunch there!'

Mrs Brotherton entertains most hospitably. She has lots of Yorkshire friends. She gives house-parties for York races. To young officers stationed in the north of England in the early 1950s she was particularly kind. One, Captain Tim Forster, who became a trainer of renown and of his own Grand National winner Well to Do, warmly recalls those visits. 'We'd go after York races. Few of us had properly been round a leading trainer's yard before. It was a *tremendous* excitement – just after Freebooter's 'National – to see all these marvellous horses owned by Mrs Brotherton, Lord Rosebery and Mr Jim Joel!' They were indeed owners of a magnitude to whet the appetite of any trainer in the land.

'Bobby Renton was very quiet, very dry,' says Forster. 'He said to me "When you go to buy a young horse you want to be able to fit your bowler-hat neatly between his forelegs". I've never forgotten that – as a measure of whether it's likely to be wide enough.' It conjures up, too, in the bowler-hat, an image of a racing world which died quite suddenly in the 1950s.

When Red Rum arrived at Oxclose Mrs Brotherton,

though thinking him on the small side, 'Still thought he'd make a 'chaser'.

Bobby Renton chipped in: 'I said, "This is a Liverpool horse. You could run him in the 'National".'

Mrs Brotherton added, correcting him, 'I said "At seven he ought to run in the 'National".'

Yet she sold him when he was seven....

'Well, the year before I'd sold two of my horses,' said Mrs Brotherton quite testily, to emphasize that the culling of Red Rum was part of a strategic policy, 'and then Red Rum was the oldest, so he had to go.'

'He won three hurdles and five 'chases when he was here,' said Bobby Renton firmly. 'Eight races.' He was right to reiterate the successes Red Rum enjoyed under his official training and then under his wing. For the money he cost, he had done well. It is just that his stakes of £3761 earned in four seasons from forty-nine races at Oxclose, does not stand up very proudly against the £65 666 he would earn from nineteen races in his first two seasons in Southport.

'No doubt, I've been very lucky anyway,' said Mr Robert Renton briskly, gathering himself together. His wits were very much about him. 'I've had some beautiful horses. . . . But the labour got very difficult. And I had rheumatism. Towards the end I became rather a "soft" trainer.' He meant in the degree of work he gave his horses. He added, 'I got a bit tired of it.'

'You used to get up at eighty-three at crack of dawn,' said Mrs Brotherton indignant at his mild self-criticism.

'Well, I did all my own feeding,' said Renton, 'I always trained my horses "by the manger".'

He and Mrs Brotherton would always stay at the same guest-house for Cheltenham, 'Greenways'. 'Once I had the most awful rheumatism and the manager recommended his own physiotherapist. I went along one morning before racing,' Renton recounted, 'and a man in a white coat opened the door to me and asked "Have you ever tried a woman?" '

The old man watched me gleefully for signs of shock or mirth. 'Rather early in the morning to be offered that, I thought.' He explained, 'He meant a *masseuse*. . . .' Suddenly he chuckled with delight. His mind came looping back to Red Rum. 'His isn't a *story*,' he said. 'It's a fairy tale.'

15. 'I loved the horse from the start'

Three very different people, typical of racing's contrasting strands, were working for old Mr Renton at Oxclose when Red Rum arrived from Tim Molony's in the spring of 1968. There was the sharp young Irish jockey Tommy Stack, who had just turned professional. There was Renton's head lad, Charlie Wright, a local man who had served in the Yorkshire Hussars during the war and was then fifty-five. And there was the young stable girl Sandra, also from nearby Ripon, who had been riding with Renton's string since she was thirteen and a half and playing truant from school on her beloved little pony 'Tammy'.

Sandra Kendall as she then was, first saw Red Rum in his box at Oxclose. 'I loved the horse from the start. I loved his head – so full of character. So full of life, he was, and yet so kind.'

But she had been hearing about the horse for some time before he finally arrived. 'I knew Mr Renton was very interested in him, because he came back from Doncaster races and told us he'd seen this horse and had been trying to buy him out of a seller.'

Was the inscrutable Bobby Renton then the mysterious bidder who had done the not-done thing at Doncaster and run up Tim Molony in the bidding? Such was Sandra's impression. Mr Renton does not say.

Sandra added, 'Then Mr Renton said he'd had to pay a bigger price for it and thought he'd got it.' Bigger? The mystery thickens. Sandra continued, 'He was very excited. Next morning he told us "I've got him!" He loved the horse.'

So it seems the deal was done with Maurice Kingsley as swiftly as that. In the astute world of business, articles are often not bought until the buyer has already 'pre-sold' them.

Bobby Renton wasted no time on the new acquisition for which he had been straining for so long. He allotted Red Rum to young Sandra because he had just given away one of the three horses she had been 'doing', St Willie, to Mrs Brotherton's daughter Anne.

Such is the lottery of a racing stable. One lad or girl may by ill-luck 'do' three bad horses and suffer financially by getting no presents for winners, and suffer in morale by tending animals who constantly, publicly fail. Yet there are lads like Fred Winter's Vincent Brooks, known as 'The luckiest lad in racing', because he 'does' the two stars Pendil and Bula.

In a happy fairy tale Sandra, who first schooled her 'Rummy', who 'did' him for four years, who rode him out more than 1000 times, would have been the one who took him to Aintree for his triumphs.

As it was, she drew him by accident. St Willie had gone lame and been sent hunting. Very well, Sandra should make up her three with Mrs Brotherton's new horse, this three-year-old off the flat.

The morning after Red Rum arrived Sandra rode him out in the back paddock immediately behind the stables. It was here on her first day of paid work for Mr Renton as a girl of fifteen that she had taken her first fall. 'A horse reared over on top of me over the little hurdles.' She always schooled all 'her own horses', meaning in stable-lad jargon, the horses she 'did'. 'Several fell with me over fences and hurdles,' said Mrs Sandra Miles cheerfully six years later and securely married in her bright comfortable house in a smart street on Ripon's outskirts. What happened to Red Rum finished the joys of racing for her for ever.

'So the first morning I rode him out in the paddock. Gosh! I've sat on some horses, but by jove – he bucked, he kicked, he did everything but stand on his head! In fact I think he did that, too! I didn't know *what* to think. Then Mr Renton calls out, "Pop him over the hurdle!" So I did. He just *flew* it – never even hesitated. He was great. But I had a job to pull him up.' Sandra's eyes glow with the thrill of it. 'I really got used to him. Touch wood, he never dropped me once.'

Girls do really love horses. Sometimes with a very special horse, a girl can love the horse to the exclusion of all else. That spring morning in the paddock Sandra and Red Rum instantly clicked. Sandra had a steady boy friend, older than she, who for years wanted to marry her. But that came about only when, four long and loving years later, Rummy (pronounced in Sandra's Yorkshire voice as 'roomy') was dispatched from Oxclose to be sold.

From little Sandra's schoolgirl start old Mr Renton nicknamed her 'Dandra' and called her nothing else. When Sandra was fourteen she was sneaking days off school to go racing with her brother in the horse-box. She even used to lead the horses round. 'One day at Manchester we had three winners and ever since then Mr Renton and Mrs Brotherton took me all over the place! Then, when I left school, Mr Renton badly wanted me to work there. I loved horses and my parents knew I loved them.'

Like the parents of a hundred thousand horse-mad children, Mr and Mrs Kendall, though living in a town and quite disinterested themselves, indulged their children.

Walter had a horse which he sold when he went to work for Renton. Sandra had little Tammy on whom she rode out with his racehorses. The pony was bought by her brother for Sandra's thirteenth birthday and was only put down at the age of eighteen in the spring of 1974, with chronic laminitis.

Sandra started with Mr Renton at £4.50 a week. 'He liked to start you low. Then the next week he gave me £6.50. We had a good home life though: we never gave mother anything, but lived at home and we biked to work. I had six ponies at home, and I had to do them before I went up to work and after I'd finished.' The length and labours of her days would be strenuous for a grown man. For an ex-schoolgirl of fifteen they were Herculean. But such is the passion of girls for horses.

Early in her stable girl's life she had the first inkling of the pain of parting with a horse. The girl or lad tends a horse all day, sometimes for years, feeding him, tending him like a maid or valet, caring for him like a nurse in sickness and in health, riding him out on biting winter mornings in the dark, and on spring days when riding is a joy. They take the horse racing, sharing the trepidation of the journey out, and the occasional triumph and general disappointments on long journeys back. They get to know their horse far more intimately than anyone else can know him. Affection, even for awkward horses, is inevitable. Love, in many cases, blooms.

Yet the absentee owner who foots the bills and sees his horse for perhaps ninety minutes in a year, decides absolutely to sell the horse – either at a profit or to cut a loss. And the stable lad or lass suffers the parting.

Sandra's first winner as a stable girl subsequently went under, struggling to give two stone away to a lightweight in a handicap. 'And then they sold him and that broke my heart. Next they gave me Dagmar Gittell.'

After his initial success on leaving Maurice Kingsley for Mrs Brotherton this precursor of Red Rum had disappointed for several seasons. 'Nobody else wanted to do him,' said Sandra, 'because he was a *devil*. And he could hardly win bad sellers! Then I looked after him and he won no end of races, including the Topham at Liverpool.' That was March 1962, the year of Kilmore's 'National, six years before Sandra took over Red Rum.

Renton's routine when Red Rum arrived was for the staff to start at eight o'clock. 'We mucked out first,' said Sandra, 'then rode out First Lot. Then groomed. Then rode out Second Lot. Then it was lunchtime. We rode out every single day whatever the weather.'

After a horse's lad, it is the head lad who has most to do with his care. In a busy stable the trainer is so often away racing or at sales that he may spend no more than a couple of minutes a day really looking at any one horse. The good head lad is around the place from pitch-dark dawns to moonlit nights, acting something between a matron and a sergeant-major. Red Rum enjoyed at Oxclose the care of the old-fashioned type of head lad, the sort no longer being born or moulded but who (when I first came into racing) were greatly sought after. 'Never make a *racing* lad your head lad,' several senior trainers counselled me. 'Get, if you can, the old huntin' type of stud groom – much more reliable sort of fella in ev'ry way, y'know. And doesn't think he knows all about racin'.'

Bobby Renton's head lad Charles Wright was Yorkshire born, in Masham, and lived in Ripon. By 1974, he would – had the stables been still going – have done twenty-seven years at Oxclose. He started from an advertisement in the local paper, as Mr Renton's groom-gardener-handyman. The job sounds now a peculiar jumble. But before the war most countrymen knew a little bit about horses as well as gardens. Wright still has a close-cropped military look and preserves in a crumbling age more than mere vestiges of the military virtues: neatness, loyalty, obedience, responsibility. But the stables at Oxclose are empty and tumbling down. Charles Wright preserves a beautiful album full of photographs of all those Renton winners in the past, of himself and his officers in the Yorkshire Yeomanry, mounted, going off to war on their brave horses in the days when Britain too was a place of consequence, valour and success.

Life was tough at Oxclose. 'The apprentices got ten bob a week and their grub.' But Charlie Wright progressed till he was doing a racehorse Flagrant Mac, and then one day after the old head lad, Jim Laurence, retired, Mr Renton said to Charlie, 'Just take over things till I get someone else.' Wright added, 'He advertised the job, but he didn't get any suitable replies.' So Charlie started on £8 a week plus a cottage. 'Money was always very poor till Mr Gillam took over.' He added fairly, 'But we did have free potatoes and milk till Mr Renton closed the farm.'

'I'm one of those,' said Charlie Wright 'who like their horses fed *one hour* before exercise. So I cycled to work leaving Ripon at six.'

But when Red Rum arrived at Oxclose the establishment was running down. There were far fewer gallops than there had been in the good old days when there had been horses specially to roll and harrow them – 'tractors ruin the terrain,' explained Charles Wright. 'We had a good gallop in the middle – over the river, but when Mr Renton sold the land, the agreement to the gallops ended. Then we'd only a little gallop – just like a footpath through the gates. . . .'

He thought of Red Rum when he arrived – 'He was pretty light. But he'd eat anything and he was a hardy devil.' Wright reflected, 'Best thing about Mr Renton was he'd never stint his horses on food.' When Charlie Wright was feeding Red Rum in training he gave him: '6.30 a.m. one bowl of oats with chop. [Chaff as it's sometimes called: hay cut up fine with a chaff-cutter to give bulk to hard feeds.] After work – one bowl of crushed oats.

Midday – two bowls of crushed oats and chop. Then at night two heaped bowls of crushed oats and one bowl of whole oats – oh, he'd have a massive amount of grub!'

Even on top of this extrordinarily heavy diet, Sandra would from time to time sneak a bit extra for her Rummy. He is a horse with a gargantuan appetite.

Charlie Wright considered Mr Renton carefully and said with simple praise, 'He knew his horses all right'. It is the highest accolade one horse-master gives to another. 'To know' means fully to understand. And that takes a special talent and a lifetime. Then Wright added with a sort of wary admiration: 'He was a cunning old fox, he was.' Noticing my surprise, he added, pregnant with rustic meaning, 'Still waters run deep, and the devil lives at the bottom.'

16. 'He was murderous at times'

'The cunning old fox' lost no time in getting 'the hardy devil' into action. Charlie Wright's old buff army note-book, in which, in his round and careful hand, he noted all his horses' programmes, shows that Red Rum was 'brought into steady work in May 1968'. Once more our hero was toiling while his rivals relaxed. He had now had no summer at grass since he left Rossenarra as a yearling. But Mr Renton, aware behind his back perhaps, of time's wingéd chariot hurrying near, intended to run the horse in three-year-old hurdle races very early in the coming season.

On the principle of starting at the top, he aimed for the season's first meeting at Cheltenham. This would not be the course most trainers would choose to introduce a flat-race horse to the difficult art of contested jumping at speed. No flight of hurdles at Cheltenham is really on the level. The gradients on the course are extreme, requiring the ability to jump while climbing hills and, which is infinitely harder, to jump downhill, under pressure towards the end of a race. The good Cheltenham horse must be an extremely well-balanced, well-schooled, active horse, quick to correct his length of stride as he both climbs and dives over the different flights. Jumping uphill his forelegs meet the ground sooner than he anticipates; jumping downhill he finds his foothold falling away with the impetus of his leap carrying him forward over his feet, much like missing a step on a staircase.

Mrs Brotherton and Mr Renton, however, liked racing at Cheltenham. Unlike many other northern trainers Bobby Renton had achieved more than his share of victories there, and he and Mrs Brotherton enjoyed their visits to the attractive spa. Moreover, they had been advised by Tim Molony of Red Rum's distinct preference for firm fast ground, which would be a rarity in mid-season. Molony had told Renton too that Red Rum had been jumping since a yearling. And Mr Renton had watched Sandra and Rummy fly over those baby hurdles in the back paddock the day after he had arrived.

Sandra had the roughest of rides getting him ready. 'Even trotting out with the other horses he'd buck and fool around. You could hardly go on the roads – he was *murderous* at times. He'd go into buses and all sorts! He'd never go past a car without he'd kick out at it. It took three whole seasons before he'd settle down.'

Fortunately there were fewer cars and better-mannered motorists on the lanes round Oxclose than in Britain's crammed south-east. Even so Red Rum was extremely lucky not to get killed in Yorkshire. He sometimes only just avoided the breaking of those legs. . . .

'Several times he kicked a car,' said Sandra. 'Though the motorists never bothered: I think they thought it was their fault for going past! We used to stop them, then I'd rush Rummy into any gateway I could find. We knew the roads and where the gaps were, so he was never hurt.'

But Red Rum was as dangerous to Sandra – though the ground was softer – when it came to cantering. 'He'd *never* stop bucking. He was never on four legs! We always had running martingales on, no matter what horse we rode. We tried Rummy once in a rubber snaffle, but he didn't like that. He used to throw his head all over the place. So he had just an ordinary plain ring snaffle.

'He had a *soft* mouth, though he pulled,' Sandra explained, moving her hands gently to demonstrate not the brute force of ham-fists, but the flexed wrist and give-and-take whereby, like playing fishes, a rider of eight stone may stop a horse weighing half a ton. 'He'd never tear away or anything. You just had to be very careful about his mouth.'

Sandra believed that, despite all these explosions and convulsions underneath her, she had never even 'lost a pedal'.

'No, I think he's the sort of horse that, once you get used to him, you get the *feel* of him. You just balance your hands on his neck and let him buck all he wants to. He'd buck even jumping hurdles. As soon as he touched ground, he'd buck like mad.'

It was the custom at Oxclose, as in the majority of stables, for the horses to be dismounted after work and led home to let them relax. But this proved impossible with Red Rum.

'Lead him out!' exclaimed Sandra, recollecting in her married tranquillity and motherhood the violence of those Oxclose mornings. 'Oh dear! Oh dear! He was *terrible*. He'd buck and rear and roll. You'd never come across another horse like him. He'd rear and roll and get a leg over the reins – well, that was it! So you couldn't lead him home after he'd galloped, at least not for the first two seasons he was with us. You'd have to ride him right back into the yard and right up to this box before you got off him.

'He was full of character,' said Sandra. 'And for a stranger to get on him – he knew right away. There was hardly anyone who'd ride him, even Tommy Stack.'

Tommy Stack had arrived at Oxclose from Ireland the same summer in which Red Rum was born. He had come from Ireland as an unpaid amateur with one little suitcase to work for nothing in the hope that he might one day become a jockey. He had enjoyed quick success as an amateur, had turned professional, but was still working as a stable lad when Red Rum arrived, 'doing his two' and considered to be not yet good enough to ride him in a race.

Six years later, Stack had become one of the star jockeys at the table's top. He was champion jockey with 82 winners for the season 1974–5. He painfully remembered Red Rum's arrival. 'I *hated* riding him out. He never stopped bucking and kicking. I remember one day after I'd had a fall and my back was really sore – *ow*! I had the most *terrible* ride out on him.'

Tommy added: 'Really no one rode him except Sandra. There'd be big trouble from Sandra if she saw anyone else riding her Rummy!'

Sandra recalled with justifiable pride, 'If I was off work Mr Renton used to keep him in his box!'

After his initial pop over the baby hurdles, Sandra schooled Red Rum with other horses three times over the big hurdles before he was sent on the long haul down to Cheltenham. 'I always schooled him,' said Sandra, 'and Mr Renton always liked him in front in case he hurt himself.' She meant jumping into the heels of the leading horse who wasn't as quick as he was, or falling over something in front that had blundered. 'He just *flew* over them – really fast!'

Bobby Renton had decided upon a jockey. Josh Gifford had ridden Dagmar Gittell to win the Topham for Mrs Brotherton and himself. He had inherited from Fred

Winter the plum role of stable jockey to Ryan Price and he was making great leaps up the jockeys' table in which that season he would finish sixth.

When a trainer does not retain a stable-jockey but, as young Tommy Stack would discover to his loss, shops around outside, then an association of ideas often leads to the choice of jockey. Renton thought 'Mrs Brotherton . . . Dagmar . . . Gifford', and booked him.

Josh recalled afterwards, 'Mr Renton said Red Rum was a good young horse, but that he needed "very hard riding". And,' Gifford recalled ruefully six years afterwards, 'I'm afraid I gave him a very hard race indeed.' He is yet another professional amazed by Red Rum's ability to survive the punitive rigours of his racing.

The ground was good and fast with a small field of ten: ideal conditions for a first outing had the course not been Cheltenham and the jockey had not been ordered to give Red Rum a hard race. He jumped so well he led from the second flight of hurdles to about halfway. He came to the last hurdle with the favourite Acastus (who had already enjoyed the experience of winning a hurdle race) but could not quicken up Cheltenham's severe climb to the post. He was second, beaten four lengths, by a previous winner, and in good time. He collected the first portion of the massive fund of prize money he was going to accumulate under National Hunt Rules – £74,200 by the end of the 1976 season. In his first race he earned £90, enough to pay jockey Gifford, the horse-box from Oxclose and back and his keep at Renton's for a fortnight. Mrs Brotherton and Mr Renton were satisfied. For Sandra and her brother Walter, driving Red Rum the long way home to Yorkshire, pleasure in the young horse's promise was streaked with sorrow at the punishing ride he had suffered. She said, 'I think Tommy Stack told Josh Gifford that Rummy was lazy. He had a very hard race. He had stripes on him that lasted *weeks*. And he didn't much care for Cheltenham after that.'

Next time, however, Sandra was absolutely livid. The pattern of multiple jockey changes which had been Red Rum's lot as a two-year-old (seven different jockeys in his eight races) was now to be repeated as he was learning a new craft over hurdles. He was going to have another long hard season – too long, too hard for a 'baby' some would say. He was in action without a previous summer's holiday from September 1968, until the end of May 1969. He ran in ten races and additionally travelled to Ascot to be declared for a race but withdrawn.

It is helpful for a young flat-race horse to grow accustomed to the same pilot. He receives the same 'aids' and the jockey can report on progress or deterioration, and any new tendencies. Red Rum did not enjoy those advantages when he was flat racing.

But it is five times more important for a young hurdler trying to pick up the art of jumping at speed, when tired, when pressurized, when in a group, when blinded by backsides and flying mud, when slipping, when 'wrong', to have the same man on top. No two jockeys 'press the buttons' exactly the same. With an experienced horse the good jockey swiftly senses the type of jumper he is and can go along with him. But the inexperienced novice is not yet a type. He needs guidance. He relies. And with each different jockey a horse is trying to learn each time what the new man on top is trying to tell him, instead of learning the smooth, economic way of getting on with his job.

All good jumping stables retain a jockey. Most good ones have a secondary stable jockey who will be educating the young horses when the star jockey is either riding elsewhere or on something more fancied. The stable team will keep continuity of schooling at home.

But outside jockeys no longer drove to remote Oxclose. And in Red Rum's first jumping season he was ridden by J. Gifford, A. Turnell, J. Cook, T. S. Murphy, J. Doyle, and P. Broderick. In the first two years of his racing he had perforce to make do with fourteen different jockeys. Was it purely coincidence, the time of year, or the fact that by the spring he had finally learned, that it was his last jockey Paddy Broderick who won on him finally thrice in a row?

As had been said by many experts who know something about Red Rum's story: 'The horse did it spite of all!'

After Rummy's second race at pleasant Market Rasen an enraged Sandra gave his jockey a piece of her mind. 'By Jove,' she flashed out at little Andy Turnell as he came in on the horse, 'I hope to God you never ride my horse again!' Sandra said afterwards, 'I'm not saying what else I said.' She was still embarrassed six years later about her explosion. But she justified it: 'He was last turning into the straight and he just sat there and expected the horse to win! And the horses were good that he was against. He came from *nowhere*, and the poor horse had a hard race for nothing!'

17. 'He won three on the trot'

It is hard for a stable lad or girl to watch, as they may believe (and usually from a poor vantage point) their horse's chances getting lost. Few will be as forthright as Sandra. Their chances of conveying their views to the trainer, too, are slim. Perhaps a grimace may be made on the gallops one morning, when they ask, 'Who's ridin' my 'oss on Saturday, Sir?' and the Guv'nor says 'Bloggins'. But the lad cannot pick whose hands and mind will give – in his opinion – his horse the best chance of winning.

Red Rum had started second favourite at Market Rasen after his promising Cheltenham start. He finished fourth, beaten sixteen lengths. In fairness to Turnell, then a much greener pilot than the stylish self-assured jockey he has now become, *Chaseform* observers noted that the horse made a jumping error just as Turnell started his challenge.

But more significant than the manner in which Red Rum had been ridden was the state of the going: he had come across the sort of ground which he had clearly shown Molony he detested, consequently disappointing Mr Renton and Mrs Brotherton. But the warning was not heeded.

He improved next time at Nottingham where the going was good. The winner at Market Rasen, Francophile, now finished second, but Red Rum was third and only three lengths behind him – an improvement of thirteen lengths, with Francophile carrying a 7 lb. penalty. Red Rum's running basically followed the Market Rasen pattern: he was making up ground towards the end. Unless a horse is being stopped by a dishonest trainer late progress in a race generally shows that stamina is the horse's strong suit. It is therefore better to have such a horse up with the leaders all the way. There is patently no point in holding him up for a final quick burst of acceleration. Nothing can make a horse quicken. Good riding may preserve to the right moment that little final squirt of speed. Good training can make the speed hold out a little longer. But no more.

Red Rum was already showing that, in conflict with his breeding, he possessed much more stamina than speed. The Nottingham winner was none other than Soloning, Fred Winter's cheap buy who had run behind Red Rum in that Warwick flat race. He had already won one hurdle and been second in his other start, so he had made a far better beginning as a jumper than our hero. He ended the season with five victories compared with Red Rum's three.

It is significant that Soloning was ridden in every race that season, bar one, by Fred Winter's then stable jockey, Bobby Beasley. And he was ridden in the other – which he won too – by Winter's second stable jockey, Richard Pitman. . . . Soloning on the flat was much inferior to Red Rum.

It was soft ground again at Doncaster when Red Rum with his fourth jockey change in four hurdle races started favourite, and finished third. He had, however, come up against a cracker: Fred Rimell's Coral Diver, a future top-class hurdler making his first jump race a winning one.

Red Rum was now sensibly given a long break through deep winter. He did not run between November and March. And so by way of Wetherby and more soft ground and another new jockey, the claiming lad John Doyle, and another disappointment (sixth), to the place with which he will always be linked – Liverpool.

There, running two days before Highland Wedding's Grand National, and on good fast ground, Red Rum with his fifth jockey switch found Paddy Broderick in the saddle. So far Red Rum was certainly turning out to be no juvenile star. He was easy to back in the important £1000 four-year-old Lancashire Hurdle.

He ran, as *Chaseform Notebook* dashingly put it, 'a cracking race', The winner was the brilliant young hurdler Clever Scot trained by that able Welsh businessman, barrister and former motor-racing driver, Colin Davies. His owner was the unusual and grandiloquent Mr Henry Alper, who was lucky enough to own that good Champion Hurdler, Persian War, whom he circulated among a bevy of trainers. Davies had schooled Clever Scot to a fine polish.

There were nine flights of hurdles in Liverpool's very sharp two-mile hurdle track instead of the usual eight. A scintillating hurdler may gain two lengths a flight over his more ordinary and plodding rivals. This is the basic, mathematical reason why flat-race form and hurdle-race form do not equate. At Liverpool particularly, round those dog-track bends on the hurdle track, a horse who can jump hurdles like lightning and make lengths at each flight, may bowl away in front and mock his pursuers. So Clever Scot treated Red Rum, who doggedly chased him round the bends, jumping adequately for Paddy Broderick, but losing a little at each leap to the flying feet in front. The winner was ridden by Brian Fletcher whose victory in the previous year's 'National had brought him to the notice of other trainers and owners. He was enjoying, as a result, almost as good a season as his best-ever of seventy-seven winners in 1967–68. That year he was in eighth place on the list between Stan Mellor (seventh) and Ron Barry (ninth). Not possessing eyes in the back of his head, he saw nothing that day in the race of his future partner, Red Rum.

Fashions for jockeys cruelly come and go. A few bad races in succession, a fall which puts you not just out of action but out of trainers' minds, and the winning jockey of yesteryear is soon a semi-forgotten man. A trainer, remembering him out of loyalty and satisfaction may suggest him to an owner. The owner disturbed from an office conference or television viewing will repeat incredulously, 'Put up Bloggins on my good young horse! You must be barking mad! Feller hasn't ridden a winner for bloody years. Nerve's gone they say. He's bust. Or bonkers. Bankrupt. Bent. Maybe all four.'

The dreadful slanders perpetrated by grandstand watchers and television viewers about that heroic band risking their necks out here are worse than the cruellest things ever said about politicians.

Both Paddy Broderick, who first forged a winning connection with Red Rum over jumps, and Brian Fletcher, who later did the same more famously, are based in Co. Durham, near Bishop Auckland. Broderick, eight years older than Fletcher, came from Ireland and had enjoyed his best season one year earlier than Fletcher in 1966–67, when he rode fifty winners. For all those early successes, his popularity waned. At the end of the 1973–74 season this good horseman, who started Red Rum on his winning career as a jumper, was down to nine winners from 138 rides. Two seasons later, the pendulum swung back for him exuberantly when, in the 1975–76 season, he rode 23 winners, including the Champion Hurdle on Night Nurse.

Sadly, Brian Fletcher, for all his three Grand National victories, was never, after 1968, a really popular jockey. Even in the season 1973–74, when Red Rum won his second Grand National and the Scottish 'National, Fletcher's final results – thirty winners – fell far short of his best. His remoteness, as we shall see, never helped. . . .

In the spring of 1969 the gallant Paddy Broderick had 'clicked' for the season's last rides on Red Rum. Sandra was positively delighted. 'He won three on the trot! Wetherby, Nottingham and Teesside! At Wetherby he just *cantered* home – nothing in sight – you'd have thought it was first time round! At Nottingham, only a week later, he was bucking so much going down that Paddy Broderick thought he'd never get him to the post. And he nearly dropped him after jumping the first hurdle! [Giving one of those bucks.] We thought he'd done too much, because he went off in front – Paddy couldn't hold him, he was so well – he was third coming to the bend and we thought he was going to be beaten. But then he just flew past them all – trotted in – no trouble at all.'

The good ground and the warmth of April and confidence in Broderick all combined to do the trick. Ten days after Nottingham he was off to Teesside, still in the highest of spirits and proof already that he was a horse who not only flourished in the spring but who at that period of the year could stand races very close together.

'At Teesside,' said Sandra, 'there were all these good young hurdlers, Explicit and all those.'

Lads leading up their horses overhear conversations as they are being saddled. 'Mr Shedden said at Teesside – "He'll never beat my Explicit",' Sandra recalled with glee. Shedden once upon a time had been Bobby Renton's head lad – for ten years back in 1925 – and has been one of Mrs Brotherton's flat-race trainers for years. When two trainers have horses for the same patron, rivalry is needlesharp.

'Rummy was last turning into the straight, and he just flew past the lot. Nothing could stop him!' So it may have seemed in Sandra's rosy memories. But Red Rum had had a struggle. He got home only by a neck from another previous winner, Rigton Prince. The vaunted Explicit, belonging to Lancashire pig-breeder Stan Wareing (who comes into Red Rum's story later) finished fourth, nearly nine lengths behind.

This particular victory, the last of Red Rum's treble, confused more than Sandra in recollection. Against all the pattern of his racing before and since it was gained on soft 'patchy' ground (which otherwise he hates) and he came from last to first, being ridden for speed, as if he had been a sprinter.

Bobby Renton was subsequently going to be harshly criticised from many authoritative quarters for his placing and running of Red Rum. The horse's former handlers at Wymondham would express themselves astonished by Renton's continual subjection of the horse the following season to ground he detested. But at Teesside on 25 April 1969, Red Rum had beaten a very good field on soft ground. That result rightly lingered on in Renton's mind.

Red Rum ran once more that season, a month later, when he would have been better off enjoying the best of the grass. He was sent up to Ayr, scene of his future triumph in the Scottish Grand National. His running there, too, can in retrospect only have confused his trainer.

When you are planning a campaign for a horse, your choice of race will be compounded of impressions built up over the past. You begin to *feel* the horse prefers left-handed tracks to right, flat ones to hilly ones, spring to winter, fast going to soft. A pattern is shaken out of the kaleidoscope. If some pieces do not fit, you check with *Chaseform*. And there, confusingly for the future, were the facts. Red Rum had won well on the soft at Teesside. Now at Ayr the ground was firm and he ran poorly.

Broderick was hard at him from soon after half-way, but he did not improve his position from the back of the field.

With the benefit of hindsight it is easy to see the wrong factor was diagnosed. Sandra commented, 'They blamed Paddy Broderick, but I don't think it was him. The horse had had too much. He just wasn't himself, I knew that. He'd come straight off the flat the year before to run over hurdles. Now he knew the summer grass was there. . . .'

18. 'You must be mad to keep running the little horse'

The next year was the year of the cough. The virus, as it has come to be called, has both short-term and long-term effects. A sick horse cannot run to form. And if he is run when he is sick, his wind may be so damaged as to ruin him as a racehorse for ever.

In the season of 1969–70 when Red Rum had the cough he ran no less than fourteen times. It is not surprising that he failed to win. It is not surprising that he struggled round eleven times unplaced. What is astonishing is that the horse's spirit, running in going which he plainly loathed and being subjected to punishing races, was not extinguished.

But his understandably miserable performances of that dire season had a side-effect which shaped his destiny: they planted in Mrs Brotherton's mind and in Mr Renton's the seeds of dissatisfaction. They began to feel that this was a moderate horse. They could not conceive that now he would ever be a good one. He was a disappointment: he would be no better – at best – than a middle-class northern handicapper. He emerged in their minds as a horse who might well be got rid of.

Sandra recalled: 'That season every horse in the yard had a virus, a bad cough. Rummy was really coughing. His throat was swollen and he was really bad with it.'

The virus was rampant. Anthony Gillam, who would be Red Rum's fourth trainer, was then training a handful of his own horses under a permit at nearby Roecliffe. He recalled: 'I ran Royal Charity at Perth and he should have won, but he came back coughing. Well, so did Bobby Renton's. Renton's horses weren't right all that year. I don't think he had a winner, including Red Rum and he ran fourteen times!'

Back at Wymondham, Tim Molony and head lad Jock Mayes, followed Red Rum's constant failures with increasing gloom. 'I didn't think very much of Bobby Renton for running that horse in the heavy,' says Tim Molony politely. 'I told him, "You must be mad to keep running the little horse on soft ground. He *hates* it." '

Poor Red Rum had even started the season unhappily, for he had not flourished at all when out at grass. 'I don't think he'd ever *known* grass,' Sandra suggested afterwards. 'He was turned out with a lot of horses in the field behind the stables. They were always playing together, so they didn't really get down to earth. Mind you,' said Sandra, gleefully, 'I always used to go out and give him a bucket of corn every night.'

Charlie Wright's neat old army notebook carefully records, '*Red Rum brought into work, July 19th, 1969*'. Five years later, the last two of which she had spent entirely cut off from racing, Mrs Sandra Miles remembered that exact date which, even for a girl who loved a horse, is surprising.

As in 1968, Red Rum began the season at Cheltenham and at the same meeting. No longer a novice, he had to run in an all-aged handicap. This provided the first official assessment of his ability: in a weight range extending from 10 st. up to 12 st. 7 lb. Red Rum was given a mere 10 st. 7 lb. The handicapper certainly did not recognize in him much sign of merit.

Although Red Rum was trained only a few miles as the crows flew over flat land and river from Anthony Gillam's little place at Roecliffe, this was the first time Gillam had noticed him. But this was due to proximity rather than any distinction. Red Rum made no show of any sort. He was ridden by Renton's new stable jockey, Tommy Stack, who had now satisfied the Guv'nor (he was still working as a lad) that he was good enough to ride more of his horses.

Anthony Gillam had a runner, Royal Charity, in the very next race. He therefore took some note of his neighbour's four-year-old. Gillam's horse won. It was Royal Charity's second win of that early season. After the first, Anthony's father had agreed to let him give up working in the family business to train for himself. This move, and those early successes would take place the young man in a position later to take over Renton's stables and the training of Red Rum.

That day at Cheltenham Gillam, though knowing very well what the famous Mr Renton looked like, had never addressed a word to his elderly neighbour. His own horse that day was ridden by the same young claiming jockey John Doyle, who had won on him at Southwell. It was at Doyle's father's Wetherby stables that young Gillam had worked holidays and weekends, riding out and mucking out and then going racing or hunting afterwards. 'I owe Tony Doyle a great deal for all his help then,' says Gillam.

John Doyle's two victories for Gillam on Royal Charity drew him to Bobby Renton's notice, and as he wanted a claiming lad at Oxclose, he retained him for that disastrous failure of a season. 'Poor John Doyle got a lot of the blame,' said Gillam afterwards. 'And I think quite unfairly.'

But young Doyle was only one of five more jockeys who had pushed and shoved Red Rum round over thirty miles of hurdle races in going he loathed while burdened by the debilitating, and potentially damaging legacy of the cough. There had been Tommy Stack, John Doyle, Paddy Broderick again, Roy Edwards and Barry Brogan before Red Rum was retired in May 1970, after a blinkered failure over three miles up at Ayr. By then he had experienced in his short but hard-pressed racing career twenty different jockeys of all sorts. They shared one thing though, which hurt our hero at the time and could have ruined him for ever: they all subjected him, under trainer's orders, to hard races.

19. 'Could I come to work for you free . . . ?'

The jockey who rode Red Rum most frequently that dreadful season was the keen young man from the remote beauties of Co. Kerry, Tommy Stack, who was later briefly to train him. Irish-born jockeys usually dominate our steeplechasing scene, though for every Tim Molony and Ron Barry we have had Fred Winters, Mellors, Giffords and Davies'. At the end of the 1973–74 season one Irishman, big Ron Barry, topped the table for the second time and another, just behind English Richard Pitman, was third: Tommy Stack who became champion in 1974–75.

Most Irish jockeys spring naturally from a background of hunting, point-to-point and racing. It is only in a story as unusual as Red Rum's that his third trainer and stable jockey should have had a most unlikely start. Mr Thomas Brendan Stack, born 15 November 1945, worked in Dublin's fair city as a clerk in an insurance office. His mother, totally disapproving of anything to do with racing, had wanted him to be either a vet or a priest. The order of priority was given to me by Stack with a grin.

Stack's father had a 160-acre dairy farm in Kerry which Tommy's elder brother has now taken over. His sister married a butcher in Co. Limerick who, through some cattle dealing with old Mr Renton, possessed that single tenuous contact with the English racing scene which Tommy Stack exploited.

Unusual for an Irish farmer's son, Tommy hardly even hunted as a boy. He was sent away, aged twelve, to Mungret College, in County Limerick 'to be taught by the Jesuits. But there I met two racing people: the future jockey Barry Brogan and the future trainer Bobby Barry who married one of Lord Harrington's daughters.' The dark, mercurial, unfortunate Barry Brogan, sometimes superlative, sometimes nerve-shattered, was the young man who led clerk Stack from the straight way of an insurance office down the primrose paths of racing.

In the jockey's world of shared dangers and shared changing-rooms, shared holidays and ambulances, shared hospitals and parties, the characters of the gladiators are well known to one another. Two jumping jockeys have so far had the greatest influence on Red Rum – Tommy Stack and Brian Fletcher. Except in one trait, a cautious reluctance to spend money, they are in everything else direct opposites. Stack is shrewd, careful, business-like, calculating and ambitious. He is cool and assured in manner. Several beautiful and talented girls appeared to adore him before he married one, Liz Townson in June 1975, despite his nonchalance and the business-like tempo of his life. He had quite easily more rides – in races – than any other jockey during the season 1973–74: 458 rides for his seventy-six winners, compared with Pitman's 316 rides for his seventy-nine winners. In 1974–5 he rode an incredible 577 horses for his 82 winners which topped one list. Stack earns big money. He breeds horses – he bred and profitably sold the high-class flat-racer Brook – and he makes money. He salts it away. 'Stack's worth a fortune,' other jockeys say. They laugh, 'Old Stacky never spends any money,' but he is greatly admired by his colleagues.

Barry Brogan, his oldest racing friend, recounted with delight, 'When Tommy first came to England he bought a little, very old black Austin for thirty or forty quid. He ran it for two and a half years – thousands and thousands of miles – and then he sold it for £70. That's really typical of Stacky!'

Against his family's objections the schoolboy Stack hankered to get into the horse world. 'One way seemed to me was to join the Irish army and get into the army equitation team and go show jumping round the world!' But he was not accepted at his interview in a Dublin barracks.

'So I went home and helped out on the farm,' said Stack, 'till it became necessary for me to go off and earn a living.' He and Brogan were not only school chums: they went on holidays together. 'Oh, Ballybunion!' exclaimed Brogan of the famous holiday resort. 'What girls there were! And what "cracks" we had down there. . . .'

But the Phoenix Assurance Company at £7 a week for a junior clerk and a small flat shared between five in Drumcondra Road, Dublin, was Stack's next move. 'We'd a lot of fun, but no money. Some days we went without food entirely.'

The pipes of the horse-world continued to call him softly. He would go off to Barry Brogan's father, Jimmy, at weekends to ride out. 'He could,' said Brogan, 'hardly ride at all, but he was willing to learn, and prepared to have a go at anything.'

'I knew nothing about riding,' says Stack frankly now, 'but I was very keen to model myself on a combination of Pat Taaffe and Bobby Beasley. Taaffe sat over fences better than anyone I've ever known. And Beasley was *the* stylist. Even as a little lad I thought this. I'd go home to jump things on my little pony with the *style* of Beasley, but sitting as if I were Pat Taaffe!'

When Jimmy Brogan died suddenly, Barry was forced to take over his father's yard. Tommy Stack thus found himself at weekends riding out with his old school-friend now suddenly the trainer. Brogan's owners opposed his risking his neck by schooling bad jumpers. He had one such, 'a great big clumsy brute of a horse called Irish Steel', says Brogan. 'It'd fall over anything. So more as a joke than anything I asked Tommy Stack one morning, "Why don't you have a go and school this horse?" I thought Irish Steel would bury him! But Stacky had the guts to get up and have a go. And the horse jumped really well for him – better than he had for anyone else. And I thought then, "Tommy Stack might really make a jockey!" ' It takes one to spot one. . . .

A few months later Barry Brogan had to sack his head lad. His stable had three runners over at Liverpool at the National meeting and he would have to be away all week. So he asked Tommy Stack if he'd take a week off from his insurance office and come up and act as head lad.

Stack was not only delighted to come. After the week he loved the work so much that he resolved to pack in the insurance job. 'I gave them a month's notice. My mother was furious. "You're making a great mistake giving up this good job," she said, and it was true that I'd just had a rise. But I felt I must cut loose.' Barry's mother, Mrs Brogan, also told him that it was the height of folly to embark on a riding career 'which would very likely end in nothing'.

'The chances of getting to be a top jockey,' Mrs Brogan warned Tommy Stack 'are the same as winning the football pools.'

But nineteen-year-old Tommy sat down with a copy of *Horses in Training* and selected ten different English trainers simply because they listed a large number of horses. He knew none of them and indeed nothing about them. He wrote the same letter to each. He explained that he was so keen to get into racing that he wondered if he 'could come to work for you free, just for the chance of getting a ride, and the possibility of becoming a jockey'.

Of the ten leading trainers the lad had so addressed only one had the time, courtesy and kindness to bother to reply. Captain Neville Crump wrote back. But he regretted that he couldn't help him.

Tommy was disheartened. Then his brother-in-law, the butcher from Limerick, said he would write to Mr Renton of Ripon to whom he sold cattle. Bobby Renton telephoned Barry Brogan whose name Tommy had given as a reference. By good chance Tommy was in Brogan's house at the time, 'Barry did me a great favour,' says Stack smiling. 'He told Mr Renton I could ride quite well.'

Bobby Renton arranged to interview Tommy Stack in the Hibernian Hotel in Dublin – 'I found Mr Renton a very charming old gentleman,' and the arrangements were made. Tommy Stack's father gave him £50, saying gruffly, 'When this runs out I expect you'll have to come back.'

Like a Kerry Dick Whittington, Tommy set off on his first visit to England and his first entry into those weighing rooms he hoped might be paved with gold.

With what was left after paying his fare, and carrying one small suitcase, young Mr Tommy Stack, future champion jockey, arrived to work for nothing at Oxclose near Ripon on 13 July 1965. He was immediately pitched into the deep end.

20. 'Oh, we'll just have to run the brute!'

Like most new ventures, Tommy Stack's start at Oxclose under the elderly Mr Renton was a mixture of high hopes and early disappointments. 'I remember,' Sandra Kendall recalled, 'the day Tommy came. He only had the clothes he had on, and Bobby Renton bought him an old bicycle!' The stables were so shorthanded that they were taking a third lot out in the afternoon, a time in normal stables when the horses rest and the staff have three hours off. Stack had no sooner arrived than he was riding out. But he impressed Bobby Renton from the start. If he had slightly codded his way into the job, the end justified the means. He was given his first ride – naturally for Mrs Brotherton – as early as September at Newcastle. Four rides later Mr T. Stack, the unpaid amateur, rode this horse a winner – the first of his life and the start of hundreds on the way to the jockeys' championship.

'I remember,' Sandra said, 'I took his first winner away to Newcastle: New Money, he was called, a great little horse.'

Sandra watched Tommy Stack develop. 'He was very keen when he came. He still is. He's as cool as a cucumber – a businessman. But he's a good lad. And a very good jockey on certain horses.'

Sandra considered that Tommy Stack never really got on with Red Rum at that time, 'because I think he got at him too early in a race – never kidded him on. . . .' She reflected on all those races Stack had ridden the horse and added justly, 'I think Tommy rode him one of the best, although he didn't get on with him!'

Mr T. Stack stayed an amateur for two seasons and was then instructed by the authorities, reasonably enough, to turn professional. He was still a humble paid-lad 'doing his two' horses at Oxclose and getting the odd spare ride when Red Rum (who had been born the summer Stack left Ireland) arrived. Stack was already restless. He had discovered too late that Bobby Renton was not a trainer who 'made' jockeys. He had hoped that, after his good start as an amateur, Mr Renton would give him more and more chances on his stable's horses. This gives a broader, more enduring benefit to a young jockey than simply the granting of opportunities and the giving of experience. It demonstrates to the racing world that the trainer has real faith in his young jockey. In such a way did Ryan Price 'make' Fred Winter, in spite of all the future maestro's early tumbles and blunders. To hold a jockey's licence and to work as a lad in the yard, and then not to get rides on the horses, is tantamount to the trainer declaring that the jockey isn't good enough – yet so it was with Mr Renton. He continued to shop around for different jockeys and left Stack in the wings. Stack was not just a passive witness, as when Josh Gifford gave Red Rum that first hard race over hurdles at Cheltenham; he also had to engage other jockeys. He himself booked Barry Brogan for a ride on Red Rum. Brogan remembered the horse well: 'A *big* "little horse". Always happy and giving a buck and a jump. A real character. He was super over hurdles and always jumped well.'

During the dreadful season of 1969–70 Stack rode Red Rum most of the time. 'He ran fourteen times without winning,' said Stack. 'I wasn't impressed. After a bit we all thought he was ungenuine.' The notion now seems to be so ludicrous that the astonishment showed in my face. 'Yes, we did,' Stack said. 'After all, fourteen times nowhere. So they tried him in blinkers.' Wearing these, Red Rum and Stack were second at Catterick on New Year's Eve. Much more significantly, the ground that day was not heavy, nor holding, but good. . . . *Chaseform Notebook*'s modest prognostication has a nice ring, read in the light of his future triumphs of maximum stamina. Of this two-mile hurdle race performance, it commented, '*A longer trip would probably suit him better. . . .*'

Otherwise it was, with the relics of the cough, more jockey changes, more soft ground, blinkers on and blinkers off, a change to three miles, a depressing business. . . . 'He did,' says Stack looking back, 'definitely seem to be running without interest.'

It was at that point, the nadir of his career so far, that our hero's spirit came closest to breaking point. Another month or two like this and even he would probably have been crushed.

Red Rum must have felt the greatest relief when his season was finally permitted to end in May and he could at last relax unmolested at grass. 'This time,' said Sandra, 'he did very well. He came up really big.' '*Brought into steady work 16 July 1970,*' reads Charlie Wright's notebook.

Sandra suggested, 'With him being raced so young, he hadn't grown into himself before. Nor was he getting better with age – bigger and bolder like a stallion. That was the year he was going to start in novice 'chases.'

Red Rum's first school over Renton's fences by the canal was a disaster. The two obstacles were no longer well-built, nor were they well-sited, being jumped away from home (every horse does things more boldly homeward bound) and having their left flanks exposed to a vacant belt of grass and then the gaping canal. Most horses duck out left rather than right (a legacy of riders generally carrying sticks in their right hands) so that schooling fences are best built with their left wings against a hedge. And facing homewards, too. . . . There was no reason for Mr Renton in the last years of over half-a-century of training to rebuild or resite his two broken-down schooling fences. Plenty of other horses had done their schooling there before Red Rum.

Stack recalled the morning. 'He was due to run in a

novice 'chase in October, so a few days before we tried to school him.' This might seem leaving it a trifle late. . . . 'However,' Stack went on, 'the two fences were only little bush things, very low, but he just *scraped* over the first one, and he'd already begun to refuse as soon as he saw the second one, a little open ditch! The second time we schooled him he was even worse. Bobby Renton groaned, "Oh, we'll just have to run the brute!" '

What Tommy Stack did not know was that after this shambles Sandra schooled Red Rum the following day. She remembers, 'The first day he was very bad with Tommy. He never hardly took off over the first and he refused the open ditch. But the ground *was* very boggy. Next day Mr Renton says, "Put Dandra up" and we schooled him again and he was *brilliant*. He never looked back. Tommy never did get on with him.'

If Tommy Stack did not 'get on with him' at that time, it was mainly because the horse really did not impress him. His early experiences on Red Rum, pushing and scrubbing him along in those hurdle-races and generally getting nowhere, convinced him the horse was very moderate. The judgement lingered on, making what Red Rum subsequently did incredible to Stack. So it is when plain dull schoolgirls are suddenly heard of luring husbands away from other homes, wild sirens of delight, and when stupid schoolboys are said to have become tycoons. You see the caterpillar still where others glimpse the butterfly. Red Rum's metamorphosis between Yorkshire and Lancashire was as great as that, and Tommy Stack, even when he came to ride Red Rum 5 years later for Donald McCain – found the change incomprehensible.

This deep-rooted early judgement may even, as we shall see later, have cost Red Rum his Grand National treble in 1976.

The lads and lasses 'doing' horses see their charges through rose-coloured glasses. They may grumble themselves at the horses, as mothers berate their children, but woe betide outside critics. For Sandra the season of 1970–71 was proof positive that her Rummy was a good one. 'Winning those *three* novice 'chases and except, for the once, never out of the first four all season! You must have thought then that this horse was something quite exceptional. They knew this.' The use of the somewhat sinister sounding '*they*' in relation to doings at Oxclose, invariably means Mrs Lurlene Brotherton and Mr Bobby Renton. Sandra concluded, exasperatedly, 'This is why I *can't* understand why she wanted to sell him.'

Stack, more objectively, conferred qualified praise. He had not been particularly nervous he said, after that fiasco of a 'school', about riding Red Rum in his first steeplechase. Jockeys depend more on the judgements of colleagues they respect than on any glowing reports from the stable. Thus Stack recalled that his friend Stan Murphy had told him after riding Red Rum over hurdles – 'This horse will make a good 'chaser.' The opinion of Murphy registered and lingered on.

Mr Renton 'ran the brute' as he put it, at Teesside. Tommy Stack said, 'I thought after that school that the horse might well refuse the first! But he was good. He jumped like a cat. We finished third. The next time we ran him at Doncaster – big fences at Doncaster – in a two-mile condition 'chase, and he beat a high-class horse called Orient War – a horse with a touch of class.'

Stack did not go overboard. He summed Red Rum up sensibly: 'We thought then the horse would make a good "North Country" horse.' This is racing shorthand for the equivalent of football's Division Two. The standard of racing in the north is markedly lower, perhaps 10 lb. on average, than at Cheltenham, Newbury, Sandown or Ascot. As Arthur Stephenson consistently proves with his hundreds of winners a season nearly all north of the Trent, races up there are easier to pick up; the average North Country winner does not sally southwards.

Red Rum won that season at Doncaster, Sedgefield and

Ayr, over two miles, three miles and two and a half miles respectively. He came south three times: to Cheltenham in November (third of four finishers on yielding ground. Soloning was second) and again in March to run in the two and a half mile Mildmay of Flete steeplechase. The ground was so heavy that fences were omitted. He was never in the hunt and finished fourth of six finishers, beaten nearly twenty-five lengths. 'A good class race,' commented Stack, 'and the going was all against him.'

His other southern attempt was at Newbury in February eight days after he had rather luckily won his first handicap at Ayr. The favourite Bandarole went lame on the run-in while fighting it out, and Red Rum went on to win his third race of the season by half a length. He was made favourite to win Newbury's Compton 'Chase. It was the Saturday of Cala Mesquida's Schweppes Gold Trophy.

Doping to stop horses winning occurs far less frequently than it did a decade ago. Improved security – good on most racecourses, fair in most trainers' own stables – has made it harder for the felon to get in and offer the hungry horse the heavily barbiturated sugar-lump. But the favourite in any race remains a tempting target if it is your business to 'lay' horses. There are plenty of avaricious people who will sell something valueless to the mugs born every minute – and it is a feature of racing that it embraces some of the sharpest as well as some of the stupidest people. If you are a bookmaker and know that the favourite *cannot* win because he has been 'got at', you have a licence to print your own money for that race. Financially, but quite amorally, it is 'good thinking' to spend a few hundreds to 'buy' someone to stop the favourite. Dopers can still occasionally penetrate – and their targets most often are favourites on Saturdays: more 'mug money' about!

There is just a possibility that Red Rum might have been 'got at' by some stranger that day at Newbury.

Certainly his adoring Sandra would happily have broken the neck of anyone trying to harm her Rummy. Moreover, she was very strong. The stable legend is that she was a Judo Black Belt. She laughs about that. 'No, I'm just strong. Any tearaway I could hold. It's all the bad pullers I was given to ride. My brother's just as strong as me, but he couldn't hold some of them.'

One day all the lads at Oxclose bet her a pound that she couldn't pick up a twelve-stone sack of corn and carry it up to the top of the barn. She flicked it up on to her shoulders and whipped up the steps.

Sandra would have as quickly disposed of any intending malefactor she caught at Newbury. But she reported, 'Something was wrong that day, definitely. Rummy didn't jump well. He was like a drunken horse. Tommy said he was got at. Tommy said he was like a drunkard. He told Mr Renton. I said to Mr Renton, "He was bucking and kicking before the race and he slipped on the tarmac. Perhaps that shook him up, I don't know." But he was definitely wrong that day.'

The 'bucking and kicking' sounds most unlike a drugged horse. At the yearling sales he had made himself lame by slipping over. Later, in McCain's care, taking on Crisp again at Doncaster in the autumn of 1973 he was going to hurt himself before the race doing the same thing. It is worth noting (but without attaching too much significance to it) that though he started favourite he eased a little in the betting from 3–1 out to 7–2, and that the winner (but a very lucky one) was well-backed from 7–1 down to 11–2. *Chaseform Notebook* which had given Red Rum a rave notice for his previous Ayr victory . . . 'plucky individual . . . gave his all to gain the upper hand . . .' commented darkly on Newbury: 'Proved disappointing. He dropped right out of the race a mile from home and there seemed no valid excuse.'

If he was doped that day, only the perpetrators know,

and neither the doer of the deed nor those who paid him are likely to announce it.

Thirteen days later Red Rum ran again up at Teesside. 'We felt,' said Sandra, 'that maybe he'd had too much after that Newbury race. Then he went, less than three weeks later, on the soft going at Cheltenham. He doesn't like Cheltenham and he hated the soft going. He had a hell of a race.'

The recollection of seeing her Rummy struggle round at Cheltenham provoked Mrs Sandra Miles into a rage three years later. 'Mrs Brotherton,' she burst out, 'was a difficult woman to please. If she came into the yard and saw Rummy bucking – he used to buck in his box when he was well – she'd say, "What on earth is he bucking for? Can't you shut him up?" Shut him up!' repeated Sandra, bewildered, as if her pet dog had been booted into his kennel. Sandra was nearly crying.

For Bobby Renton, more than fifty years a trainer, Red Rum was one of thousands of horses through his hands. He had fallen a great way short of his best winners. The old trainer had warmed both hands upon the fire of life. It was sinking. Was he now criticizing himself for not having recognized the spark inside Red Rum? For not having been able, as Ginger McCain was to do, to fan that spark into a blaze?

Mrs Brotherton, too, has had many better winners in her colours than Red Rum. Yet his character seems not to have meant much to her, and that is strange for a woman owner who knows about horses. She seems to have tried to ignore Red Rum, and even to have been annoyed by him. Did she suspect then that much more lay in him than would come out at Oxclose? Did she take his bucking and kicking as a sort of mockery? Did she suspect that the horse might have the most triumphant last laugh?

21. 'He looked as if he was hating it all the way'

With the exception of Red Rum's race at Wetherby on Boxing Day when Macer Gifford rode him, Tommy Stack rode him in all his other twelve races that first steeple-chasing season. The keen man from Co. Kerry was really making his name. He was getting rides all over the north of England and would end up the season with around fifty winners. He won on Red Rum three times, one novice chase, the good condition race at Doncaster, and the lucky handicap at Ayr. He was also third on him six times: at Teesside, Cheltenham, Wetherby in November (Macer Gifford was third on him in the £2000 handicap on Boxing Day), at Teesside in February, Wetherby in March, and at Perth, his last race of another busy season, on 20 May.

The blinkers were not put on Red Rum that season. He ended it half-way up the low-class staying handicaps (11 st. 2 lb. at Perth when third of four) and towards the bottom of the better-class three-mile 'chases (10 st. 6 lb. at Wetherby when fifth of eight). He was finishing, on going he liked, in the spring and early summer of 1971, about five to ten lengths behind the winner, plugging on, without being able to accelerate and win.

Discounting Sandra's loving bias, Red Rum's performances in his first season over fences ended up distinctly lower-middle class. After the mysterious Newbury flop, he did not live up to the considerable promise he showed against Orient War at Doncaster and when he was third next time out at Wetherby in a high-class Wills Premier 'Chase qualifier – *'Ran splendidly'*, applauded *Chaseform Notebook.*

In that race tall Mr Anthony Gillam finished fifth, well

behind Tommy Stack on Red Rum. Next time at Sedgefield, Anthony Gillam on his Fooasaboot (trained by Jimmy Fitzgerald) was again riding in the same race as Tommy Stack. By now the contrasting pair, the lanky Yorkshire-born amateur and owner-trainer and the little professional jockey from Co. Kerry, two years his senior, were not only the firmest of friends: they were living in the same house.

Anthony Gillam, then a bachelor, was living in Ivy Farm, Roecliffe, an attractive cottage looking out on to one of the prettiest village greens in Britain. A cosy line of six boxes converted from the original cowshed and a few paddocks on the lane to Boroughbridge made Ivy Farm an ideal base for a young man anxious to train and ride his own horses. This was the course on which Gillam was now set, and which would, by a series of coincidences, result in his becoming very soon yet another trainer of Red Rum.

The smallholding at Roecliffe had once been part of Anthony Gillam's grandfather's Copgrove Estate, and had been bought from the estate with a Trust Fund which came to Anthony when he became twenty-one in July 1968. His grandfather was one of the largest and most successful owner-breeders in modern racing history, that fierce, but much respected millionaire, the late Major Lionel Holliday.

Major Holliday's daughter married another foxhunting Yorkshire industrialist and their son, Anthony, grew up in well-to-do, horsey, but strict surroundings. His parents have a stud in Co. Limerick and live there for part of the year. Their Yorkshire home is Healaugh Old Hall, near Tadcaster, and it was from here that Anthony hunted as a boy and later worked at weekends with Tony Doyle, the trainer at nearby Wetherby. He was hooked on racing from his schooldays. But his parents did not permit him to embark on it lightly or wantonly. Anthony was put to work on the shop floor of one of his father's factories, punching his card, like everyone else. 'I used to get to the factory early, like most people did, to sit in the lavatories and read the paper! They used to read the *Daily Mirror* and I read the *Sporting Chronicle*.'

There are as many ways into the kingdom of racing as there are holes in a sieve, and though young Anthony Gillam, the businessman's son, did not have to pass through the eye of a needle, he had to work quite hard for his admission. He progressed steadily from riding in point-to-points to winning point-to-points, to riding under Rules, then training under a Permit, to winning with Royal Charity and thus coming across Tommy Stack.

'One spring Tommy just turned up one night at Ivy Farm,' said Gillam. 'He was then living in digs in the bungalow at Oxclose. We saw more and more of each other and went racing together. Then in the summer of 1970 four of us went on holiday together in Corfu and had a tremendous time. When we came back I said to Tommy, "Look, instead of living over at Oxclose in that rough old place, why don't you come and live at Ivy Farm?" Which he duly did.'

They rode together in races, the professional almost invariably finishing in front of the amateur. Then at Sedgefield on 5 December 1970 Gillam found himself again, as at Wetherby in November, riding in a race against Tommy Stack on Red Rum. Gillam was on his own horse, Fooasaboot, and as they galloped round three miles of Sedgefield on that darkening December afternoon Gillam had his first real close-up of Red Rum in action. 'He looked as if he was hating it all the way,' Gillam recalled. 'I saw Tommy Stack sitting there and scrubbing him along. Red Rum had his ears laid right back as if he was loathing it all. And I was just cruising. I thought, "that's one horse I *will* beat!" Then he came past me and I thought, "Well, he can't keep *that* up". But they just went away from me, laughing, and won.' That was the picture of Red Rum he held in his mind for years. A smallish horse, evidently lazy or reluctant, being scrubbed along by a hard-working jockey. Gillam had had a close-up of Red Rum, but that was the impression the future Grand National winner gave in those days to all northern racegoers.

Two insults were added to the injury of being beaten in the Sedgefield race. *Chaseform Notebook* reported baldly on Fooasaboot – 'He needs really strong handling,' and Tommy teased Anthony after the race: 'It took me all week to persuade Bobby Renton to *run* the horse here, for he and Mrs Brotherton don't like coming to Sedgefield.'

Gillam commented with irony, 'Well, thank you very much indeed – and with you living with me at the time – very kind.'

Stack, through his butcher brother-in-law, made the link with Renton. Gillam, in the factory, learns he's got his start in racing. The two young men meet. Through their friendship the unfortunate Anthony Gillam was about to be drawn into the most distressing chapter of Red Rum's adventures, in his last, dramatic, season at Oxclose.

22. 'I'd bitten off more than I could chew'

Red Rum was the joker in the pack. If he had maintained the promise of the first half of his first steeplechasing season, eighty-three-year-old Mr Renton would probably have postponed what was for him a most unfortunate decision.

But one late morning at Oxclose Renton asked Tommy Stack to come in to see him in the house at lunchtime. Stack went into the sitting-room wondering what was so important as to be unmentionable out in the stable-yard or on the gallops. The old man said abruptly, 'I'm going to give up training. It's all getting too much for me.'

Stack was astonished. Bobby Renton seemed to have been a trainer as long as steeplechasing had mattered in Britain. He had grown into as permanent a part of the scene as an old oak. But he explained to Stack that he was bored with the travelling and with the paperwork. He asked directly, 'Would you be interested in taking over the stable?'

Tommy Stack boggled. It was less than six years since he had arrived at Oxclose, an ex-insurance clerk, knowing nothing of racing. He had now made his name as a jockey, but training was an entirely different kettle of fish. It needed years of pupilage and experience. Many senior jockeys fail every season to make a successful change from riding to training. What seem at first sight to be similar branches of one profession are soon harshly revealed as requiring very different qualities. And Tommy Stack was not yet twenty-six.

Renton said persuasively, 'I'm sure Mrs Brotherton would leave the horses with you. . . .' He had without doubt already discussed the matter at length with his old friend and had obtained her assurance. Without her horses there would be really nothing left at Oxclose to be trained.

Young Stack still hesitated. There was a domestic complication too. He was no longer living with Anthony Gillam at Ivy Farm, but much further away on a farm near Tadcaster belonging to Gillam's parents. They had liked him and his then girl friend so much that they had offered them a vacant smallholding, Wighill Lane Farm, Healaugh.

Stack asked Renton for a week to think over the proposition and went away shrewdly to weigh the pros and cons. 'It was,' commented Anthony Gillam, 'a hell of a decision for him to make.'

As it turned out, Tommy Stack made the wrong one. He went back to Mr Renton and said, 'Yes'. It looked at first as if it was going to be all right. He took over the staff, including head lad Charlie Wright and Sandra. He paid their wages and he paid old Mr Renton a lease for the yard and the gallops. In return he collected the training fees. 'I quite liked it,' he said afterwards. 'I wasn't too worried about it and it was nice to be the boss.'

He started with a winner and he trained two more winners during the first three months of the season. But when Anthony Gillam returned from his honeymoon early in October he could tell immediately that Stack had by no means settled into his new life. 'Things weren't at all the same as when I left. Tommy was very unhappy, because he wasn't getting half the amount of rides. He'd ridden fifty winners the season before and now the rides were dwindling because he was training.'

Stack, never one to mess about when complications threaten his ambitions, had realized his error. 'With all the travelling there is in England,' he said, comparing it with Irish racing, 'you can't both ride and train.' So he went directly into Oxclose and said to Renton, 'I'm sorry, I can't do both. And I'm going on riding, so I'll have to stop training.'

He had found Red Rum 'a very easy horse to train and a very good "doer". But his form was only middling.' The horse had come up from grass slightly later than usual on 1 August 1971 when Tommy Stack got his brief trainer's licence. He ran twice in October, ridden by his trainer, at Southwell and Kelso, finishing fourth and fifth. Tommy thought him 'thoroughly disappointing'. He declared, 'I don't think he's trying'. So he decided to put the blinkers on him again for his race at Newcastle, a three-mile high-class contest, on 6 November. Quite unfancied, he ran a very much better race and finished second, beaten four lengths by the useful Slave's Dream, who had led throughout.

This was his last race when trained by Tommy Stack, and his trainer-jockey made a reasonable but wrong deduction. He was sure that the blinkers had done the trick. But there were three other less obvious factors. First, the ground on Newcastle's 'chase course was, surprisingly for November, just as Red Rum liked it: firm. Secondly, he had missed Sandra during October. Thirdly and far worse, something was going wrong with him.

His beloved Sandra had been off work after a horrible smash during his first two disappointing races. She thinks that her Rummy missed her badly. She had been riding a horse of Mr Renton's called Naughty Story – 'he was a mad-head, no mouth!' said Sandra succintly.

Tommy Stack said to her, 'You ride him, nobody else will'. They set off over the hump-backed bridge across the land in the loop of the canal to gallop on Ripon racecourse, for they were by then acutely short of anywhere to work the horses. The manager of the racecourse came out and said, 'You shouldn't be on the course!' But Tommy told Sandra to set off galloping.

'I don't think,' she said, 'that I've ever been so fast in my life. Round the bend his feet went from him completely. He skidded round and round and round on his side. I went into the railings and smashed my collar-bone and all my muscles. Finally I got up and walked back. Tommy said "You'll be all right". But I went to hospital and I was off three and a half weeks and I shouldn't have come back then. But Mr Renton said to me, "If you're not coming back, we're going to take Red Rum out of training".'

When Sandra got out to Oxclose again she saw to her horror what had happened. 'Red Rum was a shadow – an absolute shadow. I've never seen the horse look so rough. He'd gone to *nothing*.'

Sandra flushed with recollected fury, 'I turned to Tommy and I said "I'm leaving". He said "Don't be so daft".

'The horse was sour. He was heartbroken. But I coddled him up and we built him up. And he won for me at Catterick.'

Red Rum's new trainer, Anthony Gillam, did not agree with Sandra's view. He comments, 'The horse was perfectly well when I took over in November, and Sandra was already back at work!'

Red Rum at Catterick on 11 December 1971 was Anthony Gillam's first victory as a public trainer, for the stable had suddenly changed into his hands. When Tommy Stack had informed Renton that he couldn't go on training, he told Anthony of his decision.

'What are you going to do?' asked Anthony. 'What will *they* do?' Tommy didn't know.

In Anthony Gillam's mind over the last few months a thought had been growing. He says now that it never occurred to him when he started point-to-pointing that he would end up a public trainer. He may not have recognized the intention, but the steps he had taken suggest that it was at the root of all his decisions. He had progressed from point-to-pointing to proper racing with some success but only privately and for himself. The next step up in the racing game had to be to become a public trainer, to have patrons, to grow. . . .

He heard himself hesitantly ask Tommy Stack, 'Do you think they would even consider *me* training?'

Tommy said he would ask them. Afterwards Anthony Gillam recalled with surprise (for he is modest) and gratification (for it seemed a great honour) and with sadness (for it had been an error) that Tommy came back with the verdict: 'They'd be delighted.'

Three years later Gillam said, 'I wish in retrospect I'd never done it. I'd bitten off more than I could chew.'

From eight horses of his own close by (about which no

one could blame him if he blundered) he had now taken over eight more in someone else's stable. Oxclose was twenty minutes' drive away in the opposite direction from Wheatlands Farm, where his own horses were still at Ivy Farm, Roecliffe. The new horses, furthermore, were owned by a lady of formidable racing experience and stabled on the doorstep and in the private yard of one of the cleverest jumping trainers of all time.

Gillam had stuck his head into a hornets' nest. He comments mildly, 'I did find it difficult living here and training there....'

He took over the staff as it stood: 'Charles, the head man, Sandra of course, and four lads. And Red Rum. But he wasn't the main attraction. I didn't rate him very highly. The talking horse was Polar Bear. He'd run in only four novice hurdles trained by Denys Smith and he'd won three of them! Polar Bear was the attraction of the job. He might well have run in the Arkle 'Chase at Cheltenham next spring, he looked that good.' Gillam added sadly, 'But he was a disappointment'.

He also caused the first difficulties between the owner and the new trainer. Gillam reported, 'Tommy had built Polar Bear up so well that I just *couldn't* get him fit. But Mrs Brotherton kept wanting him to run. Then come 1 January Mrs Brotherton said "He's going novice 'chasing. We'll run him." But we'd had a lot of frost and bad ground and I had only got about one and a half schools into him. I knew he shouldn't run. Tommy knew he shouldn't run. But she insisted. And of course he came to the open ditch and went head over heels....'

Young Anthony Gillam did not find it easy to train for Mrs Brotherton or to understand her attitudes towards her horses. She found him – not surprisingly for he was roughly a quarter of Mr Renton's age – less wise and experienced than her trainer of thirty years' standing. Mr Renton, moreover, was still living on the place. Some of the horses he had trained remained in his own boxes. The staff whom he had engaged and paid were still there. The horses belonged to his very old friend and special patron. The new trainer lived miles way. In those circumstances it was absolutely natural, though not necessarily helpful to young Gillam that old Mr Renton was very much around.

Worse, by far, and more specifically, there were also almost immediate doubts about Red Rum. The third factor, after the blinkers at Newcastle and the absence of Sandra, had secretly started to work against him. Something was going wrong with Red Rum's feet.

What was starting invisibly would threaten not only Red Rum's future racing career, but even his ability to walk about without pain. The dreaded bone disease of pedalosteitis had begun.

23. 'Very few horses, I'm afraid, get over it'

It has been one of racing's best-kept secrets that the famous horse was ever a sufferer from what, in loose terms, is the equivalent of arthritis of the main pedal bone of the foot. The forcc and shock which this bone must endure is immense: at instants when galloping and jumping half a ton of horse strikes the ground at speeds between 30 and 40 m.p.h. The first main brunt is borne by the foot. Pictures of dummies being flung through car windscreens in 30 m.p.h. impacts reflect the violence involved. . . .

One would expect the career of a human athlete or football player to be finished if he developed arthritis in his feet. He would be hobbling about on sticks. Yet Red

Rum went on racing. And he had other complications, too: ossification of a cartilage, arthritic growths, the emergence of a spur on the bone and so on in a dread array. With the full help of Red Rum's professional advisers, official reports from the horse's veterinary surgeon and physiotherapists follow on pages 127–8.

The gravity of Red Rum's affliction may be summed up in the reactions of three prominent equine vets in the south of England when I told them about it. One said, 'Impossible. The horse could never have gone on racing.' The other said, 'My God! He's finished then. How awful!' And, when I explained the period of pedalosteitis had occurred *before* the first of his Grand National victories, he shook his head in awe. 'What a horse,' he said reverently. The third remarked, 'If you had been writing fiction, no one would have believed you. . . .'

But then, as old Mr Renton sagely said, Red Rum's story is a sort of fairy tale.

'In my opinion,' said Anthony Gillam, 'the very first time I ran him, he was beginning to feel his feet. Even though it was soft ground at Haydock he came back with a bit of heat in his off-fore. He wasn't lame, but the heat had come up into the joint. At first I just hosed the foot and joint like mad. Then Bobby Renton gave his advice which was, "Slap on clay and cow dung and lots of Stockholm Tar. Try to cool him down that way".'

Red Rum's first two races that season had also puzzled his jockey and his then trainer, Tommy Stack. 'Tommy had bunged a lot of work into him,' said Gillam. 'He couldn't understand why he hadn't done better. So that's why he put the blinkers on him at Newcastle.'

Sandra commented on the three trainers' different methods. 'Mr Renton left it to us more or less, when he was getting old. He used to watch us, but he'd let us do what we wanted. Tommy used to take notice of me with Red Rum – no doubt about that, but he couldn't get out of his head that the horse needed bags of work. Anthony

Gillam was very good. He used to ask, "Well, what do *you* think, Sandra?" '

Gillam would not have run the horse at Haydock on 1 December had he been a weather diviner. But the forecast was for going to be good. It rained all day and became soft. Red Rum then ran moderately which, in those circumstances, Gillam could understand. The winner was the same horse, Red Sweeney, of Gordon Richards' who had beaten Red Rum in his second race that season at Kelso on firm going. At Haydock Red Rum ran by comparison at least 10 lb. worse. That could be the ground, Gillam thought. What was mysterious was the heat in the foot and the joint. A trainer would expect this from jarring on hard ground, or bruising from a stone pressed into sole or frog or heel by hard ground. But why the heat after the soft turf at Haydock? Could it be from some inflammation starting from his fetlock joint which was creeping downwards? Heat from a point of strain may move either way. But if the heat sprang from a strain of the joint why wasn't he lame?

In Gillam's position two external influences were at work. Mrs Brotherton, judging from her pressure over Polar Bear, was not likely to consent to his wasting time. And Mr Renton from his vast experience did not seem unduly worried: 'Clay and cow dung and carry on.'

So because Red Rum had blown quite heavily after the Haydock race, as horses do when they are in pain as well as when they are unfit, Anthony Gillam assumed, as Tommy Stack had, that the horse was still unfit and that he needed an inordinate amount of strenuous galloping or racing. This would not be the treatment doctors would prescribe for arthritis – once they had recognized it. And equine patients cannot talk. So Gillam kept Red Rum hard at it and ran him again ten days later.

Horses are born to confuse us, as Red Rum did next time out at Catterick. If there was anything wrong with the foot, he would surely, on firmer, faster, more painful ground, run even worse.

No one had yet allowed for the horse's courage. Rather the reverse. Tommy Stack had doubted it. But time was going to show that all those races, struggling on to finish fifth or sixth in mud he loathed, under goading boot and thwacking stick were the product of bravery over disability. So now he overcame the pain in his feet. Galloping three miles one furlong and eighty yards in the Charles Vickery Memorial Cup, a valuable race, Red Rum blinkered and driven along as hard as Tommy Stack could manage, took up the running going to the third last fence and hung on to win by a length. He earned Mrs Brotherton £930.70. 'Mrs Brotherton came, which was very nice,' said Anthony Gillam, pleased that his owner had watched his first victory as a public trainer. 'She doesn't often go racing.'

Tommy Stack had special reasons for happiness. He had cast off the weight of being a trainer. All the anxieties were now young Gillam's. As if to celebrate the lightness of his spirit he rode a treble in a row at Catterick on 11 December, two outside rides for Shedden in the one o'clock and the one thirty then Red Rum at two. A splendid day for a jockey.

The trainer's worries, however, begin again as soon as the jockey gets off. The rider may be carefree till the next day's racing. The trainer has immediate worries about his horses. For Anthony Gillam the pleasure of victory did not extend into the evening. 'Red Rum came back level in his action,' said Gillam, 'but there was that heat there again. And I didn't know now if it was in his foot or in his joint.'

A trainer, however old and experienced, who starts to have doubts about one of his horse's health and soundness, becomes aware – even from the kindest and most patient owners – of pressure. He feels obliged either to find out what is wrong and to cure it, or run the horse. At £36 a week and more, racehorses are not for looking at.

Moreover, by winning at Catterick Red Rum seemed publicly to have removed the need for caution. Whatever a trainer's doubts – and Anthony Gillam's were now increasing – you cannot tell the owner that you are seriously worried about the horse, if the animal comes out and runs and wins. So Anthony ran Red Rum again at Catterick on 22 December. The ground was suitably firm, except that now, unknown to his trainer, the firmness was hurting his foot. 'It was,' said Gillam, 'a similar sort of race to the one he'd just won there.' In fact, the class was not quite so good. 'He should have won,' Gillam said. He finished third, *Chaseform Notebook* commenting, 'Found the pace a little too fast from three out.' So it must have seemed.

From what we now know it is almost certain that his off-fore was beginning to hurt Red Rum more and more from each concussion landing after every fence. In the last half mile or so the pain, even for a horse of courage, became a little much. 'I didn't tumble to anything.' Gillam unhappily admitted two and a half years later. 'We ran him without blinkers. But Tommy said that didn't make any difference: that wasn't why he was beaten.'

Both trainer and jockey knew then that something was going wrong with the horse. But what was it?

The result of his next race seemed to confuse the issue even further. Because the ground at Catterick was generally firmer that winter than anywhere else in the North, Anthony Gillam kept entering him there. He had won the Charles Vickery on 11 December, been beaten into third place in a less valuable race on 22 December, and now reappeared there in another well-endowed contest, the Zetland Handicap 'Chase worth £651 on New Year's Day 1972. It would be his fourth race in a month. Tommy Stack energetically drove Red Rum on from start to finish in the four-horse race over the same 3 miles 300 yards of his two previous races there. He won by seven lengths and a distance. In three runs at Catterick in three weeks he had earned £1622.30. He had paid the cost of all his keep for a year. For a heavy tax payer his tax-free earnings were particularly valuable. His two victories in Yorkshire in valuable races would help considerably to establish his young trainer in his first few months as a professional. They were two more hard-earned steps up the ladder of Tommy Stack's climb to the top.

But Red Rum came back from Catterick definitely lame. He showed it plainly the next day. He stayed really lame for several bad days on end.

There was in the yard at Oxclose at that time a certain Yorkshire physiotherapist of renown who was treating one of Gillam's horses for shoulder trouble and another for back trouble. Gillam, now deeply anxious, asked if the physiotherapist could help him diagnose what was wrong with Red Rum. The gentleman, who lives not 100 miles from the Yorkshire town of Richmond and who on ethical grounds must be called merely Mr A, very properly said that he should first be called in by a qualified veterinary surgeon. He recommended a man with whom he had often worked. So it was that a certain Scots vet living not 100 miles from the Border town of Hawick arrived on he scene at Anthony Gillam's request.

The vet took X-rays of Red Rum's feet and, after he had examined them, said, 'I'm very sorry to say that he has chronic pedalosteitis in his off-fore.' He added glumly, 'Very few horses, I'm afraid, get over it.'

24. 'He's still feeling his off-fore'

The racehorse is heir to a thousand ills and accidents. His chances of survival depend on the combined wisdom, patience and solicitude of the trainer, his professional advisers and his staff. Red Rum was thrice lucky. He had an anxious, conscientious, young trainer who bothered, and who was keen to call in the best advice. He had in the vet from Hawick a man who combined experience with advanced views. He had in nearby Richmond a leading equine physiotherapist. And he had the love of his stable girl Sandra.

Without this united care and treament the future Grand National winner would have become a cripple. As it was, the horse remained quite lame for nearly two long months. Anthony Gillam remembered the outline of the treatment which appears below (with the permission of the two practitioners' respective professional societies) as their two official reports.

'The vet said, "Put him on a course of cortisone, intramuscular, to relieve the pain". We kept that going for six weeks. The vet arranged that Mr A would come three times a week to give him ultrasonic treatment round the coronet band. He also told us to "put special Swedish hoof pads on him".'

These 'pads' are made from a mixture resembling putty which comes in a small tub. You add a 'thinner' to it, mix it, and paint it right over the sole of the hoof and the frog. You then put a piece of thick plaster over it. Finally you get the blacksmith to reshoe the foot through the plastic pad and the rubbery Swedish mould.

'Our blacksmith,' said Gillam, 'was awfully good about it, because there was a lot to nail through, and he did think at first that it was rather a new-fangled idea!'

Sandra said, 'Rummy had terrible feet, shallow feet.

I used to put Stockholm Tar on them three times a day. They got better with the treatment.'

Gillam remembered, 'After about six weeks the foot pads rotted – slightly Sandra's fault, because she was determined to put Stockholm Tar on his feet and the brush penetrated the pads and rather rotted them: it didn't matter. They were still doing the job.'

Sandra said, 'Red Rum was petrified of the vets, but they did a lot of good. They said they would completely cure him.'

The veterinary surgeon from Hawick reports as follows:

During Nov./Dec. 1971 the horse was observed to be intermittently slightly lame. The condition gradually became more apparent over this period of time. There was no evidence of tendon ligament or other soft tissue involvement. Searching of the affected foot revealed dry corns which were pared out without any improvement in action. The wall of the hoof had become brittle and by January 1972, heat was present in the region of the heels and the area sensitive to pressure. The hoof was markedly smaller than its opposite fellow, and contraction was occurring at the heels of the off-fore, and the horse was untrainable.

X-ray of the affected part revealed pedalosteitis to be present, localized osteophytic formation on the lateral aspects on the angles of the pedal bone and also ossification of the lower part of the lateral cartilages, and the presence of a spur on the proximal border of the lateral angle of the bone, were observed. No lesions, fortunately were to be seen on the navicular bone.

The trainer was advised that physiotherapy was the best line of treatment and not to rest the horse but to give him long slow exercise daily on the level roads and soft going. The horse was to be let down on his heels and hoof pads were applied to both fore-feet. To alleviate pain a supplementary course of corticosteroid therapy was administered over a period of six weeks.

Ultra-sonic treatment was prescribed to retard ossification and to assist absorption of the spur and microwave to assist in the pedal circulation.

Mr A, the physiotherapist, reports as follows:

I saw the horse in November 1971, in conjunction with the veterinary surgeon.

Various forms of palliative treatment for soft tissue lesions were tried with success.

We jointly saw the horse again in January 1972. Because of persistent heat the feet were X-rayed.

This confirmed the veterinary surgeon's fears and he passed the horse over to me for an intensive course of physiotherapy. Having previously dealt with similar cases using a combination of the normal treatment for gout and osteoarthritis I followed this pattern using ultrasonic microwave and interferential therapy.

The 'long slow exercise daily' prescribed by the vet was in the careful hands of Miss Sandra Kendall. Anthony Gillam gives her full credit. 'If he'd gone out with the others he'd have gone berserk, he was so fresh. So for two months Sandra hacked him quietly round the fields, quite on his own.'

So daily as winter reluctantly gave ground to spring Sandra and her Rummy rambled round the fields and quiet lanes together for hours. 'He loved that. I used to round up bullocks on him – anything like that. I used to go all over the place.'

'Eventually,' said Anthony Gillam, 'he came right.'

The vet from Hawick reported:

A prognosis was given that there was every reason for optimism and that he would eventually be able to give his normal performance when returned to work free from pain. By mid-February the condition was much improved and the horse recommenced training.

And the physiotherapist reported:

The veterinary surgeon re-examined the horse and recommended full training to be resumed.

Gillam had Red Rum shod in light steel shoes – 'I always race my horses in light steel plates, so we don't have to keep changing them as you do with aluminium plates'. Over both soles they nailed a protective leather-pad between shoe and hoof.

He ran the horse again at Catterick on 6 March 1972, and for the first time in his life Red Rum hit the deck. He was lying third, and being ridden along when David French (D. Atkins) who was leading, fell at the fourteenth fence and Red Rum, unable to avoid the sprawling body, tumbled over him.

Tommy Stack was very disappointed. He reported to Gillam, 'In no way would I have won.'

Gillam recalled, 'Tommy was very depressed. At that point he finally lost faith in the horse. It was a bad race and he was favourite and he should have trotted up. I said to Tommy. "Don't worry. It's not your fault. I don't think the horse is right." He was sound, but he just wasn't striding out.'

Gillam thought he had given the horse enough work to run him – 'but as it turned out, nowhere near enough to do himself justice. I would have given him lots more time,' said Gillam. 'But Mrs Brotherton was very keen to run him. If he'd been mine, I don't think he'd have run again that season. But that's a fault of mine. I'm too easy with horses.'

If Red Rum had not run again that season after his lameness he would either have stayed on with Gillam or he would have been sold for very little money. There would be few buyers the next August for a horse which had not run since January. The racing world and his wife would have known there was something gravely wrong with him. Who could have bought him?

After Catterick Gillam had the trainer's unenviable task of telephoning the bad news to the owner. Mrs Brotherton took it extremely well. She said, 'He was probably short of work. Better luck next time.'

But the Catterick accident had wrecked the plans for 'next time'. It had been the intention to imitate Dagmar Gittell and win the Topham Trophy with him round Liverpool. Earlier that season Tim Molony had come up to Gillam and said so himself. But now they felt they could not take to Liverpool for a first cut at those huge fences a horse who had just got knocked over. Furthermore, Stack reported after Catterick, 'He's lost all his speed'. Jockey and trainer conferred. 'We knew he stayed,' said Gillam, 'so we agreed to go for the Scottish 'National.'

Tommy Stack had, however, no retainer from Gillam's small stable: he simply had an arrangement that he would ride when he could. The Olivers from Hawick – Ken, 'the benign bishop' and co-founder of Doncaster Bloodstock Sales and his able and charming wife Rhona, now offered Stack the ride in the Scottish 'National on their grand mare Young Ash Leaf. Tommy accepted.

Mrs Brotherton suggested Josh Gifford's younger brother Macer. Macer therefore rode Red Rum at Nottingham in his next race. Macer commented in the paddock, 'He *is* a tubby little fellow, isn't he?' Gillam said, 'Well, yes, and I'm afraid the ground won't suit you either.' Nor would the distance: it was only two miles six furlongs.

The horse finished third to Nom de Guerre who had beaten him thirty lengths in their first race that season. This time, and on the same terms, Red Rum was only two and a half lengths behind. Gillam recalls, 'Macer felt that if he had kicked on hard from four out we might have won'. Confidence may have ebbed in Stack's mind; in Gillam's its tide was strongly turning. He felt the horse was on the way back. This was going to make the coming parting that much more painful.

In his last race before the Scottish 'National he ran such a good race at Wetherby in a £3000 'chase against three really good horses. Ballysagart, who won, Jomon (second) and Supermaster (fourth) that even Tommy Stack was impressed that Red Rum finished a close-up third; beaten two lengths and one and a half lengths. 'He ran a hell of a race,' said Gillam 'and on soft ground too. I was thrilled to bits and I thought we *must* have a chance in the Scottish 'National with only 9 st. 7 lb.' Well, yes, as the historians may drily note, for two years later he was to win it, a mere twenty-one days after winning his second English Grand National, carrying a 6 lb. penalty to make it 11 st. 13 lb. . . .

Unfortunately an airport strike stopped Macer Gifford flying up to Ayr. 'So I seemed stuck with no jockey,' said Gillam. 'But Martin Blackshaw made sure I saw him! He could do 9 st. 8 lb. without wasting, but he had only ridden in a few 'chases because he was fresh off the flat. He *rode* the horse beautifully. The only thing was that I said, "Stay close up and kick on from the *top* bend" but he must have misunderstood me, for he kicked on from the *bottom* bend and so tried to lead for all the last circuit.' Red Rum led to three fences from home and stayed on well to finish fifth about seven and a half lengths behind Quick Reply. Slave's Dream and Esban were second and third. Tommy Stack, well backed on Young Ash Leaf, was impressed by Red Rum's running.

Mrs Brotherton watched the race on the television. 'She played hell!' said Gillam. 'She said "If *only* he hadn't made so much *use* of him – " I defended the boy. We'd set off being laughed at: "What are you taking that useless horse up to the Scottish 'National for?" sort of thing. And we finished up leading over the third last, and bloody nearly wiping their eye!'

The judgement of two people who had observed Red Rum's running in this race now affected his future. The Scottish vet from Hawick watched his ex-patient all the way and noted quite clearly that in the last three-quarters of a mile, the horse kept changing legs. Plainly he was still feeling his foot. He observed, what was more, that over the last four or five fences Red Rum was jumping to the left every time, towards the rails (which is most unusual) and thus away from the damaged off-fore. He said to Gillam, 'He's still feeling his off-fore, I'm afraid,' and Gillam told Mrs Brotherton. Her gloom increased: there was still grave doubt about her horse's recovery. . . .

Trainer Donald McCain in his third season as a public trainer and still looking for his 'One Good Horse', had also watched the race. Knowing nothing of Red Rum's mid-season bone disease and being not too impressed by his jockey's tactics at Ayr, he made a strong mental note about the horse he'd first seen win a seller at Liverpool five years earlier. This, he thought, is a real stayer, a possible Grand National horse. If he was ever for sale, he thought, I'll mention him to Mr Le Mare. . . .

Red Rum ran only once more for Mrs Brotherton, Anthony Gillam and Sandra. Gillam says with his splendid honesty, 'I made a serious mistake by running him a fortnight later at Market Rasen. He was over the top. So he ran really badly behind rotten horses and finished fourth. He really did collapse.'

A blow of a more dreadful nature was now suspended over the stables. Mrs Brotherton had made her mind up. She was about to issue her edict.

25. 'The best proportioned horse you'll ever see'

One May day Mrs Brotherton told Anthony Gillam, 'I'm going to sell Red Rum'.

Gillam was horrified.

Mrs Brotherton said calmly, 'I've got to sell him, because he's the oldest'. Her other horses at Oxclose were either younger and thus with apparently more potential or had leg trouble and were therefore unsaleable.

To Sandra the news tolled like the knell of doom. 'Mr Gillam came and told me "I've got some bad news for you, Sandra. She's thinking of selling Red Rum." I just went potty,' Sandra exclaimed. 'I thought it was the last horse on *earth* they'd ever sell!'

She burst out at Anthony Gillam. 'That's it then, I'm going.'

Gillam said, 'He might not go'. Sandra looked puzzled. Hope flickered. Anthony explained. '*I* might buy him. I'll try.'

Gillam recalled, 'Every time I saw Mrs Brotherton during the summer I worked on her. Originally he was only going to have a 3000 guinea reserve at the sales. During June and July I was trying to get her to raise it to 5000 guineas. I thought I'd be nearly safe there. And I did have two buddies and we'd agreed we'd try to go into the horse together. Of course, we hadn't much money, and after a certain point we'd be beaten.'

Certainly the worry about Red Rum's feet was a contributing factor in Mrs Brotherton's final decision to sell. As her son David Brotherton understood it, looking back with a friend in 1974 over the fateful decision, ensuring that Red Rum got right might mean months more of expensive treatment: 'Thousands of pounds' were somewhat loosely mentioned.

Gillam himself placed 'a hell of a lot of significance' on what the Hawick vet had reported after watching the Scottish 'National, but Mrs Brotherton, said Gillam, was 'rather unsympathetic'. She didn't understand all of what was going on about the foot trouble. 'As far as she's concerned,' said Gillam, 'vets are sometimes eyewash! She thought Bobby Renton's old-fashioned remedies marvellous. But she thinks vets' bills are terribly expensive. However, this treatment proved to be a triumph for modern veterinary methods.'

She would not be alone. Vets' fees soar like inflated balloons. For some it is a matter of a quick glance at a horse's leg; squeeze – squeeze; tch-tch; 'poultice, Good Morning' – and that's eight guineas plus VAT plus mileage! One southern vet places upon the bonnet of his car a ticking clock, so that the trainer can both hear and see the golden guineas ticking away.

Like coalminers and express-train-drivers, equine veterinary surgeons have soared up the incomes league and up the social scale. They are no longer garbed as labourers, gumbooted, in old cords and patched coats. The top men can justifiably purr up in Jaguars in flannel suits dictating notes on tape recorders and calling their office on radio-telephones. These things have to be paid for by racehorse owners. . . .

'Quite frankly,' said Anthony Gillam, 'I didn't give Mrs Brotherton half the bills I had for Red Rum! I paid them myself.'

Ironically, the horse did better that summer at grass than he had ever done. Something kept telling Gillam that Red Rum was at last coming to himself. He kept front shoes on him in the field and kept his hooves well rubbed with Cornucrescine to promote new growth. When Red Rum came off grass at the start of July he looked magnificent. Much more important, when he started trotting along the roads he was absolutely sound. The doubts of the Scots vet rang in Gillam's mind, but the horse seemed cured. Gillam wanted to buy him, and he had these two friends with whom to share him. He asked the vet, 'Do you think he will stay right?' and got an uncertain answer. 'It's fifty-fifty, and if I was you,' advised the vet, 'I wouldn't spend too much money on him.'

Gillam concurred. 'Of course he was right. And I hadn't the money anyway. I did say he might be a 'National horse. But I never *dreamed* he'd be such an exceptional one. . . .'

To sell a horse at a fair price you must either send him to the sales with a vet's certificate, which gives a professional opinion of his soundness, or you must warrant the horse sound. Vets are growing very chary about signing certificates of soundness. They fear legal comebacks. Several partnerships now refuse to issue any. At Doncaster a horse sold either with a 'clean and unqualified veterinary certificate' or 'subject to re-examination' can be examined by a panel of vets in the sales paddocks at the request of the buyer (who pays £15) as soon as the horse is sold. The sale is contingent upon the horse passing the panel.

In Red Rum's case he was thoroughly examined at Oxclose, found to be completely sound, and his V S Certificate was announced when his entry was made for the sales.

The horse was entered in Doncaster's good August sales, their 'Great Annual York Race Sales', probably the best market in the British Isles for both made and prospective National Hunt horses. Because Mrs Brotherton was a well-known vendor, she drew an excellent place in the catalogue. The auctioneers in their offices in Hawick prepared Red Rum's particulars with their customary care. But they omitted from their printed copy one important piece of information and strong selling point. Red Rum had qualified himself for the Grand National, as one or two keen prospective buyers, like sharp-eyed Ginger McCain, could work out for themselves by going through the form-book and checking the value of his races won. But neither the sales catalogue nor the advertisements said that Red Rum was so qualified.

Nobody came to Oxclose to look at Red Rum before the sale and only a few people bothered to ring Gillam up about him. 'And they were only people who were curious, like Guy Cunard. I never had anybody sincerely interested.'

Gillam, like any trainer in danger of losing a horse he wanted to keep, found himself in an invidious position. He is a straight man and could not therefore even suggest to enquirers that there might have been anything gravely wrong with the horse during the previous winter. He had, moreover, to enthuse, against his own interests, about the horse's health and prospects.

The fact that Red Rum had not run for over two months would have looked more suspicious to the complete ignoramus than to the man who knew something. It was the usual case of a little knowledge being dangerous: those who knew a little about Red Rum had heard he hated soft ground, so they assumed he had not run in January and February for this excellent reason. Nor was it a question of his not having run since, a fact which would have deterred anyone. He might not have shone on his last race from Oxclose at Market Rasen, but he had finished fourth and sound. And a great number of people, Ginger McCain included, without the inside knowledge and thus the sharpened observation of the Scottish vet, had watched his Scottish 'National at Ayr on television, and thought how well he'd run. He *seemed* a hard, tough, sound horse.

Army training, which teaches the frequent senselessness of orders from on high, is good practice for modern state-meddling life. 'Upset?' repeated old Charlie Wright, reflecting in his potting-shed (for he was helping out in summertime in Mr Gillam's garden) on the departure of Red Rum. 'I've been in racing long enough not to get upset. You've got to get used to it, when horses have to go.'

Wright's old army notebook records, as the last entry against each of scores of his former charges, the sad order of their going: 'Sent to Mrs Mears Oct., '70 . . . Sold £900 Doncaster May, '72 . . . sent to Doncaster sales Aug., '70, sold £1700 . . . sent hunting . . . sent to flat . . . returned to owner . . . destroyed . . . lame after work, sold July, '67 . . . sent to Stud Paddocks, Destroyed June, '72 . . . Sold Doncaster . . . sent hunting . . . Destroyed . . .'

Sandra's love for Red Rum transcended Charlie Wright's reconciled philosophy. Mr Brian Miles, now her husband, had kept the nice house in Ripon waiting for her for six and a half years. 'Brian wanted me to get married. But I never would while Red Rum was there,' said Sandra, and so it turned out. This sort of priority may seem ludicrous to people unbitten by the horse bug. But the strength of Britain in all its horsey fields in show-jumping, Eventing, as well as in racing, is built upon people as passionate about the animals as Miss Sandra Kendall, now Mrs Miles.

She then received the final blow. She had suffered the

shock of hearing that her Rummy was going to be sold. The hapless Anthony Gillam now had to approach her with even more unpleasant news.

'They're not going to let you take him to the sales,' said Gillam. He was acutely embarrassed.

Sandra exploded, 'I've taken horses to those sales, and they've had the top prices for them! They've had top prices there for *rubbishy* horses. And they won't let me take Rummy.' She turned away.

It was her belief that another of Mrs Brotherton's flat-race trainers, Mick Easterby, had influenced Mrs Brotherton's decision. She went off immediately to telephone Mr Easterby. 'I told him what I thought. He said, "Have a drink". I said "I *won't* have a drink!" I went mad at him. I said to him, "I know as soon as I put this phone down you'll go and ring her up. So the best of luck".'

Sandra was not yet done. She strode off to find Mr Renton. He was quietly digging in his garden above the still waters of the dark canal. Sandra demanded, 'What's all this about?'

Bobby Renton replied, 'It's nothing to do with me. It's between the two of them.'

'Apparently I upset him,' she said two years afterwards. 'But it was the way they treated *me* after eleven years, that's what upset me. Years of hard work. I'd done them I don't know *how* many winners! But you're no better thought of. . . . This is why I cracked up. . . . I think Easterby rang Mrs Brotherton up and she rang Bobby up. So I went off down into Wales on a holiday with Brian.' Sandra blushed.

In Sandra's absence, Charles Wright took over Red Rum for his last week at Oxclose. On the Sunday evening before the sales, Anthony Gillam was sadly going round his horses. Bobby Renton was in the yard too. He had several times over the horse's four years at Oxclose remarked to Gillam that Red Rum was too small for a Grand National horse. That evening, however, he went into the horse's box and stood there staring agog at the bright bay. He called across the yard to young Anthony Gillam.

Old Mr Renton cried, 'Come here and look at this horse!' Gillam went into his box. Red Rum was in the straw standing, as Gillam too vividly recalls, 'just right and looking super.' The wise old trainer said to the young man with the emphasis of the elderly who, recognizing the shape of something immeasurable, try to pass on some yardstick before it is too late, '*You remember him*. . . . Because this is the most perfectly balanced and best proportioned horse that you'll ever see.'

The old man looked again at the horse and turned his gnomish eyes back again towards Gillam. The horse, oblivious of his fate, turned that splendidly bold head and fearless eyes towards the tall thin young man, and the little hunched old one. He was aware, as all animals are, of tension. It shimmered in the summer evening air.

'I *know* he is,' Anthony burst out in anguish, 'so why the something something are you selling him?'

Renton wagged his old head, 'Well, Mrs Brotherton says . . .' he began.

'And it was that night I got her to put his reserve up from 3000 to 5000 guineas,' said Gilliam. 'And at that I didn't think I'd lose him.'

26. 'Who's McCain?'

From Mrs Brotherton's point of view the luck of the sales ring ran sweetly for her. Bloodstock in the summer of 1972 was a soaring market. The absurd relation between the cost of a jumper and what it might earn had not impinged on steeplechasing's supporters. Like the millions who do their weekly football pools hoping for a miracle, the thousands of jumping owners and buyers realize that one horse each year wins the Grand National. Why not one year then it could be them. . . ? Money in those halcyon days was easily available.

Doncaster Bloodstock Sales which had started in 1962 were booming in their tenth year. They had turned over one million pounds in 1970 and were rising to a record of £2¾ million in 1973. Their Great Annual York Race Sales reflected this glitter. The turnover in 1971 had been 170 000 guineas; at Red Rum's sale it was going nearly to double at 320 000 guineas. The delusion of the British that one flourished because one borrowed was at its craziest height.

Mrs Brotherton was a regular seller. There seemed therefore nothing suspicious about her off-loading three of her older horses. Several of her weed-outs, as Sandra said, had sold well there in the past. The third senior partner in the sales company, Harry Beeby, son of the renowned ex-trainer George Beeby, is the most polished bloodstock auctioneer now operating. No one is more adept at making the good points in each Lot sound almost irresistible and then, when he has spotted a serious bidder, mesmerizing him with full conviction: 'Just your type, I know, sir,' delivered, bright-eyed and glossy-haired from a beseeching position, half-way out across his rostrum, so that it takes a hard unflatterable heart to deny Beeby that further nod which can cost you 100 guineas. That sensual combination of authority, flattery and the need for help, to which many women succumb, is equally effective in the skilled auctioneer.

As a vendor, it is one's good luck to have Harry Beeby selling your horses. Mrs Brotherton was lucky that August day in 1972. Beeby commented, 'Red Rum looked really well after the spring grass, and I believed that he would sell well, as he formed part – he was the first of the three

– of Mrs Brotherton's annual consignment. For some reason,' added Harry Beeby carefully, 'her horses-in-training always attracted a lot of interest.'

Harry Beeby is a friend of Anthony Gillam. He stays with Anthony and his wife 'Pandie' on his way south from Hawick. They had talked about Red Rum that summer after Mrs Brotherton's edict. Other people too asked Anthony if he had anything to sell. 'I'm losing my best horse,' he had replied with gloom.

Red Rum was placed at peak sales time, about noon on the first day. In Sandra's absence in Wales, he went off with a lad, behaved beautifully and, said Gillam, 'Looked super. I didn't stand by his box, so I didn't see McCain or any other trainers come to look at him. I stayed away as much as I could, because it was a sad day for us. Obviously I had to be loyal to Mrs Brotherton. But I also had my personal feelings.'

Gillam was hopeful that the new reserve of 5000 guineas which he had given to Harry Beeby would be too high for the horse to be sold and that Red Rum would return to him. He supposed that the highest bid for Red Rum would be about 4000 guineas. He had his reserve plan, however. His two friends William Owen and David McConochie shared a good young hurdler with him called Mountain Dew who won on the first evening of that new 1972–73 season at Market Rasen just before the sales. In doing so, however, he had 'got a leg', and would be out of action. His co-owners and Anthony now resolved that, should the bidding exceed Red Rum's reserve, they would then come in and go to 5300 guineas to try to buy him. It was as much as they could possible afford by sharing the horse in thirds.

Harry Beeby summed up his valuation. 'The horse had been in training from the very start of his two-year-old days. Although he was only a seven-year-old, he had been in action *a very long time*. Prospective buyers might have been excused for wondering whether he had had enough racing.' There is a racing euphemism here. The implication is that the horse may be getting fed up, and that he may be no longer genuine. Tommy Stack's opinion would be quite well-known.

So much for Red Rum's drawbacks. 'On the other hand,' Beeby continued, 'he was a proven stayer and a really good jumper and he'd run a marvellous race in the Scottish Grand National that April. *And,*' Beeby added quickly, 'he was qualified for the Grand National – a point which I brought out during the auction.'

Two years later even Harry Beeby could not recall all the bidders who had had a go at Red Rum that August morning – 'But I certainly remember there was no hesitation throughout.' The bids came swiftly and he capped them, one step up, as the price ran swiftly up towards the reserve. 'I believe Jack Doyle was in at some stage,' Beeby said, referring to that flamboyant dealer who rose from being a very small trainer indeed to controlling probably the biggest turnover of any one-man-band bloodstock agency.

Doyle bid up to his precise estimate of the horse's value. At 5000 Red Rum was on the market and in direct danger of going. 'I know that Anthony Gillam bid,' Harry Beeby remembered, 'as he was anxious not to lose him.'

There was another bidder now, standing in his accustomed place, tweed-capped Tim Forster of the mournful mien, who had once trained for Mrs Brotherton. He had another well-to-do and mature lady owner in Mrs 'Vi' Henriques, widow of that good author Robert Henriques. Captain Forster had done very well for Mrs Henriques. His training of the bad-legged Denys Adventure to win the Arkle 'Chase at Cheltenham was a triumph of patience over weakness. She was looking for another horse. He had spotted Red Rum in the catalogue and a less honest man would now declare that he picked him out and bid for him 'because I knew he'd win the 'National'. Not so, Captain Tim, racing's perpetual pessimist: 'I rather thought,' he said, 'that Red Rum would be a "fun horse", which we could run on hard ground at places like Ludlow, Worcester and Devon & Exeter. . . . I *did* wonder why Mrs Brotherton was getting rid, but I thought how rare it was to find any decent three mile 'chaser up for sale. I went to look at him in his box. I thought that he might be a bit small, a bit "flat racey", except that he'd *done* it. . . .' He meant the three mile 'chasing.

Mrs Henriques had about £5000 to spend on her 'fun horse' and though Tim Forster had not specifically mentioned Red Rum as a target, 'I knew at the back of my mind she'd have it.'

From the 5000 guineas point the bidding, like duelling swords, sparked left and right between Anthony Gillam and Tim Forster. But both were quickly running out of ammunition.

Watching them with hawkish eyes was a tall man with ginger hair who had learned the auction business in the hard world of second-hand cars. He had bought a few cheap horses in his time and bid in vain for expensive ones. In a last throw for a rich old man whom he had driven in his taxi he had been empowered to bid, for him, an enormous amount. With one exception (which cost £1500) no horse previously bought by Donald McCain of 10, Upper Aughton Road, Birkdale, Lancs, had cost more than £1000. Now he had up to 7000 guineas to spend to find a Grand National winner for Mr Noel Le Mare, son of a penniless missionary, who had made a fortune and was then approaching his eighty-fifth birthday. The 7000 guineas had not been enough to buy Kippie Lodge in a previous Doncaster sales. McCain had also failed in the past to buy for Mr Le Mare several other expensive horses which he had hoped might win a Grand National for his elderly patron. Fair Vulgan, for which Josh Gifford outbid him, was one.

He had told Mr Le Mare that he thought Red Rum would make 4 or 5000 guineas and Le Mare had said boldly, for he trusted McCain, 'Go to seven'. McCain planned to come in at 4000, because he believed that that was the horse's reserve price. Such was the first point of his technique. 'He went up steadyish,' said McCain, doing as he planned. 'Then at 5000 a new bidder came in.' We know now that this was the start of the Tim Forster–Anthony Gillam duel. 'That rather worried me. New bidders don't come in at that money just to drop out again. And with only 7000, I hadn't much margin. But the more I look at the horse going round, the more taken I am with him. And he gets better looking all the time!'

So McCain, the car-dealer, pulls a gambit he's often used successfully in the motor marts. He resolves in an instant to depth-charge the opposition by suddenly jumping the bidding upwards in a huge stride. Gillam had fallen out. Forster was weakening at 5500 and Harry Beeby's beady eyes are fixed on McCain's face. McCain holds up one hand spread out and the thumb of his other and mouths the word 'six'.

'*Six* thousand I'm bid,' announces Harry Beeby, quite astonished, but keeping surprise well-hidden in his pale face. He looks around. But McCain's car-dealing ploy has worked: he has torpedoed his rivals. Red Rum is his. 'It did the trick. We got him. I was delighted. And scared to death! Bar the one, it was six times more than I'd spent on any other horse in my life.'

Red Rum is led out and back to his box, but McCain has to stay in the ring a little longer, for he has orders to buy for Mr Rimmer, another patron of his – and at much more his sort of price – a horse of Ken Oliver's called The Tunku. (He's going to win with that, too, that season.) He buys him for 940 guineas and hurries round to the stable-yard where Red Rum is standing, waiting for his next move.

Anthony Gillam is hovering, desolate in Red Rum's box. Ginger McCain said with genuine sadness. 'Poor old Tony looked so sick. He looked really choked. I felt very bad about it, because I knew how I would feel if I had to lose a nice horse like him.'

Gillam asked, 'You've bought him, have you?' He asked McCain what he was going to do with him. McCain said, 'Win a few races, I hope'. Between the two of them the phrase 'a Grand National horse' emerged and hung in the air over Red Rum's bright intelligent head. McCain said, 'That's what I bought him for'. Gillam began, 'I'd always thought. . . .'

McCain remembered the sadness of the scene. 'Poor Tony was very upset about losing the horse and he said so. He said it was Mrs Brotherton's decision to sell, not his. I felt very sorry for him – a bit guilty really. He was very honest and open, and told me what he knew about the horse.'

Gillam recalled, 'I told McCain about his feet. I said, "Don't bash him on hard ground, because I don't think he'll stand up to it".'

And McCain remembered, 'He told me everything, how far on he was in his work and so on. And off Red Rum went home.'

Friends at the sale tried in vain to cheer up the miserable Gillam. No one there knew anything about the man McCain. Gillam did not even know what he looked like till he stepped into Red Rum's box. It is any trainer's dread that a horse which leaves his yard will improve so markedly in someone else's hands that his own deficiences as a trainer will be publicly laid bare. So Gillam's friends said to him in the grey and drab-red surroundings of the sales ring, 'Who's McCain? You've nothing to worry about there. Now if he'd gone to Walwyn, you'd have had sleepless nights. . . . But McCain!' exclaimed his friends, 'He's only got a few boxes behind a garage in some town!'

Anthony Gillam, however, was not reassured. That spring watching Aintree on the television he had had what he calls 'a premonition'. He watched a horse called

Glenkiln run in the Topham Trophy. 'The horse ran a stormer. And I knew that horse. He'd been with the Olivers. I was thinking of buying him at one time, but we all thought he'd got a "leg". But this McCain bought him for a Mr Le Mare and produced him to run in that Topham and to show such tremendous form. When I saw that night who McCain had bought Red Rum for, and read the name Le Mare, it all came back to me and I had this strange premonition again.' He knew then that McCain was not just a taxi driver, but what he could do, and that he *would* do well with the horse he had just lost.

Down in Wales the unhappy Sandra on her enforced holiday bought all the papers to find out whether her Rummy had been sold. When she read the awful news she said to faithful Mr Brian Miles, 'Well, Brian, we'll get married now, and I'll get out of racing.'

The sale of Red Rum broke Sandra's heart and finished her for racehorses for ever. It seemed a long time back to the days when schoolgirl Sandra, full of hope and happiness, rode up to kindly Mr Renton's place on her little pony Tammy.

27. 'My God! I've bought a lame horse!'

Red Rum crossed more than the Pennines when he left Yorkshire for Lancashire and for his fifth trainer in seven years. He moved from a drowsy yard in the country's quiet green heart to a tiny stable converted from a brewer's yard behind McCain's used-car showroom in a town's bustling side-street. The back-windows of tightly embracing houses peer down into the little cobbled oblong and its solitary tree. Half a gear-change away buses stop and traffic whines and hums. A few clickety-clicks and rumbles further and the trains from Birkdale clank across the level-crossing. Red Rum had moved to the wrong side of the tracks. The straight run of the street is completely flat and lacking in perspective. The stables lie within an amble of the sea, and some of the cold washed sea-light is reflected in the skies above Southport. Birkdale feels itself a superior suburb, but you would not expect much to be trained there except budgerigars and – in its tiny gardens – runner-beans. Nothing about the length of Upper Aughton Road suggests even the passing of a livery stable nag; the existence of steeplechasers behind the traffic seems surrealistic.

Rummy had changed his Sandra for a Liverpudlian lad. Miss Sandra Kendall of Ripon had tended and loved him for four years at Oxclose. Now Billy Ellison, born on 8 August 1945, took over. He was just twenty-seven when Red Rum arrived in the yard. Billy, square of body, square of face with that mop of square dark hair and squeezed-up naughty eyes became, through Red Rum, a nationally-known figure in the racing world. He admitted frankly that he was for years 'a layabout', and has had his troubles, too, with the law. His parents were, as he said, 'ordinary working-class people. Me father's a clerk and I was born very small. At fifteen I was only 6st. 12lb., so people said, "Why don't you go to be a jockey?" ' Doug Smith was a childhood hero: his life looked glamorous.

Billy rode the coal-merchant's pony, and hung around the local riding school. 'They helped me write to some trainers. I went off to Ron Barnes at Norley near Warrington. The head lad there was Johnny Handes, a little Irish bloke and very helpful. The first horse I ever looked after was an old horse called North Light. I used to run down to the village with a leading rein to meet the horses coming back from exercise. Then I'd be put up on North Light and Johnny would lead me back.'

Such was the manner of young Billy Ellison's riding instruction. He 'did his two', stayed five years with Barnes and rode in four races. He was second in his first race – one-and-a-quarter miles on the flat at Redcar – riding Th' Boggart. 'Never forget it – jet-black horse – butterflies in me stomach – the owner had £100 each way on us at 8–1. I was beaten half a length. He give me drink afterwards. But Ron Barnes told me off. He said I should've won. One season I was there we had twenty-three winners from fourteen horses!'

Billy was smitten by his first sight of jump racing. It was at Liverpool, where he had taken a horse he did, Cold Comfort, to win the seller there on the flat, the same sort of race for which Red Rum subsequently deadheated on his first sight of the famous steeplechasing track. 'I saw Josh Gifford win there and it seemed much more fun watching a horse go for two miles over flights of hurdles than a five furlong flat race – if you drop your race-card in a flat race by the time you pick it up it's all over! I liked the class of people with the jumpers too.'

So Billy went off to work for Frank Mason, who farmed at Little Budworth, near Tarporley in Cheshire, and had been training since 1936. 'Didn't go with the intention of riding. Actually I got married there for the first time.' He was married again in 1974, after a lively interval. For five months every summer Billy worked nightly in the bar of the local Pontin's Holiday Camp.

He used to ride out for Don McCain 'for a quid a morning when I was a bit of a layabout and he was just a permit trainer'. McCain interposed, 'One morning after the end-of-season party at Pontin's – it never stops for two or three days – Billy was late for First Lot. He arrived swaying and grey. I said "Don't ride that good horse!"'

Billy grinned wickedly. 'Best thing in the world is that beach after a hangover! First time I rode on the sands I thought, "If we get run away with here it'll take six miles to pull up."

'I'd kept in touch with Mr McCain, so when I was separating from my wife and wanted to get back from Cheshire to Southport – 'cos it's close by home – I went up to him at Haydock races and asked him for a job. It was 1969, the first year he had a full licence.'

Billy was doing Glenkiln, the first horse McCain bought for Mr Le Mare in the hope of winning a 'National, so the young lad saw the elderly owner (who in his youth had been a bold lad, too) several times around the yard. 'I won "The Guinea for the Lad" from "*The Racehorse*" for Glenkiln,' said Billy rightly proud of the way he turns his horses out. 'We heard the Guv'nor was going to the sale to buy another 'National horse for Mr Le Mare, owing to old "Glen" not being qualified then.' Of which dire administrative blunder more later. . . .

'I'd just finished stables and I heard the horse-box arrive and Jackie Grainger, the head lad, walks into the yard with Red Rum. Aye! God! He did look super! An' I thought "I'd love to do that!" '

Derek Critchley, a nice young 'claiming' lad then in the yard who held a jockey's licence, had been given several rides on Golden Blue, one of Billy's horses. Critchley had brought Red Rum back from Doncaster sales and so it seemed that he would 'do' him. Billy said slyly, 'Derek was hopin' for a few more rides on Golden Blue, so I offered him Golden Blue back for me to do Red Rum.'

So it was that Billy Ellison came to do a horse which in his first two seasons under his care won twelve races and was placed five times from only nineteen starts and earned £65 666 for his extremely generous owner. . . . Vincent Brooks from Fred Winter's yard, nicknamed 'the luckiest lad in racing' because he does Bula and Pendil, had had his position usurped.

Billy was thrilled with his swap. 'I knew the horse had some useful form, so next day I went across the street to

Steve Makin, the bookie, and got all his form-books out and studied them.' As with a company's balance-sheets and profit figures, you can read a lot into and out of the form-book. Billy Ellison is a carefree optimist, who keeps coming up, bouncing. He had just manoeuvred young Critchley into handling over this smashing new horse. He devoured Red Rum's form with soaring enthusiasm. 'It was fair old form and tho' he'd cost six times more than any other horse in the yard I couldn't understand why he was so *cheap*!'

Two days later, the first time Red Rum came out of his box, everyone in the yard thought they knew. Robin Greenway (son of McCain's vet, Ted Greenway of Little Budworth) came to the yard to ride out. He had ridden Glenkiln an easy winner at Cartmel in an amateur race at the very end of the previous season, and was due to ride him again shortly at Hexham.

Don McCain, overjoyed by his expensive new acquisition, put Robin Greenway up on Red Rum. Trainers with new horses are like children with new toys or boys with new girls: they need their friends to admire them. They walked down through the town to the beach.

'And as soon as we start to trot out on the beach,' says McCain, still appalled in recollection of the scene, 'Red Rum is lame. Without any doubt at all, he is going short. I thought, "My God! I've bought a lame horse!" Yet his legs were like bars of iron. I felt *sick*. I shouted, "Bugger off with him into the tide then!" The others worked and cantered. Red Rum just walked about in the sea. 'And when he came out of the water,' said McCain, fixing me intently to convince me of the miracle, *'he trotted sound*! Mind you,' McCain ended cautiously, 'horses do do that – with the cold water taking out the pain – and then get worse again after. But I think the horse has never been lame since, except the day after his first 'National when he'd struck into himself.'

McCain still winces at the narrowness of that squeak.

'We just started to go steady with him. I said, "We'll take it more quietly". We've never trotted him on the roads from then on for two reasons. One, he's a bright fellow and he could slip. The other, he might jar his feet.'

Billy chipped in, 'He doesn't *like* jogging on roads. He'd *rather* walk. He's different on the beach. Down there he'll still give a buck and a kick.'

Miles away in Scotland the clever vet who had diagnosed Red Rum's foot trouble and prescribed with the physiotherapist the right cure for it in Yorkshire, marvels at the luck by which the horse, out of all the stables in Britain, happened on one by the seaside. He says bluntly, 'Red Rum would have been *unraceable* without treatment – I'm a great believer in ultra sonics, they're the thing of the future – but I was *not* happy when I saw the horse changing feet in the Scottish 'National, as if they still hurt him.' He said, 'That off-fore foot is *still* contracted and shallow. So if he wasn't going to continue our treatment, where could he get something like it? In the sea. Sea water is a great thing, cooling off after exercise, stimulating the circulation. . . .'

Ginger McCain had not known the well-kept secret about Red Rum's generally incurable pedalosteitis, though he had made, as we shall see, several enquiries via a friend for whom jockey Stack rode. McCain remembered though, as a child, watching those broken-down old horses pulling the shrimping-carts through the tide off Southport beach and returning after two summers miraculously sound. 'All cripples and crocks,' says McCain, 'and after a couple of seasons – perfect legs!'

Mrs Brotherton's son, discussing in the summer of 1974 the equally miraculous cure of Red Rum, made the point to a friend, 'Of all the hundreds of people who could have bought him, it just happened to be a man who had only the beach to train on!'

And Mrs Sandra Miles that same summer recalled a single event when old Bobby Renton was training Red

Rum, the significance of which was ignored at the time, because only in retrospect has it become pike-staff plain.

'Once – and only once – when Rummy was at Oxclose, he went to Redcar Sands. He went with two other horses. Bobby had had a strip properly harrowed by the people on Redcar racecourse. We saddled up on the racecourse and rode down to the sands, Tommy Stack, my brother Walter and me. Mr Renton stood on the beach to watch us. We cantered two miles down, then turned to gallop the two miles back. I was in front. At first Tommy kept calling out to me several times, "Sandra! Can't you go any faster?" I shouted back "I can't! I can't!" But,' said Sandra, eyes amazed, 'when I got to the end of the gallop I was that far in front that I'd pulled up, turned round and *walked back to Mr Renton*, before the other two horses had reached him!'

Everyone had been instantly astonished by this extraordinary performance by Red Rum. It is, of course, now plain that the horse relishes galloping on sand, that he needs time to warm up (Sandra had guessed this in her criticism of some of his jockeys) and that the further he goes the more powerfully does he travel. Would five miles be too far for him to race? It is obvious now that he required miles more cantering first and then twice as much galloping on sand than he would ever find on ordinary gallops. It is probably true, too, that he delights in the wide spaces of the beach, that his spirit rejoices by the wild wintry sea, and that he works phenomenally well there because of it.

He never went back to the sea again during all those four years at Oxclose. It was difficult to get to Redcar sands. It took one and a half hours in Pickersgill's horse box. The amazing gallop that Red Rum had done there was soon forgotten, not to be remembered until a new season of fabulous victories had come, and the racing world was asking 'What has this man McCain, this taxi-driver, done to make Red Rum so marvellous?'

Primarily it is the beach and the sea. And if Don McCain, for whatever reason, had to move Red Rum from his miles of soft sand and the cold splashing sea, then I do not believe that the horse would be as good again.

28. 'I was absolutely brilliant with a catapult'

The man McCain, whom hardly anyone in racing knew when he bought Red Rum, has lived nearly all his life in Birkdale. He was conceived just over the road from his present stables and born five hundred yards away. Bar his army service and jobs with horses in Cheshire, he has never moved away. Born a townsman, brought up in streets, he has yearned all his life to be a countryman. His wife Beryl surmises, 'He'd really have liked to be a gamekeeper.'

He is not sure whether his blood is originally Scots or Irish, but something in it, as often happens in the urbanized citizens of our island, yearns for nature and country things and animals. Horses are McCain's magic carpet out of the grey streets into the green fields. 'My life's ambition is to live in the country. I've always wanted to. I've never had a lot of opportunity to – getting a living – but I have a thing about badly wanting to own some land of my own.' He adds with that steely intent of purpose: 'And I will do.'

The yearning did not come directly from his parents. His father worked for forty years in the despatch department of Marshall & Snelgrove's. 'He plays about with pigeons,' said Ginger affectionately, who used to race pigeons himself. Bill and Sally McCain live in Liverpool Road, Birkdale, and mind Ginger and Beryl McCain's two children Joanne and Donald when needed. 'My mother,' said Ginger, 'still treats me like a small child.' He has two sisters (one a nursing sister at Eastbourne) and one younger brother. 'Father comes back after the war from the air force and, of course, there's another brother, sixteen years after me!'

Birkdale still enjoys the ranking of being Southport's smartest suburb – those wide and leafy avenues and richly garden-girt Victorian houses still wear slightly superior smiles. But McCain says dourly, 'Some of Birkdale's smart right enough. It's also had the muckiest slums ever.'

Ginger, born on 21 September 1930 – the year of Red Rum's breeder – was a schoolboy in the war. With his father away in the RAF and his mother working on munitions – 'Sometimes days, sometimes nights, obviously they didn't have a lot of control. And with the war on, if you didn't go to school, they didn't chase you very hard.'

Ginger spent most of his schooldays with dogs. 'I've always had a whippet or decent coursing dog – Waterloo Cup's only just down the road, eight miles away. I used to go there as a boy as a beater for 7/6d a day.' He did a tremendous amount of poaching: 'Pheasants, rabbits and hares – mainly with dogs and I was absolutely brilliant with a catapult! We made our own.'

In wartime Lancashire horses and ponies of every sort trotted down every street. The grey roads of Birkdale clattered with tradesmen's carts. 'The Cooperative Dairies had about forty horses on the road. The laundry had two dozen horses. The dustcarts were pulled by heavy horses. The tradesmen, the butchers and bakers, had tremendously smart little outfits.' McCain's mind's eye sees those spinning wheels, the bits a-jangle, and he hears again the squeak and creak of leather harness.

His grandfather drove two horses in a cart delivering goods for a provision company. When Ginger was thirteen, his grandfather had an accident, and the schoolboy played truant to do his job. 'It was the horses that attracted me. I used to ride them bareback down to the blacksmith's forge and in the summer we used to ride them around the fields.' It sounds like a picture of Edwardian England. But it was only thirty years before Red Rum won his first Grand National.

Young Ginger longed to have a pony of his own. His grandfather was always saying, 'I'll buy you a pony.' So the boy built a shed for the pony at the bottom of the garden. The pony never came. His grandfather's promise was not kept. In McCain's voice now there lingers still the trace of an acrid tang. His face suddenly takes on its grim, forbidding, fortress look. Much of our adult motivation springs from childhood's frustration. Much of McCain's burning – and often financially crippling – desire to own horses, sprang from his grandfather's broken promise and the little empty shed waiting in vain at the bottom of the garden.

Young McCain took lots of jobs: 'milk boy on the milkcart, perch-boy on the theatre working the arc-lamps, and worked in a confectioners where I hated every minute. And I made a living fishing and poaching – which I loved.' A family friend started a riding-school and offered Ginger lessons. 'I think I was only on the leading-rein once, and then I went on the beach.' So he must have had a knack. He was very keen, and soon advanced into a good young rider, for when he was fifteen a local butcher asked Ginger to ride his horses. 'Arty Edwards was his name – bald-headed fellow and a tremendous character. He had show-jumpers and did a bit of dealing.'

Ginger jumped Mr Edwards' horses in the cemetery behind the butcher's stables. 'He had a sharp little pony which could really stop. One day he stopped with me so quick he put me off right into a gravestone. I was knocked out dizzy, and I came round feeling a bit sick lying on the gravel by this gravestone. I can remember this "*Rest in*

Peace" bit gradually looming into focus just above my head.'

Arty Edwards used to enter his butcher's van and hackney horse called The Colonel at all the district shows which then abounded. He had seen a hackney show-jumping, so he said to young Ginger, 'Here, you get up on The Colonel.' Ginger said, 'The super old horse had never been sat on in his life. I climbed up and he just stood there, trembling. We got him going finally – a tremendous ride, but only trotting! He wouldn't canter.'

McCain's first sight of a racehorse was riding out with Frank Speakman's stables near Tarporley. The place remained a sort of dream. Years later he would drive his wife around that part of Cheshire, breathing it in and trying to infuse her with the delight that countryside and those horses had once granted him. He schooled an old hunter over hurdles with them on an airfield. And then quite suddenly he lost all interest in horses. He bought a motor bike and started racing it. He spent all his time in the army on motor bikes – 'I enjoyed every minute of it and thought seriously of signing on'.

But he left the army when his time was up, and decided to spend the summer at home 'fiddling my time away. But they got me a job via the local labour exchange – in a wallet factory.' Sometimes a phrase uttered in kindness intending to open a door to a happy future, unintentionally becomes instead a portent of doom (if you recognize it) and a sudden glimpse of hell. If you observe it, and turn the other way, the course of your life is altered.

So it happened to McCain at the wallet factory. 'Look after this job,' the man said to him, 'And you've got a job for life.'

McCain recalled, 'I thought what the hell's it got to do with him – the thought of a job for life in a wallet factory was diabolical!' He saw the gloom through that door and immediately noticed, for such is life, the opening of another. 'On the Saturday morning someone came to the house and said Frank Speakman wanted a man to work in his stables. I had my bags packed and I was gone to Tarporley that afternoon. I never gave notice to the wallet factory. I was working with horses again for £3 a week and my keep. And when I was twenty-one I got £3 10s. because I rode schooling. I did three horses in a small yard of sixteen to eighteen horses, picking up the racing side of things from the senior boys. I was as happy then as I have ever been in my life.'

He was not too old at twenty-one – for he is a romantic – to have heroes to worship. 'Dick Francis and Tim Molony used to ride for us. They were so special to me. I'd been around a bit, but I still thought this was all absolutely marvellous.'

Then his weight beat him. 'I was 11st. 7lb. to 12st. Too big and getting bigger. . . . So I went a mile down the road to Mrs Chambers who owned a hunting and point-to-pointing stable.'

He learned a lot there about horse management from the stud groom, old Jack Cook then over seventy, who had been stud groom to a Duke of Westminster. 'Marvellous old fellow, rather like Pickwick, very round, very red face. He always wore a black apron, breeches and a stock.

'I was happy enough there,' said McCain, 'For a time. . . .'

At this vital point in his life McCain was rising twenty-three and the course of his life was veering away from racing. He could never be a jockey. He was too heavy now even to work in racing stables as a lad. He might have jogged along in the hunting world a little longer when something happened, half way through his second season at Mrs Chambers which booted him, temporarily, out of the horse world all together. 'I got into a bit of trouble with a girl and came home and got a job working for a local taxi firm.' Ginger McCain is a tall, dashing-looking fellow now. He was certainly a gay dog then.

McCain, driving his taxi, missed the horses, but he was never bored. 'I was meeting people all the time and getting tips. I could always go out with a pound in my pocket.' Then his firm decided to close. McCain borrowed some money – 'I took the car out on HP, got a telephone, went in with a friend, and took over.'

To anyone with only a casual interest in horses McCain's sudden switch of jobs would seem certain to have put him out of the racing world for ever. But if you are as hooked on horses as some people are on more harmful things, then you simply cannot do without them. Driving a taxi, too, may seem to combine oddly with owning a racehorse, let alone training one. McCain did not think so. If he could not work with racehorses, he resolved to buy one.

So, in addition to the taxi, he now acquired his first racehorse. 'I couldn't go back to riding rubbishy horses.' The horse, Scottish Humour, was one he had 'done' at Frank Speakman's. The horse had been placed on the flat and over hurdles. He would turn out later to be a half-brother to the great Irish 'chaser Flyingbolt, who one year was challenging his stablemate Arkle. But Flyingbolt was not yet around, and his elder half-brother Scottish Humour had not only 'got a leg', but was tubed. McCain, taxi-driver, and now taxi-owner bought him from Mr Speakman for £25 to include the tube, a sweat rug and a head collar.

That was the start of McCain the trainer. And as to it being an odd job to share with taxi-driving, time would splendidly reveal that it was only by driving a taxi that McCain could meet and talk to rich men who, captive audiences, must listen to his passion for racing and perhaps echo it. One of these, he imagined dimly, might one day entrust him with his One Good Horse. It was the vaguest of lovely dreams: the rich man, the shared interest, the faith, the purchase, the winning of the Grand National. . . . He did not know that one such elderly person was really living a few furlongs away from him in a big house on the good side of the railway line, and nursing a sixty-year-long dream of winning the Grand National.

McCain had to make a beginning. No one who subsequently became a trainer of fame, can have started any lower at racing's roots than with one tubed, broken-down old racehorse in a rented stable in an unlikely street. McCain rented a box in Westbourne Road. Months passed, the horse's leg improved and McCain thought, 'Why not run him?' He applied for a permit to train and got it. He had told himself he had wanted a racehorse to *ride*, but the wish to race one was nudging him on.

He started his racing career in officially unrecognized 'flapping' races, the way Brian Fletcher began beyond the Pennines. McCain's jockey was a local man, Jackie Grainger, later his head lad, born in Southport in 1917 and who, like Ginger, had been a lad at Frank Speakman's out at Tiverton, near Tarporley. With Jackie Grainger on board, Scottish Humour set out for the unauthorized race-meetings. 'They were just tracks on the outside of football fields,' says McCain, still somewhat sheepish about those activities, involvement in which technically bars you from performing under the Rules of Racing.

The flapping races were run in heats and on a track beyond Manchester the horse and Jackie Grainger *'murdered* the opposition. Somebody started squealing about professional horses and professional jockeys. We'd had a few bob on,' says Ginger. I was standing on the top of the gents toilet, which was a tin shed, to watch the final. Jackie wins it and never even stops. He gallops up to me and roars "Come on! Let's get off! Else we're in trouble!" I go to move. And these bloody miners are after me and the tin roof flew off the shed. . . . Somehow we got to the box and the horse into the box and off we went – never drew the money or anything.'

Grainger also drove the box part-time for McCain. 'Then Don asked me to come as head lad.' He accepted cheerfully and went to Doncaster 'to fetch Red Rum home.' Jackie Grainger has a splendidly gravelly Lancashire voice. He added sardonically, 'When I first saw Red Rum I thought he was too good lookin' to leave Mrs Brotherton's!'

Old, tubed Scottish Humour was the first of many racehorses he was going to ride work on for McCain. Frank Speakman's bad-legged reject was the first racehorse Ginger McCain owned and, if you count 'flapping' round football pitches, his first winner. The horse taught him several things of lasting value (there's no better way to start than with cheap and dicey horses – you have to be good to keep them sound), and literally by accident one essential pre-requisite about using the beach for galloping. If this accident had not befallen him, he might never have struck upon the secret of training on sand. When McCain was getting the horse ready to run under Rules a friend came to gallop him on the beach. 'In those days we didn't harrow the sand first.' McCain watched his horse galloping with those of another local permit holder. Then he saw him suddenly falter, drop right out and pull up. The horse had partially severed his tendon on a piece of broken glass left on the beach. 'He never quite came right after that,' says McCain. 'And he was a grand sort of horse and a damn good ride.'

From that day on McCain always harrowed a strip to clear it of dangerous débris. And so it turned out – for such is the luck of this story – that the deeply harrowed strip obviated other disadvantages of galloping on unprepared, hard, ungiving, wearying damp sand. . . .

29. 'I got a crush on him when he was down the stables'

If Don McCain's training had not hit the double jackpot in 1973 and 1974 and put his name among the famous, it would have been a justifiable criticism to say that from 1952 onwards he was trying to participate in a rich man's sport without the money, the amenities, the contacts, the background, or any real hope of success. McCain, however, even when occasionally broke, went steadily on, hoping.

Additionally, because he had perforce to buy other people's rejects with money he hardly had, he found himself with problems with every horse. He had to work swiftly to cure them too, for each bowl of corn was coming painfully out of his pocket. A young man from a racing background might spend years as pupil to a grand trainer with a yard full of good, sound horses, without learning as much as McCain did in months with his equine jetsam. Nor would they have heard whistling behind them the sharp crack of poverty's whip.

McCain the taxi-driver had put in years with horses of sorts. When he won at the 'flapping' meetings Anthony Gillam was five years old, Tim Molony was champion jockey and was eight years away from starting training, and Tommy Stack was a seven-year-old in Co. Kerry. Experience McCain had, successes very few; but hope abounding. The whole edifice of steeplechasing in Britain rests upon the under-financed but optimistic and resilient shoulders of hundreds of little permit trainers like the Don McCain of the years between 1952 and 1969. Money is being spent on horses which their loving owner-trainers cannot afford. Like McCain, they are learning the hard way, striving towards some humble target like their local selling race one Bank Holiday: (total cost of three years' endeavours: £3500; value of race £190). Like McCain, they are hoping for One Good Horse, though only one of the hundreds once in a decade will find it. Without hope, no racing.

Like McCain, struggling owner-trainers will run into trouble from wives who believe, as Beryl McCain did, that furniture and food and somewhere to live are rather more important than buying clapped-out racehorses, everyone else's discards, who cost cruelly hard cash to keep.

Beryl met Ginger when she was sixteen and says she 'Had a crush on him'. They met at the local riding school, Miss Walsh's in Southport, less than a quarter-mile from their present home between the motor show-room and the stable-yard. When Beryl left the local technical college (doing secretarial work) she got a job in an accountant's office very near Birkdale station. Outside the station sat Ginger in his taxi. And so she noticed him.

'The very first time I spoke to him was in a friend's house. I said to my friend, "There's that fellow that goes down to the stables, do you dare me to say hello to him?" She said, "yes, go on". So I said "hello" and he said "hello, there", and he'll tell you now he thought "who's that cheeky young girl?" I got a crush on him when he was down the stables – all the kids used to act the fool!' Miss Kath Walsh was, says Beryl, 'A bit of a figure-head, all the children around looked up to her.'

One day Beryl was ridng a friend's thoroughbred mare and Ginger and taxi-partner, Jeff Langhorne (who had once been head lad in a racing-stable), saw her go past. The friend could not afford to keep the mare herself, so Jeff and Ginger offered to put the mare in training for Beryl's friend under Ginger's permit. Young Beryl continued to ride her. 'I had to sit as still as a mouse on her back when she started to get filled up with corn, and she was so headstrong she'd make your hands bleed!' The mare ran unsuccessfully over hurdles and fences, but enabled Beryl to see a lot of Ginger. 'We weren't engaged, and my parents were still rather against him. When he picked me up, he used to just hoot, and I'd run down the path. Oh, there were lots of trials and tribulations!'

Jeff Langhorne and Ginger then split up their taxi business, though they were to remain friends for years – until they fell out over Jeff's daughter Christine who came to work in Ginger's yard.

Ginger took the taxis to Miss Kath Walsh's riding-stables and she became his new partner. Beryl comments, 'I was hoping to get engaged, and Ginger kept wanting to buy horses – and he didn't really have any money.'

Beryl was made responsible for exercising Kara Valley, a mare Ginger had bought for £50. She was working in the Borough Architect's Office, so got up at six, bicycled to the stables, rode Kara Valley, bicycled back, worked all day at her desk, and then every evening went down to the riding school in order to see Ginger who was running his taxis. Beryl pressed the idea of getting engaged. 'He wasn't very keen on the idea of marriage,' she says. Kara Valley became a portent. 'If she doesn't run well at Haydock,' declared Ginger McCain with more realism than romance, 'we'll get engaged.' Horses then, ruled his heart. It is the major reason he was good with them.

Kara Valley ran poorly. Ginger was as good as his proposal. 'Right,' he said, 'we'll get engaged on Grand National Day, 1959.'

'So,' says Beryl, 'we went to the 'National, and had an engagement party that evening. He had a job to get the money together to buy an engagement ring – I chose it myself, he was never any good at that sort of thing. And I said to him "When'll we get married?" he said "Two years," thinking it a long time off, "we'll get married on Grand National Day, 1961." '

This involvement with the Grand National may seem too good to be true. It is an element, of course, of what old Bobby Renton called Red Rum's 'fairy tale'. But there are two significant factors. First, it had been in McCain's mind from childhood, as it had been in Le Mare's, 'to have a go at the 'National'. The race, dominating their dreams, became the milestone of the year. Secondly – and this surprises southerners – in north-west England there *is* only one race all year and that is the Grand National. The Derby down at Epsom is ranked a distance behind.

The local bookie, Steve Makin, balding with huge, high eyebrows and gapped teeth, knows that only too well. He paid out £2600 in bets down the street the Monday after Red Rum's first 'National, and £50 000 altogether. 'He's the greatest horse in the world,' he says grinning as if he'd just come from a painful bout with the dentist. 'But I just wish he lived somewhere else. Up here, the 'National, not the Derby, is *the* race of the year.'

Looking back on his engagement Ginger recalls, 'I thought two years would be a long time, and then it slipped by, and all of a sudden you're under orders!' They'd got engaged and watched Oxo win the 'National. They got married and watched Nicolaus Silver win it. They spent their honeymoon in Newmarket.

Horses came and went. They were living in a couple of rooms on £5 a week. The flat cost £2 1s. 'We lived on Gingers' odd silver that came in from taxi-ing every day.' They looked after an old horse called Home Chief, owned by a friend who held the trainer's permit, ran him at Cartmel and he won, and so became another unrecognized 'first winner' for Don McCain. After Beryl and Don had been married for eighteen months Miss Walsh decided to end the taxi partnership. 'We panicked,' says Beryl. 'We had nowhere to go. Coming back up the road from the riding-school there was this little showroom for sale, about fifteen foot wide and twenty foot deep with a couple of rooms over it. They wanted £2500 for it.'

Beryl had ben saving her wages at the rate of £40 a month. She had £1400 saved – 'no other security.' The estate agent said, 'We'll go and see the manager of the

Westminster Bank in Manchester. He's a man who judges a person himself, whether he'll back you.' Beryl says, 'And he did. He thought we were sincere and would make a go of it.'

They obtained the loan and took the place (it adjoins where they now live), and started the taxi-business from there with very little furniture. 'We were working all the hours God makes,' says Beryl, 'driving those taxis, building up the clientèle . . . then Ginger got this enquiry about San Lorenzo . . .' Beryl sighed deeply. It had nearly meant the parting of their ways.

San Lorenzo belonged to a corn merchant in Southport. He had once been a good horse winning races for Neville Crump and George Owen and owned by Major Ainscough. But he was now old, and with bad legs. He was in Ireland with Aubrey Brabazon. The corn merchant had intended to have his old horse put down but now offered him instead to Ginger McCain. Beryl said, 'We can't afford it'.

Ginger said, 'Well, I'm going to have it'.

Beryl remembers, 'I tried everything, but as much as I argued – he was adamant. I remember sitting by the fire with my head in my hands and crying. I tried telling Ginger that if that horse came, I'd go.'

Ginger said bluntly, 'All right. Get your bags packed. He's on the boat.'

Beryl reflects, 'I don't think I could have left. The horse arrived. I didn't speak to Ginger for a week. I wouldn't go to see the horse. He was kept in an old stable at the back of a pub.'

Eventually Beryl went to see San Lorenzo. She is a generous-hearted woman and bears no grudges. She says with real pleasure, 'He was a nice bright bay, a super animal.' He was headed – where else? – but for Don McCain's beloved Liverpool.

Thirteen hard, depressing, failing years after Mr D. M. McCain of Southport first took out his permit to train, the fourteen-year-old broken-down San Lorenzo turns out at Liverpool on Saturday, 2 January 1965.

Beryl and Ginger, still struggling along, are coming up to their fourth wedding anniversary.

On the evening before the race Ginger and Beryl picked up one of their regular customers, a Guinness-drinking clairvoyant called Suzy, whom they used to collect from a pub every night at twenty-past ten. That evening Suzy said, 'Ginger, I think you're going to have a winner'.

Ginger declared, 'If the horse wins, Suzy, you can have free drinks all night'.

Beryl had been out with a friend to an Indian restaurant in Manchester and felt so desperately ill on the day of the race that she thought she would miss it.

Ginger had another type of problem. Normally he put an amateur up on his horse to save paying the jockey's fee. This time a professional, Robin Langley, asked McCain if he could ride old San Lorenzo in the selling 'chase. McCain borrowed a fiver from a friend in a pub to pay the fee. And San Lorenzo, disputing the lead to the seventh fence in the Burscough Selling Handicap Steeplechase of £192 run over 2 m 80 yds. and ridden off at 12.45 p.m., went ahead on the flat and won, hard-ridden, by half a length.

'He trotted up,' declares McCain. And there, for posterity, is Red Rum's trainer's first official winner. The name of the race oddly foreshadowed Red Rum. It is at Burscough that he spends his summer holidays.

Successful trainers start in different ways. Fame has a thousand beginnings. But can any other trainer have started after thirteen years of failures with one selling 'chase winner? Would not the Average Man, beloved by doctrinaires, have years ago given up what must have seemed, after even a few seasons, a hopeless, ridiculous struggle? But McCain, like our hero, was made of tougher metal. As Noel Le Mare had been taught as a child, as Red Rum had also been learning the hard way and as

Ginger McCain was finally to prove, it's a question of 'Try, try, try again'.

No one, however, over those early years, was more sorely tried than young Mrs Beryl McCain.

30. 'You're starving your wife and kids almost – that's horses for you'

Empty though the horse side proved, their motor business improved. There was a little money now to buy the odd 'banger' for resale at a profit. But a succession of bad old horses came and went, driving Beryl to distraction as Ginger was driven to hope. They quarrelled. They went to sales and Beryl sat across the ring, crossing her fingers and praying Ginger wouldn't get the animal for which he was bidding.

He went to Ascot sales, and rang Beryl on the way home. She said immediately, 'You've bought a horse, haven't you?' When he said, 'Yes,' she put the telephone down.

He had paid 340 guineas for a huge horse called Caspian by Crepello. He remembers the call. 'When she rang off, I muttered, "Well, sod you!" And then I had to drive all the way back from Oxford thinking of the slating I was going to get.

'It's been a struggle all the time,' says Don McCain. 'Beryl's wanted a home – which she's quite entitled to. She's wanted to live comfortably. But that's all you've got,' McCain bursts out, 'if you've got nothing else.' He means the dreams. He justifies himself, 'If you're young you can stand a bit of hardship.' He justifies his pursuit of success: 'Caspian was second first time out at Ludlow and a fellow offered me £1000 for him, and I, silly bugger, didn't take it.'

The horse never again gets placed. Beryl, against her inclinations, becomes pregnant. She was still working for the Borough Architect by day and riding out in the morning. The horses were out in rented stables on a farm. Beryl had been 'doing' the horse and towing the trailer, and at one stage when she was running a horse at Uttoxeter she stayed in very humble digs: 'I heard all these hob-nailed boots clumping up and down the stairs and there, next morning, were all these navvies with string round their pants.

'Nobody dared talk to me about the baby. I didn't want to know. I wanted the freedom to go racing, to go on riding out.' She was five months pregnant before she saw a doctor, and when six months pregnant she was still riding. 'I found my balance was going a bit.' She rode out, too, for Mick James, an ex-jockey who had been badly smashed up. A big horse of James' ran away with the pregnant Beryl. 'This horse took off with me. I couldn't do anything. I could see this five-bar gate or some sheep-wire and a ditch and I didn't know what to head her at. She wouldn't bend. Six inches off the wire, she stopped dead and I went clean over her head and into the ditch. I was soaked through.' Apart from the wetting, she was unscathed.

There were other desperate days. Ginger took Caspian to run at Doncaster in November. 'Beryl is seven or eight months pregnant, but she insists on coming. We take the car we used for taxi-ing and tow Caspian in a trailer. In the race he breaks down on *both* forelegs! On the way home over the Pennines there's a blizzard blowing and traffic piling up over Woodhead. I've got this trailer at the back and every time going round Woodhead, I'm not quite making it. The wheels are spinning. I couldn't see ten yards in front of me through the snow. I've got a broken-down horse in the back and I've got a heavily pregnant woman in front. And I think, "What the *hell* am I doing this for? What the *hell's* it all for?" '

From then till Glenkiln there were terrible times. Times when, as Ginger says, 'Everything had gone wrong and you're starving your wife and kids almost.' He adds, 'That's horses for you!'

The ray of light was still the hope that one day they'd get the One Good Horse. They used to drive out to Cheshire to look at Eric Cousins' stables, to have tea and goggle at his lovely horses and dream of what it might be like. Beryl remembers, 'Ginger used to talk about beautiful places. He said it needed only one good horse to get a place like that. I didn't understand what he meant. But he had the foresight to know. He'd seen it happen.'

McCain was still hoping to meet that someone who would give him his public chance. On several Saturday evenings he had the pleasant job of driving a charming and sprightly old gentleman from his comfortable house in Birkdale to the Prince of Wales Hotel and then to bring him home. They talked horses and racing together. Ginger was desperate now to find someone to pay him to train. He had bought a horse called Cambuslang at Doncaster. Beryl was so furious she would not speak to him all the way home. 'We just hadn't the money to pay for it. But Ginger always seemed eventually to find the money to meet the cheque.'

It took seventeen years from Ginger McCain's first permit to train for himself until 1969 when he first had official paying patrons and could apply for a licence to train publicly. Even then his misfortunes were enough to knock a lesser man not just out of the ring, but out of the business. In his first public season he took three horses to Bangor-on-Dee. The first runner finished half way back. The second, of which they had the highest hopes, jumped only two hurdles, dropped out and had to be pulled up. (It transpired later that it had a 'soft palate'.) McCain was summoned before the stewards, who included Lord Leverhulme and Robin McAlpine, and asked – before he could run his third horse – how he could explain this flop.

Ginger couldn't. He 'felt sick, choked and said so'. The day had cost him so far with transport, entries and jockeys' fees about £50. He was sent out. The Stewards' Secretary said kindly to him, 'Don't worry'.

He went out to his jockey for his third horse, Robin Langley, told him of his abrasive encounter with the Stewards and said 'Now for God's sake put up a good show on this one'.

And at the second fence the horse ducked out through the wing. . . .

Eric Cousins, to help Ginger, sent him a horse called Bardolino. Ginger persuaded the sprightly old taxi-fare from Birkdale, Mr Le Mare, one Saturday evening to buy both Cambuslang and Bardolino. 'They were cheap horses,' said McCain, ' a couple of hundred pounds or something.' They were disasters. Cambuslang had a heart complaint and ran very badly at Liverpool for Mr Le Mare. Bardelino, having run second in a decent handicap, broke down so badly that he had to be put down. Cambuslang was given away. 'So I thought,' said Ginger McCain, cast back into outer darkness again, 'that that was Mr Le Mare gone for ever.'

He was sure of it. Rival trainers of experience, rivals with success, lay everywhere in wait. Rich and elderly gentlemen with a passion for racing find it remarkably easy to attract potential trainers. A horse called Busty Hill had been bought for Mr Le Mare in Ireland. Dour Alex Kilpatrick from Collingbourne Ducis down in Wiltshire had bought Furore II for Mr Le Mare and the horse had sailed home in a three-mile 'chase at nearby Haydock carrying top weight. 'I thought I'd had my chance,' said McCain mournfully, 'and that it had gone.'

Ginger still taxied Mr Le Mare about and they would still chat about horses. 'But it wasn't ever suggested that I should have another horse for him.'

The unfortunate McCain, in his first year as a public trainer, achieved a solitary winner. There can have been few worse starts. Nor had earlier intimations blossomed. Mr David Rosenfield, 'a wealthy fellow', as Ginger puts it, 'with some good horses with Eric Cousins had suggested that if I got a public licence he might send me a couple of horses. But he didn't.'

Worse still – and the biggest blow to any struggling trainer's budget and morale – one of his new owners removed his horses. Mr Frank Tyldesley, a builder from Llandudno, had two horses with Ginger McCain. One horse 'did a tendon' the first day McCain took him schooling. The other, Ashgate, had two runs for experience. Both went home to their owner's place for their summer holidays, and never came back.

'I don't think,' says Ginger frankly, 'that Mr Tyldesley had any confidence in me as a trainer. Which would be fair enough in those times.' It was five years before he won his first Grand National. The first season's one winner was followed the next season by no winners at all. In McCain's third season he achieved two winners. It was now nearly twenty years since McCain had taken out his first permit to train. The record was worse than dismal: it seemed forlorn. But still McCain was not disheartened. He still kept on trying.

One trainer's misfortune is almost invariably another trainer's gain. McCain had now not so much a change of luck, as a peep of daylight. Opportunity belied its adage. In the shape of Mr Noel Le Mare it now knocked twice. His god horse Furore II had broken down. He was, as Ginger McCain put it, 'a bit fed up'. The McCains, furthermore, had a staunch ally in Mr Le Mare's household and at his elbow. Mrs Doris Solomon and her late husband had been close friends of Mr Le Mare and his late wife. Death had diminished the foursome to a trio and now to a pair. The attractive Mrs Solomon, mother of a judge, had moved from her position on the sofa facing the Le Mare's fireplace to the vacated arm-chair facing his. She calls him with affection' Pop'. They share, among many pleasant things like cheerful gin drinking, a mordant sense of humour, a support of things Lancastrian, and a dislike of the idle. Both admired the struggles of their taxi-driver.

Mrs Solomons used to keep in touch with the embattled McCains. She would say, 'Come and have a chat with Mr Le Mare. I think he might buy another horse'.

Ginger kept at it. In November 1971 he put an advertisement in the *Sporting Life* under Box 308 seeking a horse qualified for the Grand National. He got one viable reply from, coincidentally, another motor-dealer. Alfred Flannigan of Station Garage, Berwick-on-Tweed offered McCain Fair Vulgan for £5000. It was too much.

In addition, and to Beryl's agitation, Ginger kept combing through the Doncaster sales catalogues. Sensing one evening Mr Le Mare's disappointment about Furore II, McCain judged the moment opportune to broach the big question once again.

Le Mare had been having a bad time with his horses. His family had clubbed together for his eightieth birthday to pay 7000 guineas for that horse in Ireland called Busty Hill. This had been a complete flop. Furore II, for which he had given £6000, put his foot in a hole when racing and strained a tendon so badly that the racecourse vet had prescribed his immediate destruction. Le Mare had bought a horse called Zara's Grove for £3500 to stay in Eric Collingwood's stable, because he got a telephone call to France (he stays regularly at the Majestic, Cannes) to tell him that the horse (who had won five races in 1969–70) would make £4500 if sent to the sales.

'I went down to the bar in the Majestic where Doris was sitting,' Le Mare recounted, 'And said "Doris, I've bought another horse". Two fellows sitting there who belong to the faith overheard and said "*Masseltoff*". I asked "What's that?" They said it meant "Best of luck".' Le Mare commented acidly, 'It never did much. . . .'

Later he took a fancy to a horse called Lucky Streak and told George Owen to buy it for him for 7000 guineas.

'Ginger comes in that night and tells me 7000 guineas is too much. First thing next morning I get on to George Owen and say "I don't want to pay more than 5000". George came back and said "I couldn't buy your Lucky Streak, I've bought you another". I said, "Oh hell", and put the telephone down. That was 6000 odd. . . .

'So I said to Doris, "We've finished with horses all together". Then along comes this old scout, Ginger. "Oh come on, do let me buy you another horse". "Oh shut up, get out." But he nagged and nagged. . . .'

'Guv'nor,' said McCain boldly, 'there's a horse coming up at Doncaster called Glenkiln and he's qualified for the Grand National.'

Mr Le Mare looked interested. 'How much would he be?'

McCain said, 'Not a lot. About 1000.'

Le Mare considered. Mrs Solomons said warmly, 'Give Ginger another horse. At least he's *honest*.'

'All right,' said old Mr Le Mare, 'If you can get him for 1000, go and get him.'

McCain says with glee, 'So off I go to Doncaster like a scalded cat'.

As Anthony Gillam said, when he was interested in Glenkiln, racing gossip related that the horse had a suspect leg. Beryl McCain had heard that he had become his trainer Ken Oliver's hack. McCain strode into his box at Doncaster and felt his legs. 'One was definitely a fair bit warmer than the other,' said Ginger McCain. 'Everybody who came in was going for his warm leg. So I thought I'd leave it for half-an-hour till the horse was walking round the outside parade ring. Out there I checked his legs again. They were perfect. So I was sure it was only body heat.'

'I got him for 1000 guineas,' said McCain, 'Delighted, but worried to death, too, in case I'd bought a pup.'

McCain got home at ten next evening and immediately rang Mr Le Mare. 'I've got you that horse, sir.'

Le Mare asked, 'How much did you give?' McCain told

him. Mr Le Mare slowly repeated the price, 'A thousand guineas.' He said, hammering the figure home with heavy scorn, 'It'll be a bonny bugger for one thousand guineas!'

Without Glenkiln there would have been no Red Rum. Not merely that Glenkiln's good running gave Le Mare confidence in Ginger and Ginger confidence in himself. But if McCain had not made a regrettable clerical blunder about Glenkiln's Grand National entry, Mr Le Mare would not have thought it necessary to seek another horse qualified for the 'National. Though a less understanding owner than the amazing Mr Le Mare would probably have given his blundering trainer the boot. . . .

For McCain, having again got his keen rich owner, having at last bought a horse which wasn't rubbish, having finally found a horse qualified for the Grand National and entered it, perpetrated a nonsense. Quite unused to the special forfeit form, he misread its intentions and, thinking he was declaring the horse to run at some special stage, in fact struck Glenkiln out of the Grand National of 1972.

Of all the thousands of owners of jumpers only a hundred or so each season have horses good enough to be even entered in the Grand National. With an owner of only thirty-five, halfway through his allotted span, fury with his trainer over such a blunder would be justified. Noel Le Mare had waited fifty years to own his first racehorse. At the time of poor Ginger McCain's calamity over the form the spry old gentleman was no less than eighty-five. It would require singular optimism at that age to imagine you would have many more chances of running a horse in the race you'd been dreaming about for over seventy years. . . .

'I was so worried about the paper work,' says McCain, 'that I said I'd send this form off in good time. It says on the form "Declaration to Run", but it's really declaring forfeit. When I found what I'd done I said, "I can't face the Guv'nor". Beryl said "You go down and get it done now" '

Noel Le Mare remembered. 'Old Ginger came tearing down almost at midnight with his tail between his legs and said "I've made the most terrible mistake".'

Ginger McCain said, 'He took it like a hero. He was more disappointed for me, I think, than he was for himself. He was really genuinely sorry for me. He is the most super gentleman.'

31. 'Try, try, try again – The horse is like that, too'

'The most super gentleman' was born in India on 18 December 1887, the son of a missionary. His father's ancestors were originally French Huguenots and silk-weavers. After the Edict of Nantes (which had given the Huguenots religious liberty in 1598) was revoked by Louis XIV in 1685, the Le Mares were threatened with persecution and escaped from Catholic France. They were smuggled across the Channel and arrived in London with very little money. Later on one of their few gold pieces was stolen at the Coronation of Queen Anne.

Like his ancestors, Noel Le Mare started with nothing, for his missionary father became a 'New Theologian', and, as Le Mare puts it in his well-endowed drawing room (mauve carpets, green walls, Grand National Cups everywhere aglitter, sun-lounge opening off left, garden behind) 'My father got the sack', The family returned to England and the father and mother, who was a qualified teacher, started a little school in Lancashire at Fleetwood.

'But as soon as it got out that my father was a New Theologian, the parents started to take the kids away, for it was heresy in those days not to believe in the Virgin Birth.'

Before the school closed and his mother began a boarding-house little Noel with a few other children had to sing each afternoon at four o'clock, 'If at first you don't succeed, try, try, try again'. . . . Le Mare has a resonant voice, twanged lightly with Lancashire and delivers his words with the emphasis of a minatory finger. You expect a joke or a kick at the end of each paragraph. You are often gratified. He does not show his pleasure in your reaction, but like the best of comedians and wisest of men, regards you dead-pan, eyes contemplative as a starling's over his beakish nose.

'I remembered that all my life,' says the eighty-six-year-old, neat in a white shirt sipping his gin and tonic at three in the afternoon. 'If anything went wrong I tried again. If it went wrong I tried until it went right. And that's how we got here.'

'Here' has given him a total assurance. The cockiness which must have strutted in his youth has mellowed like a fine burgundy into a round authority. He is amused by life and by most of us in it.

'Here' was reached by his creation of a world-wide construction company the shares of which, after it went public, valued his family's ownership at £5 million. Le Mare laughed. 'After the first 'National, they turned to me and said, "We believe you're a millionaire, Mr Le Mare . . .!" And I said "I'd be a bloody fool to be a millionaire at eighty-five, wouldn't I?" I don't think they understood what I meant. Of course, it's all gone amongst the family.' He nodded fondly across the fireplace at bright-eyed Mrs Doris Solomon, who allows hours of conversation to proceed with sharp attention but without any unnecessary interjections. 'This girl says about me, "The world's greatest spender". And I say, "Work hard, play hard. Get all the enjoyment you can out of life.

When it was my own company and we weren't public I used to get *thrilled* about doing jobs".'

Norwest Construction Company really took off in the early 1930s, building bridges, office blocks, jetties, harbours, car ferries, oil refinery bases and pipes, gasworks and private houses all across Europe. But it began after the Great War with four young men sitting round a table in a tea-house raising £250 each to finance its initial working capital.

At the start of the century Le Mare had wanted, as a boy of fourteen, to become an apprentice engineer. But it would cost £50. 'My father and mother were beautiful people, but they had no idea about money. They had no fifty quid. So I went to sea in the trawlers.'

From the trawlers he 'crept in at the back door of the repair shop and that's how I got my apprenticeship'. In 1906 he was working with a fitter who said to him suddenly, 'Go on son, bugger off up the main street and see what won the big race.' It was Ascetic Silver's Grand National.

'I read about it that night. I pored over the paper the next day. I read about the gambling excitement, the longest race in the world, the *hardest* race in the world. And all those strange conclusions. So many different finishes to the Grand National – more than in any other race. "By God", I determined, "I'd like to win that!"' He was eighteen. He had sixty-seven years to wait and, since the fifties when he first owned a racehorse, nearly a quarter of a century to try, try, try again.

In that Grand National week of 1906 he heard of an American millionaire in the hotel in Fleetwood. 'Every time a telegraph boy came, he gave him a sovereign.' The young Le Mare concluded – 'all Americans were millionaires' – and thought 'Good God, what *would* it be like to be a millionaire?' He resolved 'I'll work like buggery and I'll make myself one. And I'll win that race. And I'll marry a beautiful woman'.

The 1973 Grand National: Crisp (right), ridden by Richard Pitman, is beaten on the line in a dramatic finish by Red Rum, ridden by Brian Fletcher. *Popperfoto*

30 March 1974: Brian Fletcher is congratulated by a fellow jockey on the way back to the winner's enclosure after Red Rum's second, consecutive National victory. *Popperfoto*

2 April 1977: Red Rum under Tommy Stack wins the Grand National for a historic third time. *Popperfoto*

(*Left*) Jockey Graham Lee punches the air after winning the 2004 Grand National on Amberleigh House – marking a fourth triumph for the trainer, Ginger McCain. *Matthew Roberts, Reuters*

The day after the third National win, and back at Ginger McCain's Southport stables horse and trainer admire the large selection of cards from well-wishers. *Popperfoto*

In November 1950 he had his first winner of any consequence. He won the Prospect Hurdle at Liverpool with The Sweep trained by Alex Kilpatrick and ridden (coincidentally, because of the future Red Rum connection) by Tim Molony. He told the press then of his three ambitions of forty-five years earlier. He pointed to his wife. '*Here's* the beautiful woman.' He pointed to one of his Norwest Construction signs and said, '*There* are the millions'. He added, 'And when I win the Grand National, the Lord can take me'.

His offer returned to him with a sharp pang a few years later.

His first Grand National runner was a horse with George Owen called Ruby Glen. His ruby wedding had dawned and in the summer Owen had told him about a horse he had bought in Ireland. Le Mare forgot about it. 'I'd bought my wife diamonds, I'd bought her fur coats. What the hell was I going to do this time? I sat down and wrote her out a cheque. She looked at it and said, "This just measures up for that horse". So we went down to George, who had the sense to stuff a couple of stiff gins into us before he took us into the yard. My wife said, "What do you think about it?" I said "I know damn all about a horse. It's got four legs – that's good enough for me". And we bought it. It won me a lot of races. We called it "Ruby" because of our wedding and Glen after the name of our horse here, Glenalmond. So it runs in the 'National. Here I am strutting about the paddock. . . . I went back to the seats and I see Ruby Glen walking in the parade with the others. Suddenly I remember: "Good God!" I think, "If this bugger wins, I've got to go". I called out to my chauffeur, "Joe! Come here, quick. You get on the telephone to God and tell Him I've ratted on that arrangement".'

From 1911 till the end of the Great War Noel Le Mare was a merchant seaman. He was sunk with his ship in the Mediterranean carrying troops out of Toulon – 'The

Germans blew us off with guns but let us get into the lifeboats'. They were adrift two days and travelled three miles in the forty-eight hours before a Belgian ship picked them up 170 miles off Malta. 'At that rate,' says Le Mare, 'we'd just about have reached Malta now.'

When the war ended Le Mare had already resolved to start some form of construction company. He had seen out in South America the tremendous British developments and investments there and in Panama and Mexico, a 'god-send to us in the war to realize those assets', he comments now. He enjoyed himself, too, out there in bars and with what he calls 'dark beauties'.

He is a great man still for the girls, claiming that pretty women and not winning two Grand Nationals, are the things which attract him most.

On that long ago trip to South America he went back to his ship on the last night of his shore leave and addressed himself: 'Noel, you're a bloody fool! Here you are a cog in a wheel on a ship. When the ship leaves, you leave. When eight bells ring, you go down below. Look at the romance of building a harbour halfway across the world – and fun with the girls thrown in at night! You be a contractor.' He had set his course. 'But it took me ten ruddy years to get there.'

Like young Tommy Stack forty years later, Noel Le Mare started after the war in an insurance office. The girl he made his wife, after a few false starts, had said: 'I'll marry you if you come ashore'. Noel earned £3 per week. His wife, working in Liverpool's electricity department, heard someone asking about engineers and put his name forward. They were really asking for contractors' site-agents. Le Mare whizzed down on Sunday, chatted the man up and started at £23 per month, having first written down the terms of his employment and showed them to the representative to confirm.

He worked a couple of years for the company, laying telephone cables. He then got wind that the department were suddenly going to split their operations, letting contractors dig the trenches while the company supplied, drew and tested the cable. He said to three friends: 'Look, this is our chance, boys'. He had £40. The four men resolved to start with a £1000 company. He borrowed the £210 balance of his £250 from a friend – 'and kept his son afterwards for thirty-five years in the office to give him employment for the thing his father did for me'.

They had their first board meeting in that downstairs teahouse in Manchester. Le Mare was the secretary. 'The chief had a soft felt on, I had a soft felt, the big fat fellow had a bowler and the other chap a cap – four of us, all friends.' They registered the company. Le Mare borrowed a hut, bought some spades and shovels, hired a horse and cart, and they were in business.

They made their errors as they felt their way, under-quoting for jobs, not allowing for the local authority's reinstatement charges and often facing bills far beyond their means to pay. Le Mare's ploy then was to dispute any big accounts sufficiently long for his firm to earn enough on other jobs to pay it. He fought a city Corporation for two-and-a-half years over a matter of £750. Years later, when his fortunes had boomed he took on the Government, claiming £290 000 for the jetty he built them at Heysham, against the Ministry offer of £216 000. He fought for months all the way and finally, sitting alone in London facing eighteen men from the Ministry and the air force, he got his money.

As a boy off the trawlers Le Mare went racing at Manchester and Liverpool so long as he had 5/-. He bet in shillings. 'When I first started work, a labourer got four-pence an hour and paid half-a-crown rent a week for his house. At night he went to the vaults. The tradesmen went to the Working Men's Club, the solicitors and professional fellows went to the local hotel, and the big pots were at the Tennis Club. You knew your position and accepted it.'

But Noel Le Mare did not accept his position. 'If there's something in you, you've got to use it and develop it.' What was the something? 'To try, try, try again.' But what made him try? 'To satisfy myself. Don't give up. Never give in. The horse is like that, too. . . .'

He had begun owning horses with The Sweep. A friend with whom he went racing had horses with Alex Kilpatrick. 'Kilpatrick would say "Why don't you have one, Noel?".' He paid £1500. 'I was in the money then!' He liked the name. 'It was a piebald. He was a big horse, used to tremble whilst he was being prepared. You bet I was proud of him when he ran.'

And thus via the other horses and trainers to his taxi-driver. He first saw Ginger McCain in the drawing-room where he now sat sipping his gin and reminiscing. 'He'd just brought Mrs Solomon back. He used to taxi for her. Then he taxied for both of us. Then after he'd brought us home he'd have a whisky with us, and we'd have a gin and we'd have a conversation. . . .'

Ginger McCain interpolated, 'I used to bring Mr Le Mare home fom the Prince of Wales on a Saturday night. He used to be a little bit flushed with gin and a good meal and dancing with all the girls. And we could talk horses. . . .'

Mr Le Mare said crisply, 'He worried the bloody life out of me. Every time I came home he said to me, "I *would* like to train horses for you".'

So, after the first two flops and McCain out in the wilderness again, it was Glenkiln. He gets fourth twice, third four times, second once, and wins an amateur race at the very end of the season. And did not run in the 'National. . . . Three weeks before the race Noel Le Mare rang William Hill's to have £200 each way on the horse (he had run well when second at Haydock at the start of March). Hill's said, 'He's not in the race. . . .' And poor Ginger McCain came tearing down at midnight to confess his blunder.

Worse than one missed opportunity was involved. The horse's Grand National qualification was running out and the race Glenkiln finally won at humble Cartmel on 29 May 1972 did not requalify him. Thus it was that Ginger came again that summer with talk of this horse Red Rum in the Doncaster sales who *was* qualified. The clouds then really flashed their silver linings, for only ten weeks after Red Rum was bought, Glenkiln, by winning the £4802 William Hill National Trial round Liverpool in October, requalified himself for ever for the 'National proper. Had he done so earlier. . . . Had Red Rum been for sale later. . . . Then neither Noel Le Mare nor Ginger McCain would have bought him. Le Mare wouldn't have needed him, as he thought, 'We were aiming for the Grand National.' He exclaims with passion, 'I didn't care a damn what I did anywhere else. *I wanted to win the 'National.'*

32. 'He relished the sea'

The horse who would as quickly as equinely possibly fulfil Mr Le Mare's ancient ambition, established himself as 'a character' within a week of settling into McCain's snug yard. He had shown much character in his youth at Wymondham. Sandra's love of him at rural Oxclose brought it out. Now, behind the used-car showroom in Upper Aughton Road, it bloomed. Respect, affection and success wonderfully increase one's confidence. Red Rum was going to achieve all these three sweet things.

He was from his arrival an object of reverence, because he had been by the standards of that little yard so enormously expensive. 'Six times the most expensive,' said little Billy Ellison, puffed up like a pouter pigeon. *'Different?'* he exploded. 'After riding selling platers every year on the beach I couldn't tell what *was* a good horse. But Red Rum's so different it's like getting into a big XJ after years of lil' ole bangers.

'You couldn't tell just quietly hacking about. But about the third or fourth time I rode him in a mile gallop – really striding on down the beach – he just crept up slowly. . . .' Billy's face scrumpled into delight. 'Every race he had, he came back, he got better. Now I couldn't hold one side of him galloping towards home.'

In the old horse-box which McCain used until the autumn of 1976 (Red Rum's 100 race marked the debut of the new one) Red Rum faced backwards and preferred the offside. He will not have the haynet dangling between his head and the window because he enjoys a keen inspection of the passing scene. So he tosses the haynet over and aside. There was an alarm button at the back of the box so that a lad travelling there may summon the driver in front to stop. It amused Red Rum to press the button from time to time with his tongue and lower lip.

As tension builds up in him his lower lip flaps and twitches – 'Bangs against his upper lip', as Billy put it, 'when he's a bit upset'. He knows immediately the difference between the blacksmith bringing ordinary work shoes and his racing plates. 'Won't even take a Polo mint', Billy Ellison confirmed, 'when he's being plated.' Recollections perhaps of past pain in those feet make him wary of the feel of the aluminium.

Head lad Jackie Grainger pronounced, 'He's a real old Christian. He's never been no trouble.' Grainger kept to the same feeding routine – 'feed him regular at 6 a.m. even if he's going racing'. Except for nearby Haydock and Liverpool, Red Rum is sent the night before to the racecourse stables. In addition to his miles of beach galloping, and the wading in the sea, these are two other points where Red Rum's training differs from that of horses in other yards. Few racehorses get full feeds on the morning of their race. And most, unless the course is several hundred miles away, travel to the racecourse on the morning. Red Rum, furthermore, often stays the night away after racing, too, and never leaves the course before two or three hours after the last race. Most lads in other stables are in a hurry to get their horses home. Red Rum gets his late night feed at 8 p.m. 'Oats, scoop of cubes and grated carrots'.

The horse's hearing is particularly acute. There may be an equine parallel with the sharp hearing and intelligence correlation doctors observe in children. The night that Jackie and Billy were down at Newbury for the 1973 Hennessy Cognac Gold Cup they were sitting in the security men's office looking out over the yard. Far away across the open space they glimpsed Red Rum's head. Jackie shouted from inside the office, 'Now Red!'

Billy said, 'And he started to weave and jump up and down, so that I thought he'd come out over his box.' He added lovingly, 'He hears your step anywhere and knows it.'

'In the paddock,' Jackie declared, 'he loves to be free. He's the King! He likes his own road. You must never shout at him.'

There was a warm ambience about McCain's little yard. It had a good feeling of age, toil and purpose and good cheer. It belonged once to a brewery. All around live people leading active lives. The throb of the traffic and the rattle of the trains orchestrate a perimeter of bustle. Facets of Red Rum's character are mirrored in these surroundings.

'Ginger's stable is so happy,' says Noel Le Mare. 'It's the happiest stable I've been near. He brings his horses back over those sandhills behind Birkdale. If I know a horse, it likes surprises. It climbs up those sandhills, thinking "What the hell's on the other side"? And in the afternoon Ginger's children are playing with a football in the yard, and all the horses' heads are out, looking at what's going on. It keeps them fresh. They don't get bored. If you can get happiness in your business,' said the man who started with £40 in a teashop and created a £5 million family construction company, 'you don't need to bother about anything else.'

Le Mare had faith in McCain. 'Look here,' he affirms simply, 'I'm eighty-six. I've had a life on the trawlers, on the deep-sea ships, a life amongst navvies, a life among insurance agents and contractors and heads of businesses and government ministers and the top people in London and all that.' Le Mare like most Lancastrians is not one whit impressed by grandeur.

Mr Le Mare looked back across that more than a life-span of knowing and testing so many people. 'After that,' he says, 'it doesn't take you long to find out what sort of fellow is talking to you. It didn't take me long to find out that Ginger was solid gold.'

His first reaction when McCain rang him at 11.30 that evening after Doncaster sales to announce that he'd got Red Rum was to grumble, 'I don't like the name'. But Mrs Doris Solomon, overhearing, disagreed. 'I think it's a lovely name.' Noel Le Mare tried it backwards: MUR DER – 'so that was no good'. He asked McCain no other questions about the horse at all. 'I wouldn't bother. I have great faith in this boy.'

Beryl McCain, too, had faith in Ginger. She believes in fate. When she discovered Red Rum's dam was called Mared, she was delighted: it seemed so appropriate that the horse should belong to the similarly named Le Mare.

Ginger McCain had rightly deduced that the horse did not like mud. He resolved to run the horse early. Red Rum had completed his roadwork with Anthony Gillam and was in splendid condition at the sales. McCain, after that first dreadful shock of his lameness on the second day, took him on slowly. 'He was a bright horse to ride and he wanted some sitting on going down through the town. But he was never dirty with it,' Ginger grins, 'and

Billy wouldn't worry. He'd be sitting up there with a cigarette in one hand, talking about his girl friend from last night, and not thinking about what the horse was doing.' He adds, assuaging my consternation, 'We hadn't started to attach the importance to him that we do now.'

Because Red Rum still felt his feet walking on cobbles or gravel he did all his long, slow exercise walking and trotting on the beach and climbing up the towering sand-hills. Certainly, as Noel Le Mare says, that crinkled ridge of tussocky drifting dunes – a sort of mini-Western setting – soared and plunged with interest. It also afforded maximum controlled exercise. The horse was keen to spring up the slopes. Thus his back, loins, quarters, second-thighs and hocks were all being marvellously stretched and exercised every other minute. The sand was loose on the hills. It was soft so that his delicate feet were not harmed, yet he had to work his body and legs harder to climb up. At the top of each dune his front set of muscles were brought into regular play. Down he must slither on the shifting sands, still gentle to his hooves, but requiring the full stretch of tendons and muscles in fore-arms and shoulders and neck and back. He was doing that best thing for all horses: exercising without realizing it, and loving the difference of it all.

When he first saw the sea, he relished it. Its vastness, its strange sound, its waves that ran baying in at him like dogs snapping at his fetlocks, never for one instant deterred him. Quite the reverse. He walked straight on in. McCain reflects, 'When I look back on the potentially good horses I've had, or the old ones that have been some-thing, they've always gone straight into the tide without arguing. . . .' It is, of course, a demonstration of courage.

'Red Rum enjoyed it immediately. In he went, belly-deep, then chest-deep. He relished the sea.'

He loved just as much galloping on his carefully har-rowed strip of sand. McCain's methods here, proved beyond any possible doubt by the almost magical improvement in Red Rum, flew in the face of all established training beliefs. It has been the conviction of trainers all my time in the sport that regular galloping on sand ruined horses. Le Mare was told by his previous trainers that 'it shortened their step.' I have been told variously and by leading trainers that working horses frequently on beaches slowed them down, spoiled their action, made them 'all at sea on turf again', damaged their feet ('very dead, sand you know') broke them down ('no give in sand'), strained their tendons ('there's no bounce in sand'), and strained their ligaments ('they go in too far').

All of these things may be true. The fact is that no other English trainer works his horses exclusively on a beach. They go occasionally when their 'proper gallops' are too hard in summer drought or winter frost, or too soft in midwinter flood. The sand, as McCain knows, having had to train there *faute de mieux*, remains the same. 'Boundless and bare the lone and level sands stretch far away. . . .'

Perhaps McCain unwittingly struck upon the secret: the continuing levelness and invariability of harrowed sand going. Certainly he prepares it carefully. He is sure that galloping on firm, unharrowed sand, is definitely damaging.

Would the beach work as perfectly for all horses as it has for Red Rum? McCain's record with most other horses suggests not. He had, until Glenkiln, a tiny stable of very little consequence. Glenkiln, from an excellent stable, improved. He would have gone on doing so, but working almost daily with the flying Red Rum – in Jackie Grainger's words – 'broke poor old Glen's heart'.

Red Rum's improvement in the hands of his fifth trainer has been one of recent steeplechasing's greatest feats. Certainly the beach has been our hero's salvation. He feet have been saved in their work and cooled by the sea afterwards. The sea and the sand saved him. He loves the freedom of that great expanse. The sea and the sand got him fit, ahead of most of the rest of racing, for his first run for Ginger McCain.

33. 'There was a bay horse, right off the ground'

Having been, as he puts it, 'a hard-up fellow' McCain is not prodigal with entries or his owners' other expenses. 'I'm getting a little out of it now, because we're becoming a lot more professional,' he said in 1974 with a modesty particularly charming after Red Rum's astonishing achievements. 'But it's not a thing that comes easily to a person who had to struggle to get a few bob together all the time.'

To save his owners expense he planned to take several horses together to Carlisle for its two-day meeting at September's end. It's a course McCain has always liked. It was only just over six weeks since Red Rum had arrived from the sales. He had been working well together with Gambling Girl. 'We'd done fairish work, without really getting after them.' The ground elsewhere on Britain's normal training grounds was very hard. But on McCain's harrowed sand gallops the going was 'absolutely super'. So they set off to Carlisle, McCain feeling 'apprehensive, having given 6000 guineas for a horse'.

When Anthony Gillam saw his ex-horse declared to run at Carlisle on going officially forecast as 'hard', he too was apprehensive. He was fond of the horse and had liked McCain very much. He had warned McCain about the horse's feet. This run, thought Gillam, might finish Red

Rum for ever. As Tim Molony had watched askance when Bobby Renton was subjecting Red Rum to heavy ground, now Anthony Gillam as dubiously regarded McCain's first adventure at Carlisle. McCain had booked Tommy Stack to ride Red Rum for the very good reason, as the horse's humble new trainer immediately declared, 'that Tommy knew more about the horse than any of us'.

McCain had altered his policy about jockeys. In the past he had given rides to young claiming lads whom he liked. He had now concluded that this was far from being in the best interests of his horses. 'I now decided to get the best possible jockeys I could for my horses.' He therefore booked Tommy Stack for both his horses that Saturday at Carlisle.

Gambling Girl was in the first race, the eight-runner first division of a novice hurdle. Nothing else had had a previous run that season and half the field, including Gambling Girl, were reported by *Chaseform* to be in varying states of backwardness. For all that, McCain's mare, always in the leading bunch, led at the seventh flight and went on to win by two lengths. She was returned at 9–2. The stable had backed her at 100–8.

Red Rum first ran for his new owner and trainer two hours later in the three mile handicap 'chase, remarkably well-endowed for early season Carlisle, for it was worth £622. Of the four runners, Red Rum was the scorned outsider. Gyleburn, McCain noted, was something of a Carlisle specialist. Proud King had been out already and been third. He should be fitter than Red Rum, and so should Lord Mostyn's owner-trained Nephin Beg who had already won on his previous appearance.

It was not surprising that Red Rum with his new, generally unrecognized small-town trainer, was not picked by the punters. His tall trainer, however, thought differently. Because of Gambling Girl's victory, Ginger said to Tommy Stack, while chatting before the race in the paddock's centre, 'I think Red Rum is going to go well.'

Tommy looked up at McCain with one of those sharply assessing glances and retorted bluntly, 'Well, I won't beat Gyleburn.' He added helpfully, 'Don't expect too much of this horse. He always needs a couple of runs before he's anywhere near ready.' He wanted to help McCain. He had frankly been surprised at the price Red Rum had made the previous month at Doncaster. There seemed to him no likelihood of the horse improving, probably the reverse. Ginger said coolly, 'I think you may be surprised'.

Chaseform bestowed its 'looked well' accolade on Red Rum. He and Gyleburn (Ron Barry) duelled from three fences out, Stack felt for, and McCain watched for, signs of Red Rum weakening, of blowing up. He and Gyleburn touched down together at the last – and Red Rum drew powerfully ahead to win by three quarters of a length. There was a murmur of surprise round the racetrack. The winner, when the outsider of four, is never exactly acclaimed.

Tommy Stack rode back into the winner's enclosure to be greeted by the overjoyed Ginger and Beryl McCain. Tommy got off, stood back, studied the horse, shook his head and murmured, 'Well, I don't know what you've done to him. . . . But what a *difference*!' He was genuinely puzzled. He had driven the horse along as usual, had been surprised to find him lying up with the favourite, and had expected him to crack as he used to in his early season races.

The little stable rejoiced in its first double. Ginger McCain slept easy: he had not bought a pup. Doubles even in medium-sized stables are joyful rarities. But the eight-horse yard behind the railway line now produced another double at Wetherby only ten days later. Tommy Stack was away riding at Cheltenham, so going for the best available Ginger booked that charming champion 'Big Ron' Barry. They won the seller with Golden Blue (no bid for the winner) and then Red Rum took on a really high-class trio of staying steeplechasers in Ballysagert,

Supermaster and Esban. They finished in that order – far behind Red Rum. He looked magnificent and won triumphantly by twelve lengths.

A fortnight later on firm ground at Newcastle Red Rum beat Ballysagert again in another valuable three mile 'chase. Tommy Stack was back on board and hard at him for all the second time round. 'Stayed on gamely to take the lead close home,' the *Notebook* praises. Ballysagert was leading as Red Rum rose at the last to tackle him like a Trojan on the flat. Don McCain winces as he recalls that race. 'They went no pace early on, which wouldn't suit Red Rum at all. I had three owners with me that day and they'd all put a fair bit of money on him – which I didn't know about! Going to the second last, my fellow was a beaten horse and Ballysagert was going away from him. Yet on the run-in Tommy got up to win on the line, and he was going away then!'

When Stack came in, he said to Ginger: 'I've been *very* hard on him. You'll have to give him a break after this.'

Ginger went round to the other side of the horse. 'He really had had a hard race. I felt a bit sick. I would sooner have been beaten than the horse get that sort of hammering. The three owners were all ghost-white, having thought he was going to be beaten. I was a bit choked. When Red Rum was in the "Sweat Box" to test him [a routine dope-test on winners] I went across to have a drink. I was worried about the horse, so I went to the stables to have a look at him.

'In the middle of the stable yard was a patch of grass. On it stood a man with his eyes popping out. There was a bay horse right off the ground, jumping and kicking. It was Billy with Red Rum. They'd just washed him off. He was so fresh and cocky you'd think he'd just come out of his box to run. Yet only fifteen minutes earlier . . .!'

Don McCain marvelled, 'I realized then that the toughness of this horse was something very, very special.' And Tommy Stack looking back on that race, declares, 'At

Newcastle I really "murdered" him. I thought he wouldn't run again for months. Yet he comes out a week later at Haydock and wins on the bit.' Stack shakes his head, astonished now by the horse's courage.

Those years of McCain failures were extinguished in a few weeks. Two doubles, three devastating victories by Red Rum and then Glenkiln turns out at Liverpool (ridden by Jimmy Bourke) to slaughter the opposition by twelve lengths in the £4302 William Hill Grand National Trial. The newspapers suddenly got the word about McCain and shouted it on: 'SEASIDE SCENE'S SUCCESS SECRET. . . .' 'TIDE TURNS FOR GINGER. . . .' 'THE GREMLINS RELENT AND GLENKILN WINS. . . .' 'McCAIN SWEARS BY SEASIDE TRAINING. . . '

And in poured the telegrams: 'WOULD SOUTHPORT AIR AND SANDS IMPROVE ME THREE STONE' wired Sam Benjamin of London. There were others like it. There had never been any before. The whole McCain training scene was greatly changing.

Nor was McCain just a one-horse training marvel. Red Rum's treble had not been three flashes in an early pan. More importantly, Red Rum had yet again improved at home after his gruelling Newcastle race. He was 'rarin' to go' again. Then Red Rum knocked up four in a glorious row at nearby Haydock by easily winning, and as favourite, too, the suitably-named Southport Handicap 'Chase. He won another £684 and a special paddock-sheet presented by Southport corporation, which he still wears. It was the first time it had even been won by a Southport owner, and the charming Mayoress of Southport presented it to a grinning Noel Le Mare and Ginger McCain embracing Mrs Doris Solomon in a male sandwich. Le Mare had said solicitously to Tommy Stack before the race. 'Now look after yourself young man – it's very greasy.' Tommy said, 'Don't you worry about that, sir. This horse will look after me!'

Red Rum's fourth victory made it five wins in Tommy Stack's last five rides and put him ahead of Ron Barry in the run for the jockeys' championship. For Ginger McCain's tiny stable it meant that, only three months into the season, he had won eleven races from eight horses. Upper Aughton Road had been flung onto the map. And the racing world was all a mutter: 'What was the secret of the man McCain?' 'Why should someone so long an obscure trainer suddenly start scoring?'

'RED RUM AND SEA ARE UNBEATABLE!' pronounced a *Daily Mail* headline. It was not only an accurate statement of fact but a reasonable forecast of the future.

McCain had run Red Rum at Haydock to test how he coped with the drop-fences there, as a picture for Liverpool. The papers had not yet seen the horse as a Grand National prospect, but McCain was working steadily towards that agreed target.

The reactions of Mrs Brotherton and Mr Renton, who had now seen their ex-horse win four decent races and about £2500 from four starts in the few months since they sold him, cannot have been ones of joy unconfined. They said nothing at the time to Mr Le Mare or Ginger McCain because they did not come across them. Nor did they know them. In retrospect, talking to me in the summer of 1974 when Red Rum's transmogrification had ceased to be a shock and become nationally accepted, they both very sportingly said they were delighted for Le Mare and McCain.

Anthony Gillam had already come up to McCain at a couple of race meetings. McCain reports: 'He kept saying "Well done" and "Great". He took it like a man – in a most super fashion. Because I know if it had been me, I would have been sick.'

A fortnight after Haydock and it was 'five in a row for Red Rum', when our hero from his fifth start for McCain won the £695 Mauchline handicap 'chase over nearly three and a half miles at Ayr on 13 November 1972. He won it now under top weight carrying a penalty. For the first time he was in the hands of Brian Fletcher. He was rising eight, and Fletcher from Bishop Auckland was closing the second dozen of jockeys to get on his back. His splendid association with Red Rum started, as these things do, partially by accident, but mainly by being in the right place while his rivals were in the wrong one.

After Haydock McCain had decided the horse should rest. 'But he came out better and better.' So he changed his mind and his plans. Thus, he could not get Tommy Stack, who was riding in the south for the highly intelligent and energetic trainer Tom Jones, who then retained him. McCain next immediately tried to get Ron Barry, but he, by his retainer with Gordon Richards, would have to ride Hurricane Rock, a fancied rival to Red Rum in the same race.

Without these two, McCain wisely did not let the immediate jockey problem obscure the long-term plan.

'I thought around,' says McCain, 'with Liverpool in view, as to who might be the best person. And I thought of Brian Fletcher.' Fletcher had only ridden for McCain once before and that was at Carlisle in October when he suddenly got the offer of two rides. One, The Tunku, bought by Ginger a few minutes after he bought Red Rum, fell with Fletcher when in the race with a chance. Fletcher does not say much. He had simply said to McCain after the race, 'He's all right. He'll win you races.' This was the extent of Ginger's communication with Fletcher before Ayr in November 1972.

McCain reflects, 'I thought Fletcher was possibly one of the best Liverpool jockeys. His record was pretty fair. I liked him as a horseman. He was quiet. I thought he'd suit Red Rum.'

So he did. The horse's appearance reflected not only the Scottish afternoon light but the greatest credit on his trainer. Five races in just over six weeks would convert most horses to hatstands and hay-racks. But Red Rum zoomed in by six lengths pursued by Ron Barry on Hurricane Rock. Quick Reply, who had won the Scottish Grand National that spring, now finished sixth of the seven runners on his seasonal reappearance, getting three pounds from our hero and coming in nearly thirty lengths behind him.

Now Red Rum burst out as a Grand National hope. While Brian Fletcher was undoing his sticky girths a pressman enquired, 'What's the programme now?' McCain said, 'A little break and then he goes to Liverpool.' The reporter intercepted Brian to ask, 'Would this do for Liverpool?'

McCain explains, 'Brian is a very quiet fellow. He just thought about this question for a bit. Then he says quietly, "This would do for me", and walked in. We had a chat about it. He said the horse would jump Liverpool and that he'd been absolutely delighted with his ride. It was left at that.'

34. 'I took days off school to go flappin' in Wales'

The press quickly seized upon this firm announcement of Red Rum's plans. 'CONSISTENT RED RUM IS 'NATIONAL PROSPECT,' declared *Sporting Life* and 'RED RUM EARNS A REST – AINTREE'S HIS TARGET.'

No arrangement was made then to retain Brian Fletcher for the horse, nor was there ever one. Fletcher in fact only visited Southport a few times on social occasions, and one of those was to parade Red Rum at Southport show in the spring of 1974. 'I had a job to stay with him,' said red-faced Fletcher, 'he was that fresh and well!'

He had no part in Red Rum's training. He had never galloped the horse at home, nor ridden him on the beach in any of his work at Southport. This was due partly to Fletcher's disinclination to get involved in the training side of horses (this sometimes worries trainers who like jockeys riding out regularly to keep themselves loosened up) and partly to McCain's disinclination to have jockeys down. Beryl McCain says 'Ginger isn't very keen on jockeys riding work here. Whenever they've come, things haven't gone well' (like Red Rum's first day of lameness). Beryl added, 'On grass gallops jockeys are passing trees. They get an impression of speed. But on the beach they pass nothing. They don't think they're travelling and they tend to do too much.'

Brian Fletcher lives in a lonely little farm painted an incongruous bright blue and perched on a bleak hillside in Co. Durham. His directions were slightly ambiguous. 'Fletcher?' asked a farmhand by the road. 'There's a reet lot o' Fletchers round here. . . . The jockey? Aye. Fest farm up t'lane an reeait'and side.' The Durham accent to which Brian Fletcher gives full rein takes a few moments for southerners to grasp.

He farms fifty-two acres and owns thirty-five head of cattle. 'When I'm busy a friend comes in to help.' He added apparently inconsequentially, 'The North's not so cold as people think.' He meant its people, I surmise. He dislikes the south and never wants to leave Durham. 'The atmosphere here is fabulous compared with the south. Nicer people, nicer attitudes, nicer everything! You're in a different world.'

He thought of a move south in April 1973 when, just after his first 'National on Red Rum, he had a shock fallout with Denys Smith. 'BRIAN THE 'NATIONAL HERO LOSES HIS JOB' a headline shouted. He was told he wouldn't be required to ride the stable's horses. 'A complete bombshell,' Fletcher called it then, although his contract with the stable had ended in 1970.

Brian was born and bred in Co. Durham on 18 May 1947. 'I was riding virtually before I could walk.' His father had a small dairy farm, but his main interest was training 'flapping' ponies. Brian at the age of ten was riding at these unrecognized meetings against full-grown jockeys. He raced as a schoolboy all over Britain, up at the old Edinburgh racecourse at Musselburgh, on the Border at Hawick and down in Wales. He used to cut out of school at four, 'fling me satchel down and away out to exercise the horses'. They had four or five racing all the time. 'I took days off school to go flappin' down in Wales.' His father loaded up the horse box and as soon as school ended away they would go to 'flap' round Westmorland.

Denys Smith, now the local recognized trainer, had once been a 'flappin' man' himself with trotting horses. He thus knew Fletcher's father and so when Brian left school – 'I neglected my studies 'cos all I wanted to be was successful with horses – ' he went to work for Smith as a stable lad.

Brian 'did his three horses' at Smith's from the day he started, and stuck it 'because I always had this in the back of my mind that I wanted to be a steeplechase jockey'.

He found Smith 'quite a good boss' and says generously that 'Tommy Wyse (one of the two head lads) taught me virtually everything I know'. After only nine months' work he got his first ride in public in October 1964 when he was only sixteen. It would be phenomenally quick progress for the average stable lad, but young Brian had those six years of race-riding experience in flapping races and was thus several seasons ahead of his school-leaving contemporaries. In his first season he rode three winners from twenty-four races, in his second season four winners. 'In my third season I had fifteen winners and then things began to materialize, and I got the ride on Red Alligator.'

'Materialize' is a pet word of Fletcher's. His Grand National victory on Red Alligator brought an obscure but able Durham jockey to the attention of trainers all over Britain, including Ginger McCain. But Fletcher was still working for Denys Smith as a lad and not getting a retainer. Fletcher grew restless. 'Denys Smith would say to me, "why did you do this? why did you do that?" and I began to think why am I stickin' this job? I was gettin' good offers from southern trainers. . . . But Tommy Wyse used to say to me that I had a good job and I would be better to stay where I was. Looking back,' says Fletcher, 'I was too loyal to Denys Smith. He really didn't appear to appreciate me at all.' He added fairly, 'But I did have a lot of winners through him, and he started me off. . . .'

Staying, though grumbling, in the North did ensure that he was around when McCain was looking, with Stack and Barry unavailable, for a jockey for Red Rum at Ayr. The luck involved in a freelance jockey's life is two hundred times greater than that in the Grand National. More than in any other profession must he be at the right course on the right day available for the race on offer, able to do the weight and in good enough form to be acceptable to the owner. He will not have a month or so to settle in to find his feet in the job. The freelance jockey 'copping' for a chance ride will have about six minutes on a horse entirely strange to him to prove himself a hit or a miss. If he rides a stinker the trainer will probably never ask him again. If he's second or third the trainer will believe (and the owner will be convinced) that any of the horse's previous victorious partners would have won. The jockey can really only ride the winner to satisfy and there is only going to be one of those.

Fletcher was anxious to please. He was on the way to re-establishing himself after some desperate falls in the previous season. He knew nothing about McCain. 'I had been told that he sold motor-cars. That's all I knew of him. Then one day at Carlisle he asked me out of the blue to ride a novice 'chaser.'

That is generally how spare rides start. Senior jockeys and those retained by big stables do not knock each other over to get chance rides for small stables on novice 'chasers. They have a lot to consider. So Fletcher came to ride Red Rum at Ayr.

For that first forging of his triumphant partnership with Red Rum, Brian Fletcher got sensibly simple orders from McCain. 'Give the horse a chance [to settle] over the first two miles. Then don't be too far out of it because he stays well. Then take it up [the running] three from home and win if you can.'

After that first of their victories Fletcher says, 'I was overcome with the horse. I said to McCain, "This is a typical 'National horse. If you run this horse in the 'National I would love to ride him." Things materialized from there.'

'Red Rum', Fletcher affirmed, 'is a much more classy individual now. He's gone from strength to strength. I don't know but what he *realizes* he's done well and won the two 'Nationals. He wasn't the *character* then what he is now.'

Fletcher is something of a character himself. When at the end of the day I rose to go gathering the tape-recorders, cameras, flashlights and notebooks he watched me sardonically from his sofa. 'I hope I've not left anything behind,' I murmured. Fletcher suggested keenly, 'Like your cheque book?'

I had asked him to telephone Anthony Gillam to say I was on my way. Tardily, but kindly he did so and remarked to Gillam, 'That chap's just left. Seems to know a fair bit about racin'.' Gillam said drily, 'Well he ought to. He's trained a Gold Cup winner, you know.'

'*Eeee*!' went Fletcher down the telephone. '*Eeee*! Did he!'

35. 'If he was a human being . . . he'd be Prime Minister'

Red Rum's Ayr victory was Ginger McCain's twelfth of the season. Things had never gone better. Morale in the tiny yard was ebullient. Hero-worship centred on the bright bay horse. His habits were prattled about. Two things always upset him: being plated for a race, and being bandaged before setting out. One other thing drives him berserk: being clipped. McCain groans, 'We've tried everything – the wireless on to distract him, cotton wool in his ears, so's he can't hear the buzzing. Even a hood over his head.' McCain says, 'It's when he feels the hair falling down. So the lad strokes him and I follow his hand with the clippers.' It takes no less than two weeks to finish clipping Red Rum, a task which, with a normal horse, is done in half a day. They can never clip his head.

The first autumn they tried to put a twitch on his nose to try to hold him for clipping. 'He *soon* sorted us out!' says McCain, a bit ashamed of trying this painful resort and proud of his great horse for seeing them off. 'Billy had to jump onto the manger and I was out of the door in a flash! He's a very fine-coated horse.' (And yet he survived those multiple cracks of the whip.)

'He's made a great difference to us going racing,' said

Billy Ellison proudly. 'People want to know you now. They're always askin' how he is.'

The 'Red Rum song' now famous in Birkdale and on northern racecourses was gradually developed by Billy and Jackie Grainger. They had heard two local singers in Southport rendering 'Old Snowball was a racehorse . . .' and adapted it to make a victory anthem for Red Rum.

> O Red Rum is a racehorse
> And I wish he were mine
> He never drinks water,
> He always drinks wine.

With customary courtesy and bright enthusiasm McCain dealt confidently with the press over future plans. His horse would now have that mid-season rest and then be prepared for Liverpool with a couple of runs. Glenkiln was headed in the same direction and preferred by Noel Le Mare, partly because of his seniority and the fact that he had bought him first (only to be deprived of his 'National chance by that clerical mishap), but mainly because of his wonderful performance round Liverpool in the William Hill Grand National Trial.

While the two years younger Red Rum was knocking up his five victories in a row, Glenkiln was failing to win again. Red Rum did not run between Ayr on 16 November and Carlisle on 31 January. McCain had a fixed target at which to aim, which must entail his horse resting at some stage of the season. He was also fully aware that Red Rum was no good on soft ground. The problem, with February fill-dyke now greyly looming, was whether any going other than soft or heavy would prevail before Liverpool.

The going on Southport sands naturally remained excellent. McCain continued to work Red Rum but, as he puts it 'on his own, nice and quietly, and not upsides. He thickened up with his break.' A week or so before Carlisle, 'we started to get after him a bit. But by the day he wasn't fully wound up by a long way.'

The going at McCain's fancied Carlisle was fortunately good. The race, though called the Cumberland Grand National Trial handicap 'chase, was only over three miles and was contested by a field of four. Our hero who a year previously would have been weighted at the bottom of this £632 handicap, now found himself sharing top weight of 11st. 9lb. with Gyleburn. This was the horse which Tommy Stack had declared caustically in September would assuredly beat Red Rum. He had then been giving 9lb. to Red Rum. Now they met at level-weights. Gyleburn was again ridden by Ron Barry. McCain had been pleased with Brian Fletcher's performance on Red Rum at Ayr, but still regarded the Durham lad from Backs and Sides Farm as having been a stop-gap there for the absent Tommy Stack. He therefore again asked Stack if he would ride the horse at Carlisle. Unfortunately for Stack, and blessedly for Fletcher, Stack thought that he would not be available. Ironically he was there, and not, as he had expected, at the clashing Windsor meeting. As McCain relates, 'We couldn't get Tommy, so I'd spoken to Brian about it. Brian had asked me if I would consider him. I'd said, "Yes, if I can't get Tommy Stack".'

With the Grand National only two months away and the uncertain availability of both Stack and Ron Barry for the big race due to their stable retainers, Ginger McCain thought the moment ripe to tie down Red Rum's 'National jockey. He tried Tommy Stack once more. Tommy remembers, 'I told Don McCain after Haydock that I wouldn't be able to ride Red Rum in the 'National, as I had a retainer from Tom Jones and he required me to ride Ashville.'

Like all able people McCain will always seek advice. With Glenkiln and Red Rum he had only just emerged from a world of humble horses and usually 'claiming' jockeys. He was not too sure about this retainer business.

So he had a word with his experienced racing expert friend Stan Wareing, the pig producer.

'Do you think,' asked McCain, 'that we ought to offer Fletcher a retainer?'

'Offer him nothing,' said Wareing bluntly. 'Tell him if he wants the ride he'll have to ride the horse in *all* his races prior to the 'National. Stipulate this.'

McCain accepted Wareing's advice. He spoke to Fletcher, who said, 'Yes, delighted. Thank you very much'.

'And that,' says McCain grinning, 'is the only discussion we had on whether he rode the horse.'

The horse after his ten-week lay off ran a thrilling Grand National trial. He went down by one and a half lengths and a short head to Bountiful Charles and to Gyleburn (a case of good handicapping). Red Rum challenging over the last half a mile, dropped back a little going to the last fence, but came again with a rousing run on the flat and was closing swiftly on the winner.

'The Guv'nor had gone to see him,' McCain relates. 'And we were really delighted with him. He literally flew from the last and in another thirty yards we would have beaten Bountiful Charles.'

The risk of cancellations in February from fog, frost and flood is onerous. At a period when trainers of good horses are working up to Liverpool and Cheltenham the confounded whims and sulks of the British weather can drive horsemen to drink and blows. Ginger McCain had given his two 'National horses plenty of engagements and he ran them both at the next Haydock meeting only seven days after Carlisle. Red Rum ran in the three and a half mile 'National Trial worth £1266 and Glenkiln 'whom the Guv'nor was *sure* was the best prospect for the 'National', ran the following day in a two and a half mile handicap 'chase.

Ginger McCain was a 'a shade disappointed' to be beaten by the unconsidered Highland Sea to whom Red Rum was trying to give 11 lb.

McCain noted that after the race that Red Rum had markedly improved over Gyleburn who, getting 5 lb. from Red Rum, now finished seven lengths behind him – an improvement of nearly a stone in our hero's form since Carlisle. 'He'd run a good race,' McCain observed. 'He'd got Proud Tarquin behind him, and Southern Lad and the 'National winner Well To Do.' Ginger had also won a £5 bet with the owner of Swan-Shot, a local friend, that he'd finish in front of his – 'which we won, of course!'

'Then the Guv'nor said after the race, "Right Ginger, that's *your* fellow. Now tomorrow we'll see what *my* fellow can do". And Glenkiln comes out to run a cracking race to be second, too.'

The strange arrangement under which Red Rum has now won two Grand Nationals carrying his owner's second colours derives from this sporting rivalry between Noel Le Mare and Ginger McCain over the two horses. Le Mare, always one for the underdog, remained loyal to the older Glenkiln in the face, and probably because of Ginger's mounting enthusiasm for Red Rum. The final decision was not made until about ten days before the 'National when Le Mare again made the point that Glenkiln had won over the Liverpool fences. 'Let him have the first colours then,' said Ginger McCain. 'It's your decision. Red Rum can have the second.' So it has remained.

Red Rum's programme was geared to include one more race, and again at handy Haydock on 3 March for what Ginger called 'his 'National prelim'. He selected the £4985 Greenall Whitley Handicap 'Chase run over three miles – 'perhaps not his best trip'. Three other factors mitigated against him: he was carrying top weight, heavy rain had turned the ground from good to soft overnight, and it was raining during the race – an element of English country life which Red Rum particularly loathes.

Brian Fletcher declared roundly, 'On a wet day Red Rum doesn't want to go to the races. He's a miserable horse. He's a horse like a person who, on a fine day, will get his shirt off and go to work and work well. But on a wet day Red Rum curls up and he has no interest at all.' Brian thought about this for a moment and added surprisingly, 'If he was a human being I'm sure he would be Prime Minister'.

In spite of the hostility of the elements, Red Rum was second to Tregarron going to the last fence. For the run-in the field switched onto the hurdle course. 'It was all cut up and heavy,' Ginger McCain recalls, 'and I could see my fellow absolutely bogged down. He was *struggling* through it. Two horses overtook him on the flat, Straight Vulgan and Red Sweeney, each carrying 16lb. less than he was, and he finished fourth, beaten seven lengths and two half-lengths. McCain declares, 'I felt a bit sick with myself for running him in that ground just before the 'National, but I was delighted with the horse. It wasn't as if he was tired and beaten. He just couldn't go through that heavy ground.'

Chaseform Notebook snapped up the point. 'Red Rum ran a great race on ground that was all against him. . . .' It began and ended with the modest prognostication, 'When the ground dries up he will be winning again'. His next race was to be the Grand National, twenty-seven days away. Knowing Red Rum's super equine resilience his trainer was not long agitated by that hard race at Haydock. He fretted far more lest the ground failed to dry up in time for Liverpool. McCain set about a firm training programme. For the first five days after Haydock Red Rum went nowhere near the beach. He merely hacked about through the sandhills. Then he went straight back into strong work. What he did was phenomenal. Except for Thursdays and Sundays he cantered two miles every day and three days a week he was galloping over two miles afterwards. 'I really started to get after him,' said McCain. 'For he was big and well and we started to step his feeding up.' The sort of mileage he was doing on the beach was extraordinary. 'But,' declares McCain, eyes crinkling up in his grin, 'he suddenly started to get better and better. He came on like a house on fire.'

The weather what was more, became mild, the slanting rains ceased, there was a murmur of spring warmth in the air. The spring burgeoned, too, in Ginger's step. 'We got quite confident,' says McCain, 'and Glenkiln was doing well at the same time.'

The local papers fizzed with excitement over their two hometown horses. Southport has always prided itself on being quieter, less brash, more retiring than gaudy Blackpool which flashes beyond the bay. It was sufficiently retiring for many followers of steeplechasing to be quite unaware where it was. In certain broad swathes of Britain, Southport now became known because Red Rum lived in it. Glenkiln set to carry 10 st. 7 lb. in the 'National against Red Rum's 10 st. 5 lb. had been 40–1, and Red Rum 25–1 during the final month. Much was made of Le Mare's support for Glenkiln, for whom McCain had engaged a young jockey he fancies will be the champion very soon, christened John Joe O'Neill, now nicknamed 'Jonjo'.

'Both my horses are as fit as they can be,' McCain announced. Fletcher forecast, 'My fellow is a brilliant jumper. I'm certain he'll give me a great ride.'

Everyone who knew the McCains liked them. Everyone in Southport knew of and respected their leading citizen Noel Le Mare. His lifelong ambition to win a Grand National became common knowledge now throughout Britain as racing correspondents of national newspapers seized upon the saga of the droll octogenarian tycoon who had made it from nothing and of his warm and profitable partnership with his former taxi-driver. Le Mare had unguardedly murmured once that he must have spent about £100 000 on trying to win the Grand National and the figure was plucked out and held aloft like a jewel to be marvelled at. Reflecting afterwards, Le Mare regretted he had ever mentioned it. It made him seem, he thought, a grotesque spend-thrift. But he supposed that if one added together the capital cost of all his horses since the fifties and costed in all their keep and travelling costs and entry fees and jockeys' fees, well then it might be going on that way. But £100 000. . . . He shook his head slowly. And nearly all of us in the racing game would have horrid shocks adding up our costs. . . .

'WILL DON McCAIN BRING LAURELS HOME TO BIRKDALE?' . . . 'LE MARE HAS FINE CHANCE. . . .' 'McCAIN IN CONFIDENT MOOD. . . .' Money cascaded onto Red Rum nationwide, and deluged the local bookmakers. He would start favourite on the day.

Beryl McCain looks back in wonderment. 'I just didn't really think we were lucky enough to have a Grand National *winner*. It was Ginger's ambition for many years to have a horse *run* in the race – never mind to have a winner. Secretly,' says Beryl, 'I didn't think he would win.'

She was not borne aloft by Ginger's effervescent confidence. It was that which had sustained him. For him those long dark years were finally cast aside. All had swept marvellously forward, come what may. 'We were,' says Beryl, 'both thoroughly enjoying it.' Birkdale and Southport being proud and self-possessed places had taken McCain's horses to their hearts. Had the stables been in Newmarket, Lambourn or in a large Yorkshire training centre similar excitement would not have been engendered. Cynical residents, having seen many great hopes rise and crash, would not have so enthused. But Grand National favourites don't grow on trees down Birkdale's avenues or behind its used-car sales rooms. It was a historic time in the town. The locals bragged about Red Rum. Ginger McCain, once an obscure citizen, had become a leading public personality pointed out when he passed by. 'He would say,' Beryl recalls, 'that the horse had a very good chance. He was *very* confident.'

36. 'They were going so bloody fast I couldn't catch them'

McCain left Red Rum's final winding-up gallop as late as the Friday, the day before the race. By the majority of trainer's standards the last long strong gallop before a major race is usually done rather earlier, often three or four days before D-day. The work immediately before the event is usually kept short and sharp. The last week running up to any big race is one of considerable strain on the trainer. In the case of an established maestro like Fred Winter, the pressure and the doubts, the urge to press on and the reluctance to risk damage, combine to pull out tensions like fraying elastic bands. In a yard before an important race the atmosphere twangs.

And here was Don McCain, very much the eager new boy in the big league, with two runners in the Grand National, one of them now antepost favourite and trained, what was more, most unorthodoxly on the public beach.

In the final weeks before the 1973 Grand National Beryl McCain remembers: 'I used to feel more strung up, because running a horse with a tremendous chance is always more nerve-racking than one that hasn't. We both got a bit strung up as the 'National drew closer. We were irritable.'

Poor Billy Ellison, the self-confessed former carefree layabout, was physically sick from sheer nerves most mornings in that last week. 'Billy used to get this terrible stomach trouble,' Beryl McCain remembers. She could hear the lad next door being sick most mornings before he rode out Red Rum for first lot. 'We thought it was an ulcer. And Red Rum was getting stronger and stronger every day.' This expanding, accelerating power beneath him was what so terrified the tough boxer Billy. Literally in his hands lay the hopes not just of himself but of a hundred thousand punters. Each morning Red Rum could get struck by a car, made to skid and fall on tarmac by a lorry, overreach himself slithering down a sand-dune, or run away with Billy down six miles of pounding beach.

'As he builds up,' says Billy, 'he frightens me to death.' He would look in every evening after stables to see whether his precious horse was all right, hadn't got colic or been cast. (He used to go out most days every summer to see that Red Rum was still safe in his field at grass.) During those last weeks racing towards the 'National the strain on tough Billy Ellison became unbearable. 'The fear he might rap himself –' he muttered. 'You wish and wish the 31st of March would come. And after his last bit of work on the last Friday – with the relief of it being over – I cried.' Trainers collect the credit, jockeys the glory, the owners the cash. All are subjected to strain. Think sometime of the lad or girl 'doing' a famous horse....

Part of Beryl and Ginger McCain's popularity stems from their unaffected ingenuousness. 'For that first 'National,' Beryl admits, 'we were rather enjoying the publicity, the television cameras – we had a lot of cameras – and all that. Even on the morning of the race when I was plaiting the horse's mane, we had a camera right in his box.' The reaction of F. Winter, F. Walwyn or F. Rimell to the merest suggestion of such an intrusion would have curdled the blood of the inquirer.

What was even more of a strain, there were cameras out on the beach to record Red Rum's final and extraordinary gallop. It would cover that fifteen minutes when the trainer's decision, as of a general at the *moment critique* of a battle, will lead to victory or defeat. At this point in a horses's preparation, when what is left undone or done too much will by tomorrow prove irremediably wrong, most trainers would not tolerate the presence of any bystander. Ginger McCain took along his great friend and confidant Stan Wareing and a television crew.

Wareing had said understandingly, 'I'll not come near him till his final gallop.' He was there with the television people early on Friday morning. Billy Ellison rode Red Rum, of course, feeling sick inside. He was no lightweight. Stripping at 10 st. 2 lb., he was probably riding out at 11 st. 7 lb. in clothes and with saddle, and that is plenty for a horse to hump at speed. Jackie Grainger was on Glenkiln.

McCain says, 'Red Rum and Glenkiln galloped over a mile and a half.' Red Rum, as always, led with his near-fore. As he hits top gear, he chucks his head down and, as soon as he gets into his rhythm, begins to dish with his leading foot, flicking it out-in, out-in like a middleweight boxer left-hooking like lightning. McCain tense, staring, watched his horses fly past against the sea. He was listening, too, sharp-eared, for the tempo of the feet hitting the scudding sand. Was it fast enough? Above the hoof-beats and the crack of the sea-breeze in the horses' sheets and against the lads' clothing, McCain strained to hear his horses' breathing. Was it a little thick? Was one of them stuffy?

'I wasn't too happy that they'd come quite a good enough pace the first time. They hadn't quickened up enough. When they came to pull up, Glenkiln stopped, but Red Rum wanted to keep on going. He started to disappear into the distance.' Billy, hanging on as if stopping a truck with steel hawsers, had his feet braced right up to Red Rum's ears.

'They came back and trotted up to us. They were both blowing a bit.' This was the instant when McCain would decide right or wrong. How much is 'a bit?' Would one more sharp spin put them over the top? Would no more work leave them undone for the morrow? Safer to underdo a horse. . . .

'I thought we'd run them again,' says McCain firmly. 'So the boys led them back.' They were going to gallop another one and a half miles the day before the race.

Modern trainers find these exertions incredible. But the tough old trainers of yore would nod approvingly on their Elysian gallops.

'I met them in the truck about five furlongs out and shouted to them, "Just let them *go*!" I was trying to go alongside in the truck, but they were going so bloody fast, I couldn't catch them. We were doing forty-five miles an hour on the clock, and Stan Wareing's eyes were going round and round, and I wasn't *getting* to them! They'd *gone*! I was making no impression *at all*! And at last they pulled up.

'Stan thought I'd overdone it. To be quite honest,' says Ginger, 'I thought I had, too. I was worried about it.'

Billy Ellison and Jackie Grainger declared afterwards that they too had both been worried for much of the last three weeks. Both had confided their anxieties to Jeff Langhorne the local grocer but former head lad: 'This 'oss,' they declared squarely, 'is gettin' too much work.'

Doubts, after that tremendous last morning's work raced through Ginger McCain's head, too. The horses, Red Rum in front as usual, walked home through Birkdale, yawning itself awake. McCain drove back in his truck with a wrinkled brow. 'We came home. I had both horses sponged down and strapped right out and fed them both at lunchtime. Neither horse could get to the manger quick enough. They were fighting to get into their mangers.'

There remained that final moment of pre-race anxiety: evening stables after a strong piece of work. This is when morning strain emerges in slight warmth and dreaded puffiness. And the McCain horses had done not an orthodox six furlongs to clear their winds, but two rousing one and a half mile gallops one after the other, and the second so fast that a truck couldn't catch them going at 45 m.p.h. Everyone worried during that afternoon.

'But at evening stables,' says Ginger, grinning again at the grand remembered relief of it, 'their legs were perfect. And both horses looked an absolute picture.' Not only were Red Rum's legs perfect – he has so far never had the slightest trouble with them – so were the feet. Since his second day at McCain's there had never been a trace of lameness. McCain was not aware that his horse had had pedalosteitis only a year before. That ignorance proved bliss. And the soft sand and the cold salt water had unknowingly effected an almost miraculous cure.

Billy Ellison had been backing Red Rum 'ever since the weights came out and I saw old Glenkiln had 2 lb. more. I backed him every week when I got my wages: £5 at 33–1, another £1 at 33's, £2 at 20–1, and so on.' He was one of hundreds of locals, as Steve Makin the balding bookie across the street ruefully remembers. His family owns the betting shop. 'Red Rum's the greatest horse in the world,' said Makin to me wryly, 'but he's caused me an awful lot of hard work and headaches.'

Ginger McCain was confident about Red Rum jumping Aintree's strange fences. 'He's a *funny* horse. He's a *steady* jumper. He does nothing brilliantly. He doesn't jump like Crisp. He doesn't give the fence six inches too much or too little. He jumps and he's down and he's galloping. He'd never match a brilliant horse like Crisp at *jumping*,' McCain said realistically.

The horse's owner was a little alarmed that something might happen to Red Rum. He comforted himself by recollecting Tommy Stack's words to him that sleeting, slipping day at Haydock – 'Don't worry. The horse will look after himself.' There are some horses like that, old Mr Le Mare encouraged himself, driving to the course. Furore had been like that, his jockeys had told him. He thought about Arkle who had never been faced with the extraordinary dangers of Liverpool. 'That Arkle,' he said after Red Rum had won his two Grand Nationals and the Scottish Grand National, 'that horse Arkle was a very famous horse. But she never risked it, the Duchess never risked it at Liverpool, like we've risked Red Rum.'

He was patently nervous being driven to the course and

someone in his car said with singular optimism, 'Never mind, Noel, if you don't win it this year, you might win it next.' Mr Le Mare retorted quickly – for everyone knew that the course was about to be sold to a strange building firm – 'I don't *want* to win next year. I want to win it *this* year while dear old Mirabel [Aintree's popular former owner Mrs Topham] is still there with all her old arrangements.' Nothing would delight him more than if his horse's name could appear on Mrs Topham's gilded roll of honour, even if it would be the last of an era.

Beryl and Ginger McCain were wafted across to Liverpool in a Rolls-Royce. To make their first runner in the 'National even more of a life-time's occasion, and also for that vital moral sustenance in waiting hours when friends are sorely needed, they had arranged to travel with Stan and Carol Wareing. They went out to the Warings' house, Holly Farm, near Halsall, and because Stan is a generous host who enjoys champagne, they downed a couple of bottles.

Red Rum and Glenkiln had made their own short way across to Liverpool leaving about 10.30. Our hero travelled easily and if Billy Ellison and Jackie Grainger felt agitated, they showed little trace of it and went quietly about their business in the racecourse stables. The horse was allowed to settle in, to rest, to 'stale', until the more frantic moment arrived, just over an hour before the race, to get him ready. Then tension makes thumbs of fingers as you unbuckle obstinate straps and bustling lads get in each other's way and curse, and the horse sniffing the agitation in the air, grows nervous too. Red Rum's eyes glowed. His ears cocked and flickered. His lips went snap, flap, snap, together.

In the stable-yard, and then in the paddock, he was the cynosure of every racing eye.

Almost before Beryl McCain knew it she and Ginger were early in the paddock's centre with Mr Le Mare and Mrs Doris Solomon watching the horses circulate inside banks of goggling eyes. Beryl explained, 'Mr Le Mare doesn't spend to long in the paddock, because he does get a little short of breath, and he doesn't want to be too short of time for getting back into the stands.'

Noel Le Mare had not conquered sixty years of commerce's tempestuous seas only to show excitement as his best chance of seizing the third of his life's triple ambitions whirled quickly closer. His friends observed him looking pale, but he hopped nimbly around and his wise eyes gazed sharply about him.

He waited until Brian Fletcher and Jonjo O'Neill came in, said to them cheerfully, 'Have a safe journey. Come back safe and sound,' which is always the sporting owner's valediction. He then set off back to the stands with Mrs Solomon. He was not, he claims, particularly excited. 'The only time I get excited,' he remarks roguishly, 'is when I go near a girl.' He was aware, however, that others might not be so calm. Because he believes that Devon Loch's controversial collapse on the run-in in ESB's 1956 'National was due to 'an ovation too soon', he had made a plea in the *Liverpool Echo*: 'Now remember Devon Loch. Red Rum is a Liverpool horse. Half Liverpool and half Southport will be on it. For God's sake keep quiet until he's past the post.'

12–1 for Red Rum on the eve of the race; 11–1 was forecast in the morning papers. He opened favourite at 12's and was backed down to 9–1 co-favourite with the mighty Australian Crisp who had opened at 14–1. The huge dark-brown horse had been given the maximum top-weight of twelve stone, which onerous compliment he shared with the American-owned, Irish-trained dual Cheltenham Gold Cup winner, the ill-named L'Escargot. This horse, opening at 14–1, was backed down to third favourite at 11–1, followed in the betting by Ashville, the horse for which Tommy Stack had originally had to decline the ride on Red Rum. Such are the falls of the game. Tommy Stack, Red Rum's one-time stable jockey and brief-time trainer, had no ride in the '73 'National at all. Injured in a fall at Kempton on the 10 March he would be watching his friend go by.

37. 'Of all things – toast and champagne'

Betting was particularly heavy, unusually accurate in its selection and, for once, quite beneficial to the punters. Those who prefer the bookie-free methods of racing finance practised in the world's other major racing countries noted that William Hill's boasted of £700 000 being staked with their organization on the race. Ladbrookes with their money-minting nationwide net of betting shops, claimed even more: one and a half million punters had wagered more than £1 million on the race. 'Undoubtedly a record,' murmured a Ladbrokes official comfortably.

Beryl McCain had no bet. She hardly ever does. Nor does she often watch a race with Ginger, particularly with Red Rum. 'We stand apart.' She went up onto the roof on her own.

'Don McCain', said Brian Fletcher, 'did not give me any orders. I just said I was going to sit in the middle on the outside on the first circuit and hunt round. Then ride a race past the stands.'

'Brian's plan,' said McCain, 'was to stay out of trouble on the first circuit to get the horse settled and running nicely. Then, once over The Chair [just coming up to the stands] to sit down and ride a jockey's race. This is pretty well what he did.'

Fletcher made another point. 'I was trying to help Jonjo, 'cos he was having his first ride round Aintree. He was on my "inner" till he fell. In all the 'Nationals I've ridden in, I always try to get a clear run on the first circuit, trying to dodge the fallers. Luck went with me.'

So did Red Rum's intelligence and his own instinct for keeping out of trouble and on his feet. He is simply that often-described but rare conveyance 'a safe jumper'. So was Arkle. So are nearly all steeplechasing stars. Without Red Rum's literally boundless stamina, even without his courage he would still be getting round and winning when the others fell. As it is, he gallops on and on, growing incredibly stronger while his ordinary rivals weaken.

'He is not in my opinion,' Brian Fletcher decided, 'a particularly brave *jumper*. He doesn't just take hold of his bit and go from A to B.' Jumping crackles with such terrifying tearaways. 'He watches what he's doing,' as Fletcher described it. 'He sidesteps any bother, provided he has time to see it. If there's any trouble near him, he'll dodge out of it. He's a very *clever* horse. This is a horse that has *brains*.'

Brains then, and a strong sense (often quite absent in moronic horses) of self-preservation. Quickness of reflex. Observance of trouble ahead. Balance – Bobby Renton's 'beautiful proportions'. These things combine to make him what he is: a natural jumper. Yet there is no vestige of 'jumping blood' in his pedigree. Battered by man he certainly was in some ways, but the tough school taught him not delinquency but survival. And he was helped. Tim Molony's little circular loose school was his kindergarten. Sandra Kendall schooled him on. Dozens of different jockeys doing different things made him, as a young man learns to cope with different bosses, utterly self-reliant. And finally his foot stopped hurting and he loved his supremacy on the long wide sands, and he found in battle-scarred Brian Fletcher someone who woudn't badger and bother him, but let him settle.

The ground on 31 March 1973 was exactly as Red Rum loves it: firm. Brian Fletcher had warmed up with a fourth in the first race, the BP Shield Handicap Hurdle. Don McCain was relieved to see him safe round and home.

Thirty-eight runners paraded for the Grand National. It was worth £25 486 and, three minutes late at 3.18 p.m., the field leapt forward at the start of a journey of four miles and 856 yards which only seventeen would complete. The firmness of the ground strongly suggested a fast pace. The jockeys had received their customary half-hearted cautionary warning against going a mad gallop early on. No one, in fact, believed that records were about to be broken.

Nothing accelerated steeplechasing's soaring popularity more than its television coverage by the cool and competent BBC. Its leading racing commentator Peter O'Sullevan is a legend in his lifetime. A victorious owner himself on the highest level both on the flat and under NH Rules, he knows the game from the muck-yard up to its rich and noble patrons. His commentaries set a standard so far unequalled. And he begins:

> 'They're off. And Rouge Autumn starts fast on the inside, with Sunny Lad and Go-Pontinental moving up on the outside with Beggar's Way, then comes Black Secret with General Symons on his outside and Richleau and Glenkiln. Crisp has gone right up there with Sunny Lad on the inside, then comes Hurricane Rock, then Mill Door over on the far side with Endless Folly, Beggar's Way and Black Secret, and with Rouge Autumn disputing it, they come to the first.'

John Hanmer takes up the commentary:

> 'Black Secret over in the lead. There's a faller – Richleau has gone at the first – and as they go towards the second, Grey Sombrero on the outside along with Ashville, then Glenkiln, then comes Black Secret, General Symons then Highland Seal. . . . Over the ditch and Grey Sombrero over first. There's a faller at that one –Ashville fell.'

Then shrewd Julian Wilson, beady-eyed, the intense and furrowed-brow'd, skilled television interviewer, takes up the racing tale:

'And spread right across the course with Grey Sombrero the leader over that one, from Endless Folly in the centre, Black Secret towards the outside, Highland Seal just scrambled over that one. Crisp is right up there on the inside, as they race down towards the fifth. As they race down towards Becher's, it's the grey, Grey Sombrero, racing wide of the field, the clear leader from Crisp in second, Black Secret third. At Becher's – Grey Sombrero over – and *just* clears it – from Crisp in second, Black Secret third, Endless Folly fourth, Sunny Lad five, Rouge Autumn is sixth and Beggar's Way is a faller at Becher's. Over the next, with Crisp *now* the leader from Grey Sombrero, then Black Secret and Endless Folly . . . they come towards the Canal Turn. Nereo has been pulled up and Crisp is the leader from Grey Sombrero, Black Secret, Endless Folly . . . then comes Spanish Steps. Highland Seal has been pulled up as they jump the next. Crisp is over it from Grey Sombrero, Black Secret. . . .'

John Hanmer resumes from his vantage point:

'As they go towards the next fence it's Crisp the clear leader from Grey Sombrero, Endless Folly, Black Secret, then comes Great Noise, Sunny Lad, then Rouge Autumn, then comes Tarquin Bid, behind Tarquin Bid is Red Rum, then Spanish Steps, then Hurricane Rock and Glenkiln as they go across the Melling Road.'

We pick up Peter O'Sullevan again as they turn onto the racecourse.

'. . . Crisp, well clear, over from Grey Sombrero who jumps it second, Endless Folly jumps it third, then Great Noise fourth, five is Black Secret, six is Rouge Autumn, seven is Spanish Steps and eight Tarquin Bid and nine is Red Rum and ten, on the inside, is Sunny Lad as they come to the next Crisp is over in the lead and clear. . . . Red Rum well in there' (he was twelfth) 'and then comes Glenkiln. . . . Coming to the Chair now – this is one of the biggest, Crisp, his ears pricked, jumps it beautifully in the lead – he just pecked a little bit, but got away with it. Grey Sombrero's gone at that one. Grey Sombrero's a faller, Glenkiln's a faller – '

Beryl McCain was staring from the top of the stand. 'I saw Red Rum on the wide outside all the way round. I saw Crisp. Then I saw poor Glen fall. We'd all got soft spots for him, 'cos he's a super and very kind horse. He fell at the Chair and I saw him struggle. He couldn't get up. His leg was stuck in the bottom of the fence. Canharis jumped over after him and clouted him on the back of the head. He got up. He was dazed. He jumped the water and fell in and the whole of his back legs were covered with the water. And he pulled himself out and they caught him by the stables. I hadn't watched Red Rum. And by the time Glen was out of the water, they'd jumped the first fence second time round and Crisp was still in the lead, but Red Rum was *second!*'

Ginger McCain was delighted to see Brian Fletcher really riding Red Rum along over the Chair and then the water. They improved five or six places very rapidly.

Thus away over the Melling Road with the giant Crisp loping along in front, turning the enormous fences into hurdles, seeming as if he was cantering ahead of a pack of galloping ponies.

Fletcher says. 'From the third fence on the second circuit, from the ditch, I was chasing this horse in front of me. I didn't know what it was. I couldn't tell it was Crisp.'

John Hammer calls the remnants as they thunder past him:

> 'Crisp at the ditch, the nineteenth, he stood right back, he jumped it well, he's right out in front still of Red Rum, second, Rouge Autumn is third, Spanish Steps fourth, Tarquin Bid is fifth, Great Noise is sixth, then Endless Folly and Black Secret.'

Julian Wilson's admiration of great Crisp sends his voice sailing:

> 'And Richard Pitman over that one on Crisp and what a fantastic ride he's having! I can't remember a horse so far ahead in the Grand National at this stage! Jumping that second was Red Rum, then Spanish Steps on the outside of Rouge Autumn, Great Noise made a mistake there, but coming to the next . . . Crisp is over that one, safely over the one before Becher's from Red Rum. . . . Crisp comes on his own to Becher's Brook for the second time, Crisp the top weight. Richard Pitman over it in tremendous style and he's about twenty lengths clear from Red Rum in second place, behind comes Spanish Steps, then Hurricane Rock. Crisp is over the twenty-third *already*, and racing down to the Canal Turn, as Red Rum jumps the twenty-third in second place. . . .

Crisp jumps the Canal Turn, clear. He's still twenty lengths clear from Red Rum in second.'

'I just thought at the Canal Turn,' says Ginger McCain, 'that we'd be second and how unlucky we were to meet Crisp. . . .'

'Seeing the race afterwards,' reflects little Brian Fletcher, 'I've often said to myself that if I'd *ever* said, "I'm going to be second", if I'd ever dropped my hands or eased off Red Rum for one moment, then I *would* have been second.'

Fletcher did not ease. Red Rum did not falter. Fletcher drew his whip at Anchor Bridge. He hit Red Rum twice, thrice, four times. The bay horse quickened. 'Knowing the horse would stay and jump,' says Fletcher, 'and had only 10 st. 5 lb. on his back, I never accepted he'd be second.'

John Hanmer saw the move, but Crisp was still, as Julian Wilson had shouted, a long way ahead of Red Rum. Hanmer called quickly:

'Crisp has got three to jump, he's well clear of Red Rum, who's made a bit of ground. Spanish Steps is third, Hurricane Rock is fourth. Over the third from home, Crisp over safely. Red Rum in second place, then Spanish Steps, Hurricane Rock just passing Spanish Steps. . . . As they go across the Melling Road, with two to jump, it's Crisp with Red Rum in second place *making* ground, but a very long gap after that to Hurricane Rock, Spanish Steps and Rouge Autumn. . . .'

Peter O'Sullevan takes up the saga of the slowly shrinking lead, Crisp conceding one stone nine pounds to his pursuer.

'It's Crisp in the lead from Red Rum, but Red Rum *still* making ground on him! Brian Fletcher on Red Rum chasing Dick Pitman on Crisp. Crisp still *well* clear with two fences left to jump in the 1973 'National and this great Australian 'chaser, Crisp, with twelve stone on his back and ten stone five on the back of Red Rum, who's chasing him and they look to have it *absolutely* to themselves. At the second last . . . Crisp is over. And clear of Red Rum who's jumping it a long way back. In third place is Spanish Steps then Hurricane Rock and Rouge Autumn and L'Escargot. But coming to the final fence in the 'National now . . . and it's Crisp *still* going in great style with twelve stone on his back. He jumps it well. Red Rum is about fifteen lengths behind him as he jumps it. Dick Pitman coming to the elbow now in the 'National. He's got two hundred and fifty yards to run. But *Crisp is just wandering off the true line now. He's beginning to lose concentration.* He's been out there on his own for so long. *And Red Rum is making ground on him.* Still as they come to the line, it's a furlong to run now, two hundred yards now for Crisp, and Red Rum *still* closing on him, and Crisp is getting *very* tired, and Red Rum is pounding after him and Red Rum is the one who finishes the strongest. *He's going to get up! Red Rum is going to win the 'National!* At the line Red Rum has just *snatched* it from Crisp! *And Red Rum is the winner!* And Crisp is second and L'Escargot is just coming up to be third. . . .

Beryl McCain was alone and shaking on the top of the stands. 'When Red Rum came back onto the racecourse I was getting excited that he was going to be *second*. This was fantastic. I started not being able to hold my glasses still. Then it became worse. And he jumped the last and I was getting very weepy and I just broke down. There was a lady stood in front of me and she got hold of me. And she let me put my head on her shoulder and I was crying my heart out. She said, "Which is yours?" and I said, "It's Red Rum". She said, "He's won. Are you all right?" and I said, "Yes".'

'She came to me afterwards,' said Beryl McCain, 'and asked, "Do you remember me?" I said, "Thank you very much for looking after me". She said, "I completely understand. I was the same when my husband rode the winner of the 'National in '69. I'm Eddie Harty's wife." '

Old Mr Le Mare was white. 'When he was catching up on Crisp, they're all cheering and shouting and bawling, and I just sit there and look. . . .' But another owner of McCain's had watched him with some anxiety. 'He was shouting and cheering. His hands were in the air. I thought he'd have a heart attack.' McCain said afterwards, bringing out all his loving admiration for Noel Le Mare, 'The Guv'nor tells me his face never moved!'

'Hope your Guv'nor's all right?' a friend of Ginger's gasped, running to congratulate him as the horse was mobbed by deliriously excited Jackie Grainger and Billy Ellison.

They ran at and round him hugging and slapping him, as if they would wrestle him to the ground. Red Rum was escorted in by the two police horses. Noel Le Mare, who claims he is only excited by women, got down in the unsaddling enclosure. They brought him a chair. He sat on it dazed with glory, his head a little slanted, his mouth smiling with the delight of having won something even more than the world's greatest steeplechase.

'All these people in my box,' said Mr Le Mare, 'jumping up and down like mad people!' He gave a twinkle. 'I never batted an eyelid,' he said.

It was only sixty-seven years since Le Mare the engineer's apprentice had read about Ascetic Silver's Grand National and seen that American millionaire spinning sovereigns outside the Fleetwood Hotel. It was a normal man's lifetime since he'd made his three resolves. It seemed to him, in that euphoria of dreams come true, only a day or so back across the troubled years to McCain's first winner, San Lorenzo, here at Liverpool. Mr Le Mare had watched that race from the rails. 'The horse looked to me like a donkey amongst a lot of good animals, but he came storming in, and I lost my breath and everything to get to Ginger.' So now when the third of his three dreams came true, he struggled back to get to Ginger.

As the horse came in McCain's grin beamed over the hubbub suitably like the Cheshire cat's: he has always loved that next-door county. There he stood all in brown with a furry collar, face alight, looking the nicest fellow in the world, murmuring, 'I'm only a glorified amateur. . . . Knew my feller would tackle him all the way . . . you can't get on top of him. . . .'

Beryl recovered, not quite tear-stained but eyes enormous and shining, was there in her blue coat under her white Russian hat. The One Good Horse that Ginger had been on about all these years, driving through Cheshire, pointing out the big places and the grand horses, had finally come.

And Brian Fletcher, scarlet-faced, sweating, gap-toothed, triumphantly grinning, was trying inarticulately to recount his victory with much chopping and punching of his left hand. His mother, a charming-looking lady, all aglow had (as Brian would say) materialized suddenly at his side and had come in proudly with her son squeezed by the mounted policemen. Brian murmured some good and loving things about her, and moistness of the eyes was added to the heated damp of victory.

McCain had watched the race from the top of the County Stand. 'I thought, honestly, we were going to win it even fifty yards off going to the last.' He said immediately in praise of Crisp, 'He didn't waver till after he'd jumped the last. Red Rum went absolutely straight compared to Crisp who definitely wandered off to the left.' The huge Australian, punch-drunk with fatigue, had tottered left towards the dolls like an exhausted explorer, at the end of his tether, struggling into sight of home. Ginger said, 'Crisp was magnificent. The weight bogged him down. But I couldn't see the same thing happening to Red Rum. I think he would have kept going come what may. Till he dropped. Because this is him.'

Red Rum had smashed the generally accepted Grand National record time set up by Golden Miller in 1934. (In some record books Reynoldstown carrying 11 st. 4 lb. in 1935 [the first year of his double] is credited with 9 mins 20.2 secs compared with The Miller's 9.20.4 secs carrying 12 st. 2 lb.). Red Rum's time, an incredible half-a-minute quicker than the *average* time, was 9 mins 1.9 secs – a speed over the thirty biggest obstacles in Britain of nearly twenty-nine m.p.h.

The corks came out of the champagne bottles in a fusillade on the racecourse. Fletcher and McCain agreed to pay for a case each to go into the weighing room for the jockeys and valets. McCain remarked afterwards, 'Somehow I seemed to pay for both. . . .' He put it down to the riotous moment of victory.

At last the McCain party set off back for Birkdale.

'We were only about five minutes in front of the box,' says Ginger, 'and when we turned up the road I saw the road block. I thought there had been an accident. I saw police-cars, and there must have been four or five hundred people and the streets were jammed. The police weren't even *trying* to get people through. Everyone was at a standstill. But everybody was being marvellous about it. Then the box comes round the corner with its headlights on and all its lights flashing and the horns going. Jackie driving and the boys are all hanging out of the cab. . . . It was *grand.*' McCain's face suddenly switches into one of sympathy. In the elation of victory he was thinking of the faller. 'But it was rather sad as well, because Glenkiln had had a desperate fall and was very, very sore.' The ramp went down, Red Rum came out and received a blast of tremendous cheering. McCain said to Billy Ellison, 'Take him up the road fifty yards for the people to see,' McCain grinned again at the delight of the greeting, then added, 'But while that's going on poor old Glenkiln slips out of the box and slides into the stable, very stiff, very sore. And he's such a good-hearted horse that I felt very sad.'

The celebrations exploded down the streets and into the little yard. A tide of people shouting and cheering swept over the cobbles round Red Rum's box, and then jostled into the McCain's small house. Strangers from the streets, magnetized by their new local hero, converged upon him and upon the celebratory drinks.

'Then everybody seemed to come into the house! I don't know where they came from.' Ginger added, abashed, 'I'd had a couple of crates of champagne brought in before the race – got a bit carried away, I suppose. . . .' He would never have admitted such confidence before.

He went on, 'They got stuck into those. Then the toast-machine got started and everybody was eating toast. Of all things, toast and champagne! The yard was crammed full. The police had a few jars too.' The rejoicing continued for an hour and a half and then McCain decided that the horses needed a rest. 'We filtered the people out quietly and some went off. The Guv'nor was having a do at the Prince of Wales so we went off there. But I didn't feel like getting to involved in a party, so about ten of us went and had a quiet meal in the dining room of the Prince of Wales. I think the Guv'nor had a bill for around £800 for champagne. I think all of Southport had free drinks on him.'

But the pendulum reaction to the greatest triumph of Ginger McCain's life began to swing. He is a quiet man, gratified but reluctant to be suddenly a hero. 'The dinner was a little bit of an anti-climax after it all. I would have preferred it to be *very* quiet with just a few close friends.'

He had moreover a small anxiety about Red Rum. During the race the record-breaking winner had struck into his near-fore and given himself a small, but very deep cut. The scar clearly remained fifteen months later. 'It was a nasty deep little cut,' said Ginger McCain, 'and he was rather sore. We bandaged it and he stayed in his box for three days, resting.'

There was no rest on the morrow for the McCains. On the Sunday Ginger's and Beryl's house filled up again with celebrants and they decided to go down the street to their nearest pub, always known to its habitués for visible reasons as 'The Upsteps'.

It was already crowded, with a thunder of voices and collection of splendid Lancashire urban faces making 'Coronation Street' seem plastic rubbish. A rousing cheer exploded as Ginger's tall frame squeezed in through the door and his now famous face beamed down on the hot, laughing throng. After a very great victory in a very great race, after defeating ill-luck and hardship, something magic attaches to the connections of the triumphant horse. Ordinary people want to touch them for luck and to record, 'Ginger had a word wi' me this mornin' '.

Ginger rashly shouted out, 'Drinks all round twice!' He said, 'Everybody had drinks twice and twice again and so on and we'd been at the champagne that morning, anyway. Oh, it was a *good day*....!'

If it had not been for Red Rum's over-reach he would have gone for the Scottish 'National that first year in 1973. With the wound, there was no question of running him again. After three days he was ridden out again deep into the sea. It cured his over-reach. It took away the soreness. He was sound again. He accepted homage as he passed through the town. 'It's not really a horsey town,' said Ginger, 'but he's about the greatest celebrity Southport's ever had.'

The season ended. Noel Le Mare toweringly topped the owner's list with stakes of £34 196 won by three horses in eight races (Red Rum had won six of them). Ginger McCain proved conclusively that he was no one-horse trainer by producing eight different winners of eighteen races worth £37 404. He ranked sixth in the trainers' table, finishing between the two large stables of Bob Turnell (fifth) and David Barons (seventh). Of Red Rum's jockeys that year, Ron Barry sailed away with the championship with a record (still standing) of 125 winners, Tommy Stack was third with seventy-one and Brian Fletcher, now established as Red Rum's partner, ended up sixth with forty-seven winners. Of the perils of the sport there was lower down the list a poignant reminder. The late Doug Barrott, killed in action, had finished his season, and his life, with forty-three winners.

38. 'And stuff you, too!'

Red Rum spent his first Lancashire summer half on a farm of Stan Wareing's on the flat land near Burscough, and half with a herd of other holidaying horses in a big thirty-five acre field which McCain rents for grazing and schooling. Windy and flat it borders a dual-carriageway. At the first farm Red Rum was turned out with the Wareings' Andy, the original shaggy donkey, an animal unattractive in appearance and personality, resembling a scruffy don and acting like a surly-minded picket. Beauty, however, lies in Red Rum's eye. For the first week he was caught every evening, boxed up and driven back to his stables. (There are naturally no green paddocks in the middle of Birkdale.) 'But,' says Ginger, 'he grew more and more bloody-minded about leaving that donkey. So after the first week we just left him out day and night, and he stayed out ten weeks.'

He switched halfway through to the other field to join the horse-herd, with which he might well have got into trouble, as their kicking-order was already as firmly established as the Civil Service's. Red Rum behaved professionally. There was no mad galloping. He cantered off a few hundred yards, picked a new pal in a jumper called Morning Light, put his muzzle down to the warm summer grass and settled down, with his beaky parrot-mouth, to some steady, serious cropping.

The blacksmith, Bob Marshall, a Lancashire craftsman and character with a tremendous nose, has the vital task of keeping Red Rum's delicate feet in working order. 'They're definitely not good feet. Can't allow myself to make any little mistakes – follow me meanin'? – If there's just a bit more pressure there', tapping the horse's hoof, 'than here. . . .' Marshall wags his head ominously. 'Look, they're still that little bit different. But they're both growin'. When he came he took a five plate – normal enough. But in 1974 after the Grand National a five plate would go nowhere near! It was at least one inch too short!' With all his years of hammering experience the blacksmith was astonished. The growth of the feet was extraordinary. It cannot be ascribed after so long to the physiotherapy and ulta-sonic and Swedish pads and Stockholm Tar of the winter and spring of 1971–72. Something had caused the hooves to grow. By growing, it seems that the pressure on those poor old bones had been eliminated.

Bob Marshall thought that the exercise over sandhills, along the beach and the total absence of trotting on the roads had saved Red Rum's feet, so far, from a further onset of pedalosteitis. When the horse starts conditioning he is out for two hours, two or three days a week, and except for shoving himself up the sandhills and slithering down, he walks all the way home.

In 1973, McCain brought Red Rum up 'a shade later than usual, towards the back-end of August'. The Grand National winner had been invited by his fellow, less-famous citizens to parade at the Southport Show. He and Glenkiln travelled together – it was Ginger McCain's charming and practical idea – and they paraded all three evenings. 'He loved it. He got very fussed over. He realizes he's not going racing and he loves this type of thing. But he got very full of himself – they had to take the band away,' said Ginger McCain. Arkle adored adulation. So now does Red Rum. There is no doubt at all that horses of intelligence and success, from children's ponies to Aintree heroes, are just as sensible of admiration as people.

Don McCain wastes no time getting the horse cantering. When most trainers are putting in four to six weeks' pounding along the roads (a percussive exercise which would cripple Red Rum) McCain has him cantering ten to fourteen days after first coming in from grass. 'But only steadily,' said Ginger, noting my surprise, 'and only for about six or seven furlongs.'

A great number of people, and many with experience, now told McCain that winning the Grand National finished off most horses, that winning a desperate hard set-to which broke Golden Miller's record would certainly finish Red Rum, and that anyway he'd need re-schooling after jumping Aintree's weird obstacles. McCain took note of the last and least depressing of the experts' opinions and boxed Red Rum out with two lead horses to school his champion over hurdles – 'to quicken him up, as these people had said'. McCain had a hunch Red Rum might not enjoy an exercise he could now justifiably consider *infra dig*. McCain made all three horses take one sweep round the field first, then the trio swept towards the first flight of schooling fences. Red Rum was upon them, had jumped them, before he realized it. Then he knew he'd been tricked and was shaking his head in fury: the mighty horse who'd sprung over Aintree's thirty mammoths, clapped on all brakes at the sight of the second tiny hurdle, declared obviously, 'And stuff you, too!' and ducked out to the side . . . McCain gave him best.

The horse knew best. He need never school again.

There was one plain and simple target that season: Liverpool again. The programme till then was sagely kept flexible: two or three runs before Christmas, 'knock him off when the ground goes, then bring him back into work, with perhaps two races before Liverpool, possibly both at Haydock,' planned Ginger McCain.

His immediate intention sprang from the best of horse psychology. Red Rum, in smashing Golden Miller's thirty-nine-year-old record round Aintree had endured a very hard race indeed. Its effects could well be longer lasting than the summer. Those experts who declared that Red Rum might now be finished, might dreadfully be right. . . . Glancing back down Aintree's roll of honour it was horribly plain that of the previous six winners, Well To Do, Specify, Highland Wedding and Foinavon had done little of any subsequent consequence.

McCain intended to find 'an easy contest and let him *murder* one or two bad horses. This would make him cock-a-hoop again and bring him right back. I didn't want to get him involved in another hard race too soon.' He intended to obey the best of all training adages: to run his horse in the worst company.

Red Rum came quickly into strong work, throve, seemed better than ever and, only five weeks after he came in from the fields, was entered in a race at Perth on 26 September. Ginger McCain had never been there, but had it in mind that it was a humble place but a stiff galloping track. When he arrived he discovered to his dismay that it was 'a very sharp round little track, not at all suitable for an out-and-out stayer like Red Rum'. Nor were his competitors the old donkeys for which he had hoped. Proud Stone ridden by big Ron Barry and trained by his retaining stable, Gordon Richards' near Penrith, had already run and won and was strongly fancied. Even with Proud Stone's penalty Red Rum, round this unhelpful track and far from fully fit, would be giving nearly a stone to the previous winner. Getting the horse ready was full of foreboding. Would he balloon over the first few fences as some horses do fresh from Aintree? Would he run without fire? McCain believed it just possible, and very much hoped not.

'He was always going well,' McCain remembers. It was bliss for him to realize that his horse had patently suffered no after-effects of Aintree. Red Rum and Proud Stone raced together, fighting it out, over the last three fences. They came to the last together. McCain watched his horse land safely and began to walk down off the stands as Red Rum, showing a delightfully new turn of foot, sprinted clear of the fitter Proud Stone to win by one and a half lengths. From Ginger McCain's mind a huge cloud was lifted. Liverpool had not harmed his horse. He even seemed – dare he believe it? – a better horse than ever. He and Beryl walked delightedly to the unsaddling enclosure, with spring in their toes that lovely autumn day in Scotland and with dreams in their heads of another fabulous season.

Thus it was that McCain was rather puzzled when Brian Fletcher said as he rode in, 'There might be a bit of trouble. . . . But we're all right.'

Gordon Richards had exchanged a quick conversation with Ron Barry in the second's enclosure. He now came past Ginger, squeezed his elbow and said, 'I'm sorry Ginger, I've got to object. My people have gambled on this horse.'

McCain thought Gordon Richards might be joking. He had seen nothing to which anyone could possibly object. And he was monopolized with joy that Red Rum had 'come back'. Then he heard the announcement that the objection was for 'squeezing over the last and squeezing on the run-in'. Ginger McCain exploded: 'The thought of anyone squeezing Ron was ludicrous!' He had clearly seen the two horses jumping the last fence with about four feet of daylight between them, and both jumping straight as dies.

The two jockeys went into the stewards' room. Ron Barry said afterwards that he hardly had to put his case, because Brian Fletcher had erupted that 'it was a disgrace that when we bring a Grand National winner here all you can think of is taking the race off him!' – and more righteous indignation to the same effect. Ron Barry stood poker-faced. He told McCain later that as soon as Brian had slapped Red Rum going to the last, Proud Stone 'hadn't wanted to know'. There was no patrol camera. The stewards upheld Barry's objection and disqualified Red Rum and placed him second. McCain commented, 'I think the stewards were very wrong'. He allowed that the horses' lines from the last fence to the post had closed together. He declared, 'The track is a distorted shape, but that isn't the *horse's* responsibility!'

McCain is far too big a man to nurse ill-will about that squeezing business. 'Big Ron' is a great friend of his. A photograph of the two horses jumping the last with room for one of his largest used-cars between them was sent to McCain after the race. Ron Barry got married to a tall and attractive blonde, Liz Young, in the summer of 1974. McCain sent him the coloured photograph mounted and framed with the sardonic caption boldly inscribed on it: 'SQUEEZE ME!'.

Most trainers of Grand National winners tend to keep them in cotton wool. They rarely appear early with the riff-raff. They emerge like leading actors making entrances when racing has become important in November, when the stage has been set, and lesser characters established, and the plot advanced. But Ginger McCain is boldly unorthodox. He left Red Rum up in Perth racecourse stables, then sent him direct from there to Carlisle two days later and ran him in a three-mile handicap 'chase the next day, 29 September. It was the programme you might consider for a hard-ground plater of no importance. But for a great 'National winner to camp out in racecourse stables, to be away from home nearly a week, to run twice in two three-mile steeplechases within three days . . . tch, tch, tch, clicked the clever old know-all's tongues. Up shot eyebrows. Heads were wagged. If anything went amiss, Ginger McCain would lose the reputation his last season had finally bestowed on him.

None of these considerations remained long in McCain's head. He had embarked on a bold plan. On it would go. At Carlisle Red Rum was made odds-on, only Canharis being remotely fancied to beat him. Yet Red Rum was again lumbered with 12 st. 4 lb. And Ginger bursts out laughing at the remembrance of that race. 'It was just as if he'd taken that objection personally – having that race pinched off him at Perth; as if he was saying to those stewards, "I'll bloody show you this time!" I've never seen a horse finish up that Carlisle hill like it. He went past the winning post – winning by fifteen lengths and fifteen lengths – and round the bend and just *disappeared.* I thought, "Oh hell! What's happened? What's the matter with Brian?" And when Brian comes back he's laughing his socks off. Brian shouts out, "I couldn't pull the bugger up after the race. He was running away with me!"

'And that,' says McCain with awe, 'was after three miles round a stiff track, and only three days after that other three miles up at Perth. It was just *fantastic.*'

39. 'A bit of stupidity on my part'

McCain now knew without a passing cloud of doubt that his horse had again improved almost unbelievably on the previous year. McCain realized, with a feeling of awe, that Red Rum was even more than a record-breaking Grand National winner: he was something quite extraordinary. The North of England was buzzing now not only with Red Rum's praises, but with those of the man McCain. The subject of speculation had become an object of admiration.

More was in store. A mere fortnight later, and again humping 12 st. 4 lb., Red Rum smashes the course record at Ayr by seven seconds to win the £1551 Joan Mackay three-mile handicap 'chase. He beats a high-class field including Straight Vulgan and Tartan Ace to each of whom he gives nearly two stone. Straight Vulgan was beaten a length, and was quite out-accelerated by Red Rum on the run-in. Tartan Ace finished fifth, seventeen lengths behind. 'I've never seen him look quite so impressive,' says McCain marvelling at his super horse. 'He just swept up to the leaders, as they turned into the straight, like a yacht with a wet sail, and took up the running really sailing away.'

Chaseform Notebook commented with a flamboyance unique that season: 'Looked magnificent . . . fantastic performance . . . truly great horse. . . .'

Red Rum had blundered at the last, picked up, fought back and gone on to win. The jumping error was, McCain said, 'Something he started to do that season. It's usually when he's headed the leader. He did it in the Hennessy three out and he did it in the Scottish Grand National. . . .' Ginger McCain is puzzled by this 'chancing' and just a little worried by it. It seems that when Red Rum suddenly has nothing to pursue his concentration slips.

The ground stayed as firm as Red Rum loves it all the early autumn of 1973, and off he went to Newcastle on the last day of October. He won the £860 three-mile handicap 'chase going away from Neville Crump's fancied San-Feliu.

Among the experienced journalists in Newcastle's press-room it was agreed that by now, if Red Rum were trained by a leading southern public trainer like Fred Winter or Fulke Walwyn, he would already be hailed as another Arkle. He had already begun similarly to spark the general public's imagination. His humble circumstances (so unlike Arkle's who had everything good going for him all his life) and his new chain of victories had started a flow of fan-mail which was to swamp poor Beryl McCain.

McCain was delighted by the Newcastle victory for another reason. One of Red Rum's hind plates had been trodden on during the race and had been partially torn off. A piece of it had been twisted inwards like a scythe. It had been scooping away as he galloped. He had cuts on the inside of his opposite hock. Red Rum's performance under this pain was particularly impressive and was another example of his gallantry. The relief that he had not lamed himself was considerable. The horse could have been very seriously injured.

Red Rum's target remained the Grand National – if there was one. The slow minuet of 'Will she? Won't she? Will it? Won't it?' was once again lilting over Mrs Topham's threatened Aintree. McCain who thinks very little of Cheltenham compared with his beloved Liverpool, began to cast his eyes towards the south. He might well take on those southern cracks in the Hennessy Gold Cup at the month's end.

Red Rum's next race was, however, what Donald McCain humbly calls 'a shade ambitious, a bit of stupidity on my part'. He was to challenge Crisp in a two-horse match at Doncaster over three and a quarter miles for £1763 at a meeting which clashed with the Mackeson Gold Cup down at Cheltenham. The ground was good.

Those scintillating superlatives so justly lavished on Crisp after the '73 Grand National had slightly grated on Red Rum's supporters. Several wrote protesting letters to the sporting papers about what they read as denigration of Southport's hero. Certainly he had been receiving nearly two stone from the bounding Australian colossus, but he had stayed and jumped and gone on and got him, hadn't he? And look what he'd done since: first past the post every time out. Fred Winter's mighty Crisp had whizzed round to be third in a hurdle at Worcester ('better for the race', as *Chaseform* nudgingly observed) and had then easily won a two and a half mile chase at Newbury in record time surging ahead when Charlie Potheen, at level weights, fell just behind him at the fourteenth fence.

To put the matter to the test, to measure Red Rum's improvement, to silence those who said he was a handicapper, Don McCain decided to take on Crisp at Doncaster at level weights. At Liverpool Crisp had carried 12 st. to Red Rum's 10 st. 5 lb., giving away 23 lb. Could a horse of eight years old improve this much in seven months? It seemed thoroughly unlikely. But it was ironically going to be the precise weight increase given to Red Rum for his next Grand National. . . .

A match round Doncaster was a different thing entirely. Level-weight races usually cut up to nothing, and there had only been four acceptors at the four-day stage. The public gave Red Rum no chance at all, and Sir Chester Manifold's highly versatile Australian was 11–4 on.

Red Rum did not improve his own chances before the race. McCain liked Billy Ellison to let the horse give a jump and a kick before he's saddled, as he had done at Newbury with Sandra in that novice 'chase years earlier. Walking round in Doncaster's deep straw undercover ring, he whipped round with Billy Ellison, slipped on the wooden boards beneath the straw and went down, feet scrabbling noisily. When he scrambled up, McCain saw to his horror that his horse was definitely going short behind. He sent him off briskly into the main parade ring. 'Get him out there where there's more room for him to fool around!' he shouted to Billy. He walked behind Red Rum frowning over his action. Red Rum's movement gradually improved. McCain deliberated: should he take him out of the race . . .? He considered. . . . If he did, wouldn't the world think him windy that he'd run away from Crisp? McCain hardened his heart. He said nothing, and his horse ran.

Crisp made all the running, waiting in front in a reasonably fast-run duel. Red Rum came at him under pressure to try to challenge, but Crisp sailed ahead in the last half mile, only weakening between the last two fences. He beat Red Rum a resounding eight lengths. The Grand National winner appeared out of his class.

McCain is loth to make too much of Red Rum's pre-race fall and lameness. But Brian Fletcher independently agreed that something felt wrong. 'That was the only race,' Fletcher declared to me unequivocally the following summer, 'that I've known Red Rum not feel himself. Perhaps he didn't like Crisp settin' that hell of a gallop start to finish, I don't know. Crisp probably beat him on merit, but maybe Red Rum had an off-day. He just lacked the *courage* that he has normally.'

Perhaps his back hurt him. Perhaps having only one other horse – and that a black giant clear in front – hoodwinked him that this was a loathed 'school' rather than a race. Perhaps he did not care to be taken along by something which he knew was quicker over the ground and quicker through the air than he was.

There was blue gloom in Upper Aughton Road. Beryl McCain was so upset she howled in the stables. The lads felt crushed. Their darling was not invincible. He had *not* apparently improved those 23 lb. The cursed Crisp had publicly avenged the 'National and wiped their hero's eye!

It was the early winter of 1973 when for the first time in the one and a half years McCain had trained him Red Rum forayed south of the Trent. Only a fortnight after his Doncaster defeat he travelled down to Newbury to run in the £7435 Hennessy Cognac Gold Cup Handicap 'Chase over three and a quarter miles. Red Rum was fairly handicapped with 11 st. 4 lb. Charlie Potheen (Ron Barry) carried a stone more (a dreadful weight in that company). Red Candle carried a stone less. The latter, trained by that interesting character, Lt. Colonel 'Ricky' Vallance at Bishop's Cannings in darkest Wiltshire, had shown some late promise in two races that season: his first outing when fourth in a £2000 hurdle race at Chepstow – 'Strong run two out, too much to do' says *Chaseform* caustically, and still more significantly in the Mackeson Gold Cup at Cheltenham.

Red Candle had won the two and a half miles Mackeson in 1972. This time at 9–1 he made some progress after the eleventh fence but did not, as *Chaseform* would say, 'trouble the leaders'. He finished seventh. In the fortnight between that race and the Hennessy the chestnut horse had evidently pleased his patient trainer. Opening an outsider at Newbury at 20–1, he was backed down to 12–1.

Red Rum was 'particularly well', as McCain recalls, and it was on the eve of the race in the racecourse stables that he so nearly jumped over his box-door when he heard Jackie Grainger's muffled shout of *'Red!'* The ground – 'good with a little bit of give' – was not exactly as he liked it, but was certainly not his detested soft. McCain savoured the parade of past Hennessy winners: 'Kirsten, Mandarin, Taxidermist, Stalbridge Colonist – how different they all looked,' he said delightedly, for he is a romantic, in love with the history of steeplechasing and all its heroes.

An enormous concourse of southern racegoers who had only watched Red Rum on television and read about his northern exploits, flocked round to examine him in the flesh. Most expected him to be little and were surprised by his size. He has been measured for us by his veterinary surgeon, Mr E. D. Greenway, at 16.2 hands with his shoes on. Arkle was 16.2⅛.

Perfect conformation makes horses seem small. It is the ill-made gangling creature who seems enormous by offending the eye until you walk in close to him. Beautifully made and balanced horses like Red Rum seem small at first glance, and grow bigger as you walk in closer: it is the test of good conformation. All the crowd at Newbury admired Red Rum's. Many were surprised by his extreme jauntiness.

Charlie Potheen was surprisingly made favourite: Red Rum was easy to back at 8–1. The big gamble was on Red Candle. Charlie Potheen, a desperate tearaway, declined to settle. By the fourth fence he was bowling away in front and led the field strongly with only one blunder until the seventeenth fence. Red Rum worked his passage through towards the leaders and now snatched up the running from Charlie Potheen who weakened as if shot. 'Red Rum then really rooted the third last,' McCain remembers. It was that 'error-when-leading' which McCain had anxiously noted before. Red Rum dropped back to third, then fourth, as lightly-weighted Red Candle, who had been waiting like a wolf in the rear, came racing through the struggling field and took up the running going to the second last. Colonel Vallance seemed at that instant to be assured of a richly rewarded victory.

Most of us had then discounted Red Rum's chance. But there he was again in an instant, worrying his way forward, and into the race. It was now Red Candle's turn to blunder and at the worst place: the last fence. As he scrambled over it, Red Rum came storming down on him. 'Red Rum jumped the last like a terrier!' exclaimed McCain. 'He really pinged it, got back on terms with Red Candle – then it was a *super* contest! I thought we got up. Then they came in and they said we were beat. Brian thought he'd *just* got up. . . .' They waited for the photograph. Giving away a stone Red Rum had been beaten a short head. 'It was the six inches from the tip of Red Candle's nose to the ring of the bit in his mouth,' declared Ginger. 'My chappie was *reaching* for his next stride, when the other fellow had taken his.' He had been beaten, as they say in the sport, 'on the nod'. Those six inches cost £5175 or £862.50 per inch. But that did not concern the Red Rum camp.

Mr Le Mare with his customary and unpublicized generosity, presented Brian Fletcher and Don McCain with ten per cent each of the stakes for being second. The yard were also rewarded. Billy Ellison's savings mounted. His new wife remarked to him (as the patient Mr Miles must have felt about Miss Sandra Kendall), 'You love Red Rum more than you do me'.

But in unpecuniary ways too, the stables were genuinely thrilled by Red Rum's great run in the Hennessy. On his first visit south from Upper Aughton Road he had so nearly defeated the best of England for the biggest staying 'chase of the pre-Christmas season. Anthony Watt, a useful young 'chaser receiving 4 lb. from Red Rum, was six lengths behind him. And then followed three sturdy form horses, Cuckolder (who would beat The Dikler two months later in the Great Yorkshire 'Chase at Doncaster), the redoubtable Duke of Alburquerque's Nereo and the persevering Spanish Steps, all of whom were plodding on while the two 'Reds' raced like tigers to the post. 'It was a great contest,' beamed the defeated McCain, and southerners who had never met the lanky man from Southport realized what northern racing people mean when they declare 'Ginger is the nicest man in the game'.

John Oaksey came up, twinkle-eyed and grinning. 'Look at him,' he said to McCain, pointing to Red Rum. 'No point telling him he's been beaten!' McCain nodded proudly. The horse indeed believed all the cheering was for him. No one could even guess it then, not even Ginger McCain in his highest hopes, but if Red Rum's nose had been six inches further forward at the end of those three and a quarter miles, then he would have broken, by the season's end, the immortal Arkle's then record for a 'chaser of stakes won in a season: £27 047.75 in 1965–6. Red Rum's fractional defeat at Newbury cost him a first prize of £7455. By the end of the following season he would have surpassed it easily. Red Rum earned £36 781.80 in 1973–4, the 'chasing record for a year.

40. 'Living it all again'

Red Rum returned to Birkdale and began his midwinter rest. He would resume his Grand National preparations at Haydock, McCain planned. But the best laid schemes of jumping trainers 'gang aft a-gley' when the weather fouls up racing.

Red Rum travelled to Haydock. It was cancelled. McCain took him on to Catterick – 'We were getting a shade desperate. We wanted to get him going'. When they reached Catterick it was sluicing icy-grey buckets from the dark sky. McCain couldn't decide whether to run. They had 12 st. 7 lb. to hump in the soft in weather he loathed. The press badgered him for an announcement. Brian Fletcher begged him not to run. Arthur Stephenson said, 'Don't run him, lad'. McCain said, 'Thank you,' and then realized Stephenson had a runner in the race himself. This was a spot of gamesmanship which made Ginger chuckle: 'Arthur came up afterwards and we had a joke about it. He said "Well, you've got to try everything!".'

Brian Fletcher rode the winner of the second race, and although after a winner most jockeys find the going perfect, Fletcher still insisted: 'Don't run him. This is no good for him at all.'

'Right,' thought McCain, 'that's it then.'

He told Jackie Grainger of his decision when they were saddling Anet's Pet to be second in the third race. Grainger wagged his head. He said, 'Red's so well, you've *got* to do something with him'. McCain said, 'No, we can't run him'. But they chatted as they were saddling and then McCain found Noel Le Mare and discussed the problem again. They decided to let the horse run but to tell Fletcher to pull him up if he was struggling.

They were now embarked upon that most awkward of situations: a conflict of interests between those of the horse and those of the punters. Every horseman will rate the animal in his hands who must race if he says so, as more important than punters who have no need to bet. Equally racing men are aware of the extent to which punters' money finances the sport. When a horse is a national hero, he has a specially large band of supporters. Yet, as a national hero, he needs specially to be protected.

Hovering over this dilemma fluttered the shadow of the stewards' intent to see that horses run on their merits and that there are no non-triers.

All of this was clear to McCain. But only some of it to Noel Le Mare. He nodded. Then he said, 'Ginger, you must make an announcement to the public that the horse isn't really trying. I don't want them wasting their money.'

McCain tried to explain that though the intention behind such an announcement was splendidly sincere, it would be by racing's rules a public declaration of cheating. Le Mare allowed himself reluctantly to be convinced. He would still have preferred a broadcast declaration of the stables' decision; and who would disagree pragmatically that, in the spirit of the law, though not by its letter, he would have been correct? He would have been proved correct, that is, provided the horse *did* pull up. As things turned out, the cynical public would have put quite a different construction on Le Mare's helpful intentions.

It was left to a brief word from the uncertain trainer to the dubious jockey. 'Right,' said Ginger to Brian in the paddock, 'Look after him and if in doubt, pull up.' Many are the good trainers who in similar circumstances have murmured the same.

Red Rum went surlily round, ears clapped right back, loathing every minute of it. To keep him out of the worst ground, Fletcher steered him round on the wide outside. Not only was he giving away over two stone to much of the opposition, but he was giving away distance, too, and in both directions, for he was at the back of the field until the start of the last muddy circuit. He then, still hating the conditions, began to grind his way angrily forward till he could challenge. Crump's horse Fanatic crashed through the roots of the last fence and Red Rum pounded on to win by eight lengths. Relief gave McCain a smattering of arrogance. 'I was a bit cocky, but with everything against him, it was a brilliant performance. So I thought, "I'll give the press something to chew on".' He announced,

'Given the right ground and a clear run this horse *will win* the 'National.' And walked away.

His outrageously confident prediction was the more remarkable because the weights for the Grand National had appeared the previous week shooting Red Rum up the maximum 23 lb. to topweight of twelve stone. 'Bloody hell! That's a bit nasty!' McCain had blurted out when he heard he news. He'd expected about 11 st. 10 lb. and would have been thrilled with a few pounds less. Typically of McCain, his later reaction was one of qualified pleasure: top weight in the 'National was one hell of a compliment to his horse, and he announced this frankly. Racing's wise official handicappers armed with their new computer had stated simply that Red Rum, the record-breaker, was the best horse in the race. No horse, however, in the history of the race had ever before been so heavily penalized for winning once. The bookmakers extended the odds against Red Rum from 12–1 to 20–1, and a number of racing tipsters advised their readers even at those odds to keep their money till the day.

After Catterick McCain reckoned his horse needed one more race. He again picked the Greenall Whitley at Haydock. The ground was soft on 2 March, but the sun shone brightly, and after Red Rum's dour victory in Catterick's mud, McCain was hoping that the going might not now be too heavy. Red Rum was however lumbered with 12st. 7 lb., a wearisome burden to hump round three miles of soft ground only twenty-eight days before the Grand National. Fate decreed that he should not do so. At the very first fence Red Rum discarded ten stone when an astonished Brian Fletcher was catapulted from his saddle by a horse suddenly crashing into him from behind.

McCain was desperate. Riderless horses are at risk. Many panic without a pilot, try to jump iron railings or concrete posts and impale themselves, gallop across tarmac car-parks, slip and break their knees, crash into cars while their eyes are on the flying field, or simply cross the other runners to bring about a débâcle of flailing legs.

'We needed this race badly. Now we wouldn't have it.' He dashed into the middle of the course, and so did Beryl, to try to catch Red Rum before he injured himself galloping loose. Red Rum however coolly decided that he needed the race and if Brian wasn't going along with him, too bad; he'd have to go round alone. He resolved as usual to win, and went to the front, jumping every fence. Soon he was cutting out the work of Glanford Brigg.

Tommy Stack had been unshipped at the first, too, and he and Brian Fletcher joined McCain in the middle. 'Something hit me in the middle of the back and I went straight out the saddle,' Brian said. (It was Noble Hero, whose jockey Macer Gifford afterwards apologized.)

Riderless Red Rum and Glanford Brigg keep bowling along in front, McCain, wonderfully relieved that his horse is unharmed and obviously taking care, called out to Alan McTaggart standing in the course's centre, 'Bet you a level pound mine wins this race'. 'Done,' says the Scotsman. They come together to the last and the piloted Glanford Brigg is switched onto the new run-in to go for the winning-post. No one has given Red Rum a revised plan of the course, so thinking that Glanford Brigg is cravenly deserting the contest, Red Rum bowls on over the next open ditch and the water jump while Glanford Brigg scurries along the flat beside him to the winning-post.

'Owe you a quid,' shouts McCain to McTaggart bounding over the mud to try to catch his precious horse. 'Nonsense,' says the Scot, 'Yours jumped two more than the winner.'

Beryl McCain had watched Red Rum running loose at first with trepidation, then relief, then pride when she saw how brilliantly he was running and jumping without a jockey. As the two horses jumped the official last fence together Beryl McCain said, 'You could see Red Rum's eyes as he turned to look at the other horse, thinking he'd gone wrong'. As the other runners finished, the course whirled alive with horses turning, wheeling and cantering back. Red Rum was loose in the throng, galloping about in immediate danger of crashing into the rails. Beryl ran out into the middle of the track to catch him.

'Don't be a daft bitch,' shouted Ginger, fearful that his wife would get bowled over into the mud by a half a ton of horse. But Beryl aimed herself at Red Rum as he came galloping past her. She shouted '*Red*!' The horse heard her, stopped, turned, came back towards her, and she grabbed his reins safely. All was well. He had run his race without the weight.

'He came home, ate up,' said Ginger, 'and acted all superior: "What do I want with jockeys?" – that type of thing.' Relief that Red Rum had not been injured at Haydock made that race a subject of jokes. But McCain was unable to weigh up the benefit which that riderless 'school' had done the horse. While he had feared that 12 st. 7 lb. in the mud might prove too severe a 'National preparation, he now suspected that carrying only 2 st 7 lb. without Fletcher to boot him along might mean that Red Rum had not had enough of a race.

The beach provided its usual superb going and Red Rum never missed a day's work in his last month. McCain had been worried by a remark Tommy Shedden had made to him when the horse ran at Catterick. Shedden had observed, 'I don't think he's carrying quite the same condition over his loins, Ginger, that he had last year.' McCain thought, 'Oh Lord! I've been too easy on him.' And he crammed the work into Red Rum. He used to stand and watch the horse every night going through those moments of calculating contemplation which every trainer knows. 'One night he'd look tremendous. Then the next you'd think he didn't. . . .' What worried Ginger much more in March 1974 was the rain continually soaking into the newly owned Liverpool racecourse. McCain fretted. Then ten days before the 'National the weather smiled again.

McCain sent a friend to Liverpool to check the going. 'The turf's like silk,' came back the word. 'If we can get four or five days of good weather, it's going to be marvellous ground.' It is fortunate for Red Rum that Aintree's wonderful old turf, now so little used, is rarely heavy.

But McCain wanted something faster than merely good ground, particularly this year when his horse had twelve stone to carry. 'You have to be pretty lucky to get fast ground at this time of the year. But we got it.' The drier the days, the more confident McCain grew.

He had backed Red Rum £50 each way at 14–1. He asked Noel Le Mare, 'Would you like the same bet?' The owner said, 'Please!' So McCain let him have his bet, 'and never bothered backing him myself.' He has so far never had a penny on the horse any time he has run, and it is most unlikely now, with racing's superstitions in full cry, that he ever will.

McCain's yard in 1973 had consisted of only eight horses and four lads and the generous Noel Le Mare had given them £1500 between them to celebrate his first Grand National victory. The stables had now been extended right up to the back wall to provide eighteen boxes. The little yard was crammed. Out of it the astonishing trainer would now produce no less than three Grand National runners, one sixth of his stable. In addition to Red Rum and his hardworked galloping-horse, Glenkiln, The Tunku, which he had bought cheaply at Doncaster just after Red Rum, would also be performing. Belonging to Dennis Rimmer he too had greatly improved on his past form, and had won a Wills Premier Qualifier 'Chase and a Doncaster handicap. Richard Evans would ride him, Reg Crank would be on Glenkiln, and Brian Fletcher naturally continued on Red Rum.

The three horses were in a string of nine galloping nearly two miles on Ainsdale beach on the Wednesday before the race. On the Friday before the race Red Rum galloped six furlongs lickety-split. And then did it again. McCain was delighted. Corals and Mecca offered Red Rum joint favourite at 10's with L'Escargot. Ladbrokes suggested 7's Red Rum. William Hill said 8's Red Rum. Glenkiln was at 50's and The Tunku at 100–1. On the eve of the race the Racegoers Club organized an Aintree walk-round: a group of leading jockeys guided a party to gape at the size of Becher's, the Canal Turn, and the grisly Chair.

Superstition insisted that the McCains follow precisely the same morning's programme as that of the previous year. As tension crackled in the yard and press photographers and television camera-men crouched and clicked, flashed and flooded, buzzed and pointed, Beryl McCain again with nervous fingers carefully plaited our hero's mane. The gods of racing were being placated with the same offerings. But the horse had become a public star.

'There were interviews in the yard with the press, with the BBC, with the television people,' said Ginger, 'then the adrenalin really got pumping when Red Rum was loaded into the box.' A local crowd had gathered in the street outside the yard as if to greet a king off to claim his throne. They set up a cheer as Red Rum walked past the used cars and up the ramp of his horse-box. Ginger and Beryl McCain got ready to drive out to Stan and Carol Wareing's. 'As we get in the car, it's the usual stuff,' said Ginger. 'Stomach turning over, feeling uncomfortable, feeling that little bit niggly. . . .' Once again they were refreshed by the hospitable Wareing's champagne. Again the Rolls-Royce flying lady was festooned with ribbons. Again they larked about with the electric windows and waved wildly at passing lorry-drivers as they careered towards Aintree racecourse.

Beryl was in a state. At Haydock, when Brian had been knocked off at the first fence, she had forgotten her binoculars. Now she found she had left them in the back of Jonjo O'Neill's car. 'I had this horrible feeling that what had happened at Haydock was going to happen at Aintree if I had no binoculars. I dived into the weighing-room and asked, "Can anybody lend me some?" Nobody could. Then she found Dennis Leah, a Cheshire training friend from Little Budworth where Ginger had been in the old days. He was standing by the television monitor and happily lent Beryl his binoculars. 'As soon as I got the glasses,' said Beryl, 'I felt better.'

Then she tried to find the same place on the stands from where she had watched in 1973. But she wasn't sure of the place. She moved around uncertainly. She didn't want to be with Ginger for that had never been lucky. She looked round to glimpse him standing only six steps behind her with Stan Wareing. She hoped they wouldn't see her. But there was a delay getting the parade started. In it Stan Wareing squeezed through the crowd to reach her and asked, 'Are you going to stop with us?' She could barely speak now. She shook her head.

Red Rum was drifting in the betting from 8–1 favourite out to 11's, in the face of frenzied punting on Scout (backed from 18–1 to 7–1, favourite) and for L'Escargot (backed from 10's down to 17–2).

The race began. The start had been delayed four minutes partially by some histrionics performed by the wilful and costly Princess Camilla. Charles Dickens led almost from the start with Rough Silk, Sunny Lad, Rouge Autumn and Straight Vulgan and L'Escargot in the leading bunch. The plan was so identical to the previous year's that Ginger McCain had not even discussed it with Brian Fletcher. For the first two miles, Fletcher would again 'hunt round'. For all that first circuit Beryl could not relax for a moment. She kept her fingers crossed in dread of the loose horses. 'There was one particular loose horse right in front of Brian and I thought it'd be sure to bring him down.'

The three BBC TV commentators had not read the race far enough back towards the rear to mention Red Rum before the field swept onto the racecourse in a dazzle of colour at the end of the first huge circuit. At the one before the dreaded Chair Peter O'Sullevan saw the zig-zagging threats of the loose horses.

> 'The two leaders – Pearl of Montreal and Charles Dickens – then Sunny Lad and L'Escargot and then just in behind them Spanish Steps, and then comes Rouge Autumn, San Feliu, Straight Vulgan – '

Fletcher here began his run and O'Sullevan spotted him instantly:

> 'And right up there Red Rum is going well, going strongly in the centre of the field. Coming up to The Chair now and as they do so it's Charles Dickens with a loose horse *perilously* near to him. Charles Dickens jumps it but he's *very* nearly brought down . . . but he survives all right. L'Escargot jumped it on the inside, Pearl of Montreal just in the lead and it's Pearl of Montreal as they come to the water from Charles Dickens and L'Escargot and Sunny Lad and then Vulgan Town. Then comes Spanish Steps, behind Spanish Steps is Rough Silk, then San-Feliu, and then Red Rum. Behind them Straight Vulgan and then Norwegian Flag on the inside of Norwegian Flag is Glenkiln. . . .'

Then Beryl McCain saw the loose horse run out towards the stables and Ginger McCain on the top of the stands felt not a worry at all. 'It was like a summer's day, warm beautiful weather and I was watching Brian's yellow cap bobbing along.' (Fletcher was still wearing Le Mare's second colours with the yellow cap.)

The fields raced away from the stands, onto the second circuit and John Hanmer took up the commentary:

> 'Almost at the seventeenth and it's Pearl of Montreal on the inside from Vulgan Town, Charles Dickens and right up with them L'Escargot is close up. All the leaders over that safely, Vulgan Town disputing it with Charles Dickens and Pearl of Montreal. Then comes Straight Vulgan. And Red Rum, last year's winner, taking *very* close order now, as they jump the eighteenth. And again all the leaders over safely except for Straight Vulgan. Straight Vulgan went at that and it's Vulgan Town from Charles Dickens, then comes Sunny Lad, L'Escargot, Red Rum, then Scout taking close order on the outside, then comes Pearl of Montreal. Glenkiln has gone at the ditch. As they go to the next fence, the twentieth, it's Charles Dickens, L'Escargot and Red Rum.'

The competent quick nasal chant of Julian Wilson seizes the running thread:

'Charles Dickens is the leader over that one from L'Escargot with a good pitch on the inside. Red Rum much closer now on the outside. Vulgan Town is fourth place now. Scout's got a good pitch towards the outside as they come to the one before Becher's. And it's Charles Dickens who leads over it from L'Escargot on the inside, Red Rum on the outside. Scout is right up there. Vulgan Town is in fifth place.'

At this instant Wilson's voice changes upwards. He glimpses the astonishing sight which will never be forgotten by anyone who saw it: Red Rum was cantering over the field as if they were riding-school hacks. Fletcher was standing up in his irons actually trying to restrain Red Rum from running away. The horse's sudden superiority scourged his opponents as if they were trash.

Wilson shouted:

'They run down towards Becher's for the second and last time, and as they do so the leader is now the 1973 winner Red Rum! Red Rum from Charles Dickens, L'Escargot, Scout, Vulgan Town as they jump Becher's. . . .'

At the Canal Turn Red Rum was mocking his pursuers. He was moving as if only at half-speed, bounding over the ground as if he were laughing with delight while those behind – Charles Dickens, Scout, L'Escargot, Spanish Steps, Vulgan Town, Rough Silk and Stephen's Society – toiled behind him like normal racehorses under pressure in a race of their own with three and a half miles gone. . . . And Red Rum was sauntering in the sunlight. He was Billy Ellison's 'big XJ among the ole bangers'. He was that day at Liverpool a horse apart, a giant among minnows – and yet those minnows were, like L'Escargot and Spanish Steps, horses of class.

Red Rum spurned them. The quick ground he loves spun behind his dancing feet. The warm sun he needs blessed him. He swaggered. Darkness lay behind him. Those awful struggles were forgotten. He played the King at Liverpool, making the rest serfs. In many old observers' minds this was the most memorable superiority ever shown round Aintree.

With only four more of Aintree's towering but tattered fences left Red Rum was four lengths clear and still on the bridle. Fletcher explained, 'I *had* to go to the front going to Becher's. I went to the front so early, 'cos if I'd restrained him any longer I'd have got myself into trouble or something.' The little jockey's pink face could hardly register the ease of his horse's forward cruise.

Running towards home Red Rum made his only mistake. Over-jumping, he pitched forward and for an instant looked like blundering. Fletcher sat right back, well and safely like the best of Aintree jockeys and before the forward pitch of Red Rum's neck and head were done, his other foreleg flashed forward to take the weight and keep him moving with only the briefest hiccup in his stride. It was done quick as a conjuror, and he was galloping on. 'Didn't lose any momentum at all!' exclaimed McCain. 'You *never* get the impression this horse is going to fall.'

Then, crossing the Melling Road, L'Escargot, dual winner of 'chasing's Gold Cup classics, moves forward closer, his blinkered head extending like a snake towards Red Rum, topped by the darkly sinister goggles of jockey Carberry. Will it be like last year now, the long-time leader getting hauled down in the dying seconds as a stag is pulled down by a wolf?

'I saw L'Escargot come to him,' said Beryl, 'and I thought, "Oh goodness he's going well: we're going to be beat". And I looked over my shoulder to Ginger and I could see he thought the same.'

Peter O'Sullevan came in quick and strong as the gap started closing.

'It's Red Rum with L'Escargot chasing him now, the two top weights, Red Rum from L'Escargot. Red Rum for England, trying to complete that great double that hasn't been done since Reynoldstown, being pressed by L'Escargot now for Ireland. Then comes

Spanish Steps improving on Charles Dickens. Then Scout, and behind them Vulgan Town and then Rough Silk. They're coming now to the second last fence in the 'National. And it's Brian Fletcher on Red Rum being pressed by Tommy Carberry on L'Escargot. The two top-weighted ones at the second last in the 'National. . . . It's Red Rum with a clear advantage there from L'Escargot who jumped it second. Then comes Charles Dickens third, and Spanish Steps. . . .'

Ginger watched L'Escargot and thought, 'Oh Lord, that's too close for a horse of that class. He's got that Gold Cup speed and we're giving him a pound.' But our horse seemed to sense it. He jumped the last absolutely flying.

The gap had closed. Then Red Rum spurted like a sprinter. He sped towards the last smashed fence as bright as a bay button. He headed into a mountainous wall of acclamation.

Peter O'Sullevan's voice rose about the tumult:

'This is the last fence now. It looks as though Red Rum has only got to jump it! But remember he deprived the winner of it on the flat last year. Now he's jumped it in the lead and it's *Red Rum!* This great local crowd giving him a *tremendous* ovation. Red Rum from L'Escargot, Tommy Carberry is trying to close the gap, but he's not going to. They come to the elbow. A furlong to run, he's got a big weight remember – twenty-three pounds more than last year, but he's *going* to hold on. It's Red Rum from L'Escargot in second, Charles Dickens third, and Spanish Steps fourth, and racing up towards the line *and Red Rum getting the ovation of his career* – Brian Fletcher *acknowledging the cheers of the crowds* as he comes to the line! *The winner of the 'National.* L'Escargot is second, and Charles Dickens third, and fourth is Spanish Steps and then comes Rough Silk and Vulgan Town. Behind them Rouge Autumn and then the gallant Duke of Albuquerque on Nereo. . . .'

'He settled it going to the last,' said Ginger McCain. 'And on the run in, it was quite a joke really, Brian *putting his hand up to wave to the crowds*! Fantastic. Getting a bit cocky, too. The horse thought Brian was going to hit him. And he accelerated so bloody fast that Brian had to bring his hand quick to grab the reins. *That horse was going to run away with him,*' said Ginger McCain, wide-eyed with marvelling at any horse who under twelve stone and after four and a half miles and thirty gigantic fences could so spurt at the end of it all as to be really running away.

'He just *ran* home,' said McCain. L'Escargot, dual Cheltenham Gold Cup winner, had got to within three lengths of Red Rum racing to the last and yet on the run-in, with Brian Fletcher stopping riding to greet the crowd and then pulling up, our hero had extended the distance to seven cook-a-hoop lengths. Behind him stretched a field as numerous as any since Fletcher had won his first 'National on Red Alligator back in 1968. Seventeen had completed.

'The jockey was so overjoyed,' declared Noel Le Mare 'that he waved to us in the box. When he came in he just said, "What a horse! What a horse! He didn't need a jockey!" Then he went on talking to David Coleman and I could have smacked Coleman's face! He said to the boy, "I think you picked up £6000 last time. Will you get £10 000 this time?" Then he turned to me and had a few words, then to Ginger who is very cryptic. Coleman asked him, "What is the future for him?" And Ginger said. "Aintree again next year. Subject to the owner's approval".'

And after the climax there was a down-beat ending of the day. McCain had his first runner on the flat in a race after the 'National. He wouldn't, he says, go round the corner to watch a flat race, but he'd drive miles to watch great 'chasers cross black fences together. His flat-race horse, what was more, ran disappointingly. McCain wandered off to have a drink alone. Then he felt a great urge to get away from the crowds into the quiet country that he has always loved. He walked onto the steeplechase course. Then he found himself walking further and further away. It was a beautiful late spring afternoon. The warmth of the sun on the turf over which Red Rum had raced had brought out the fresh smell of growing summer with a bouquet like a Loire wine. McCain had been flung into the skies by his horse's triumph. Now he drifted on, feeling again the quiet countryman who lives inside his bones. He heard the larks sing over Aintree and saw a hare crouch, then run with huge hindlegs and flattened ears. He walked on and on, dreaming, walking where his marvellous horse had galloped. He was, he said, 'living it all again. . . .'

He had no notion of the time. He was a mile away down the course when the last race had been run. The crowds had jostled home, leaving their refuse and their hopes. Tens of thousands of locals had left rejoicing in their hero. McCain kept strolling on round the course, thinking of all those hopes he had kept alive during two decades of dark years. He had known secretly that he would bring it off. Now that he had, it seemed incredible. . . . And he had in his pocket the key to Stan Wareing's Rolls. He came to, saw the time, strode back across the turf which had now made him doubly famous. The stands were empty.

Suddenly in the dusk his partner Peter Cundy and Stan Wareing found him: 'Where the devil have you been? We've been worried sick.'

They collected two more crates of champagne at Stan Wareing's, returned to Upper Aughton Road, continued celebrating, reached the Prince of Wales very late for a dinner of six which ended up as eighteen and at four in the morning were still carousing in Mr Le Mare's commodious residence. 'The Guv'nor was stuck in the middle of six attractive girls,' said Ginger McCain proudly, 'all lit up, and thoroughly enjoying himself.'

41. 'But he's brilliant'

The week ensuing was one of indecision. Was Red Rum's season over? Might they run him a month later in the Whitbread Gold Cup at Sandown? Or in the Scottish 'National in three weeks? There was even some talk about the Grand Steeplechase de Paris. McCain had always had the intention of going to Ayr if the horse was well enough. So he seemed. A week after the Grand National he was actually leading attractive Carol Wareing's Event horse in a sharp gallop on Ainsdale beach. . . .

But no one else thought Red Rum should run again. Brian Fletcher said no. Julian Wilson even wrote poor Ginger a letter explaining that horses can't come back so quickly after the Grand National as to run well in the Scottish 'National. In an interview with Wilson, Tommy Stack had commented, 'Ginger has made no mistakes with the horse so far, I don't think we should tell him what to do with him now.' But all other pundits advised McCain that, because the two 'Nationals had never been won in the same year before, it shouldn't be tried.

In the memories of some there lingered pictures of Red Rum in his old days struggling round on soft ground, hating it all and taking hidings. These people could not realize that the new Red Rum of the beach had entirely changed his attitude. They thought that to run him again, and over four miles at Ayr, would sour him again. 'Don't risk it,' they urged the uncertain McCain. 'Don't run him again.'

There was also what McCain calls a 'mish-mash' about whether Red Rum would have to carry a penalty. 'They were all quoting the rule book at me,' he grumbled, 'which I never read anyway, and finally they said that instead of 11 st. 7 lb. he'd better carry 11 st. 13 lb.' This, with most people, would have been the final straw. An extra 6 lb. penalty would have been quite sufficient on Red Rum's back to break McCain's resolve. But just as Red Rum is a special horse, so is McCain a special character. They are both battlers. McCain against a flood-tide of negative advice kept to his course. He would attempt the impossible again. He would go for the Scottish 'National.

They drove to Scotland in Stan Wareing's car. Beryl McCain did not come. Ginger drove. The atmosphere was rasping. Ginger did not utter one word all the long miles. Red Rum had gone up earlier to settle down. They took Bob Marshall the farrier to be at hand in case he spread his racing-plates. 'Well,' says McCain drolly, 'Sugar Ray Robinson used to take his own hairdresser, so why shouldn't Red Rum take his own blacksmith?' But no horse had ever won the Grand National and the Scottish 'National in the same year....

Fletcher, even on the course, was still opposed to running. 'Invariably horses that have run round Liverpool never come out the same season. It's like you having a hard day's work,' he explains. 'The next time you've got that job to do you won't put the same heart into it.'

As John Oaksey was ruefully to discover and generously to report, 'By all the rules he should have been a tired horse in need of a holiday. But to Mr Noel Le Mare's Red Rum the rules do not apply.'

Brian Fletcher admitted, 'He did look gloriously well. but he wasn't bucking and squealing.' It was his tenth race in seven months. Fletcher recalled, 'Pat Buckley leaned over to me in the parade and said, "God, that horse looks well, Brian". I said, "He's a *dead* horse. He's lost his character and charm." And throughout the race the horse wasn't as fresh. He wasn't himself.'

It was a mere two years since Red Rum owned by Mrs Brotherton and trained by Anthony Gillam had churned round this course under 9 st. 8 lb. Now he carried 11 st. 13 lb. and started 11–8 favourite. Like his owner and his trainer he had come up from rags to riches. And now, like them, he would need great courage once again. Twenty-one days before and he'd danced over thirty great fences under twelve stone. He had galloped four and a half miles. Now he must gallop four miles more.

Ginger McCain watched anxiously from the stands. They were walking round and round at the start for a seeming age. McCain scowled. He gnawed his lip. He dreaded that he had made a terribly wrong decision. Ginger's temper frayed. Most of the other jockeys during the delay, got off their horses to rest their backs. 'Bet Brian doesn't get off,' he muttered savagely to Stan Wareing. 'Bet Brian's the only one sitting there.'

Fletcher did not dismount with the rest. But McCain agrees, that it was probably a good thing: if Fletcher had dismounted, Red Rum might have played up, and got loose. At last they start. 'There he is right on the inside and third or fourth last all the way', grumbles Ginger, 'in a position to get knocked over if anything falls'.

McCain was in a torment, for he had everything to lose and everything for which to curse himself. Unless Red Rum won it, and won easily, the critics would snap him to shreds. 'Running a double 'National winner again!' They'd shriek. 'Ignorant! Greedy! Wicked! Cruel!'

He groans now, remembering the ordeal of that race. 'He was *always* on the rails. Then they were stretching out into the straight and I really got the wind up. I knew this was where it would tell. I felt sick. He jumps the third last. He goes to tackle John Oaksey on Proud Tarquin. There's this horse on the rails running on like an express train [it was Kildagin]. I thought, "He's going to do us". Then, slap, my fellow hits the second last. *Bump!* It's like the Hennessy.'

That mistake put Oaksey and Proud Tarquin back in the race. Everyone thought – and John Oaksey snatched at the hope – that Red Rum's present weight and past exertions on top of this blunder must now really stop him.

'But he's *brilliant*!' shouts Ginger. 'He's back into his

stride and gone *whoosh* like a bullet! He more or less stuck up two fingers at Proud Tarquin. And he *just ran away from him!'*

The ovation that day at Ayr was the greatest ever given to a horse there, and some said that no more clamorous din had ever been heard on any racecourse in all Britain. 'It made the Hampden Roar,' as *The Sporting Life* succinctly put it, 'sound a mere ripple.'

Red Rum won, spurting away, by four lengths from Proud Tarquin, with Kildagin third, and Canharis fourth. He had travelled the four miles one hundred and twenty yards in eight mins. eight seconds. He had won another £7922 to bring his colossal total under NH rules to £69 320 (nearly all of it earned in the last two seasons). His earnings in the 1972–73 season of £28 882 had themselves been a record, surpassing Arkle's best annual figure. Now that great sum had itself been easily overtaken. Red Rum's total for 1973–74 season had, with the Scottish Grand National slung beneath his sporran, reached £36 781.80. For Le Mare and McCain who were so lucky to find both him and each other, he had so far won twelve races and been five times placed from nineteen starts. Now he had done another unique thing by winning the two 'Nationals, and in three weeks. Oaksey had said before the race that Red Rum 'looked a sort of miracle'. Afterwards that highly admirable and just defeated amateur sportingly declared that 'Red Rum was assured already of immortality'.

The great crowd had started bellowing for him at the second last fence. 'When Brian pulled him to the outside to go,' recalls McCain, 'I got the impression there was a slight hesitation. Then he's into top gear and away he goes.' McCain's eyes sparkle with delight.

'*What* a reception . . .' Ginger breathed out. 'The owner of Proud Tarquin, Sir John Thomson, came over and said, "It's a privilege to be beaten by a horse like that". The owner of the third said something too along those lines.' Two months later and the tough Mr McCain was still blinking away emotion. 'It made me choke,' he said. 'Those good working people who came up to shake my hand, coming and and shaking, people who appreciated a good horse and who'd just come to see him win.'

'And Tommy Stack, who's ridden him all those previous races, goes past him and gives the horse three or four good old pats. And that was nice – sort of one old friend to another. Afterwards Tommy saw the lads, went over and slipped them a quid or two.'

McCain was detained by a crowd from Carlisle who seized him and bore him aloft and into their crowded coach. They were shouting, 'We've come all the way from Carlisle to see this great horse of yours, and now you're going to have a drink with us.' As Ginger was hoisted into the coach, a hoarse and beery cheer exploded, and two bottles were stuck into his hands. Nor could he leave the coach till the beer had been downed and he had signed every racecard. Ayr racecourse, sensible of Red Rum's historic achievement, commissioned a statue of him to stand on the field of glory. Only one other steeplechaser (and he is dead) has been so honoured: Arkle at Cheltenham.

Because Beryl (as Ginger puts it) 'had the wind up, too, about the Scottish 'National', she went to Bangor-on-Dee – and watched their runner there get beaten a neck. A heaving crowd jostles into a bar there to watch the Scottish 'National on a television set. At the very front of the crowd squat several portly old ladies roosting on shooting-sticks. The crowd waits patiently. Just as they're down at the start at Ayr, a fellow pushes through the crowd at Bangor to switch the set to flat racing at Newbury. Screams of protest rend the throng. There are shrieks of 'Lynch him!' The old ladies set about him with their shooting-sticks. He runs bludgeoned from the bar. . . .

Such passion does Red Rum engender. His fan-mail, which had started to stream into the McCain's small house in Upper Aughton Road after his first Grand National, became a torrent after his second Grand National and a deluge after Ayr. Beryl McCain is overwhelmed. 'Letters . . .' she sighs, 'I have all the paperwork and the accounts and the children do hinder a bit, and sometimes in the evening I just don't *feel* like doing them. I joke about having to have a secretary, but it would be nice. . . .' And the following year she appointed a press agent to cope with pleas for pictures.

Red Rum's fan-mail is enormous. Most letters beg for photographs or shoes, send cheques, post greeting-cards. Children enclose toys and coloured postcards and postal orders. The letters come from Headmasters – 'all the world loves a *real* champion' – and from children, 'Give him a pat from me; he's the greatest since Arkle'. From old disabled ladies: 'May I join the queue to have one of Red Rum's horseshoes? I could do with some luck. . . .' From old-age pensioners in Scotland – 'I put my last 50p on Red Rum last Saturday'. From a man of ninety-two: 'I've seen plenty of 'Nationals but I've never seen a finer winner'. From the sports-writer of a school magazine enclosing a written interview: *'Is Red Rum going for next year's 'National?'*. Beryl writes in *'Yes, all being well'*.

And poems, as Arkle had, and letters to the horse himself: 'Dear Red Rum I am six and a half . . .'. And letters from chartered accountants: 'I am sure this will create a great deal of goodwill for your future business . . .' . From Spillers Farm Feeds . . . 'We would like the privilege of featuring Red Rum . . .' . From an anonymous fan scrawled on a scrap of paper inside a parcel 'Thank you for winning. Hope you like these mints'. A football fan from Leicester City sent the horse a pin-up postcard of mares at grass. 'Dear Red, sorry to say I didn't back you this year, thought you had too much pud. Very well done. Your mates across the city did us too at Villa Park, they deserved it too. Best of luck. Hope you like the picture. Leicester Lad.'

The letters come from every corner of England, Scotland, Wales and Ireland. From cottages, hotels, offices, tenement blocks and manor houses. They are typed on engraved paper, scrawled on cards, printed on little ruled sheets. They start 'Dear Mr McCain', 'Dear Don', 'Dear Ginger', 'Dear Red Rum . . . I think you are a fantastic horse and your trainer must be very good. My dad backed Kildagin . . .'.

Arkle's fan-mail was tremendous, as I recall from being allowed by Betty and Tom Dreaper to tote a suitcase-full back from Ireland. Red Rum's has already exceeded it. He has become what ten years earlier would have seemed quite impossible: an even greater public hero, and a larger phenomenon in the horse world. Is he, that odious comparison, as great a horse? He would not have beaten Arkle in a Cheltenham Gold Cup. But would Arkle have stood up and stayed four and a half miles round Aintree twice? I doubt it. His connections did not consider it. And, as Noel Le Mare so proudly says, 'Arkle was not *risked*'.

The two horses are at the pinnacles of the two highest but different trees in steeplechasing's forest: the classic park course, brilliant Cheltenham winner and the Grand National horse representing an even longer road down racing's heritage.

Red Rum had, by the spring of 1977, already set up three Aintree records: the fastest time; the same season double with the Scottish Grand National; and, most gloriously, the unique feat in five years of winning three times and finishing second twice.

But the two horses are different, too, in much more vital ways. For Arkle it was goodness and light all his days, till his accident at Kempton. He was bred by steeplechasing people of jumping stock to be a steeplechaser. He was bought by a paragon of steeplechasing owners, Anne, Duchess of Westminster, and kept by her all his days. He was trained throughout his magnificent career by one wise man, the late Tom Dreaper, one of the greatest trainers who ever cast eye upon a horse. He was ridden in almost every one of his panoply of races by a superlative steeplechasing jockey in Pat Taaffe.

He was in human terms, the silver-spooned aristocrat with every advantage from birth, who could rejoice in the best education, have the right friends and flourish in a beautifully organized career.

We have seen how wildly different has been the case of Red Rum. Bred wrong, sold cheap, handled by five trainers, ridden by over two dozen jockeys, moved from Ireland to Leicestershire to Yorkshire to Lancashire, racing from a two-year-old onwards into his eleventh season so far and over one hundred races – and most of them hard ones. Arkle over six seasons ran in a total of thirty-five races winning twenty-seven of them and most with gracious ease. Red Rum has achieved his triumphs against all the odds, without advantages and very often, as McCain has said, in spite of people. He is like the man who makes it from rags: a survivor. He survived his mad mother, his sprinting father and the hard two-year-old racing which should, by all rules, have cut down his career to a couple of seasons. He survived much punishment in severe races. He survived the year of coughing. He survived one of the worst diseases in his foot. He survived because he possesses, in my experience, more toughness, more resilience, more downright, upright soaring courage than any horse I've ever been honoured to know.

42. 'Red Rum comes to dinner'

In the euphoria which followed on for weeks after the conclusion of Red Rum's magnificent 1973–74 season, those looking keenly for portents of disruption might have spotted two. Both, suitably, were connected with champagne, most northerly of wines and the drink of celebration; both foreshadowed the departure from Red Rum's life two of his closest companions.

Indeed in the two seasons following his great double there were going to be so many changes in the people whose lives were centred on Red Rum that in the winter of 1976–7, Donald McCain was going to shake his ginger, grizzled hair and wonder aloud: 'All those people going, all those things happening, bad things, unhappy things . . . and yet the old horse who's brought us all up, stays on – ' he nods across to the corner box closest to the kitchen – 'he stays just the same.'

They were little clouds arising from the sea, as the Bible puts it, like a man's hand in what otherwise seemed a sky of heavenly blue. Some crates of champagne ordered and paid for by Ginger McCain for celebrations in the changing-rooms at Liverpool and Ayr after the horse's unique Grand National double, had surprisingly not arrived with the jockeys and valets. Someone, intercepting them, had been seen loading them into the boot of his car. The report was related to an astonished McCain by a jockeys' valet wondering why the usually generous trainer had not done the expected celebratory thing. 'Left rather a nasty taste in my mouth,' recalled the trainer, grimacing over the incident several months later.

Equally suspiciously, but not quite so unpleasantly, several bottles of champagne waiting at the party, held to celebrate the 'National double on the flat terrace between the McCains' sitting-room and the stable yard below, had been surreptitiously removed. They were found hidden in Red Rum's box waiting, Ginger McCain assumed, for private consumption later.

The incidents irked McCain, but he was on such a pinnacle of fame, such a cloud of pride in his horse and relief that no harm had befallen him, that they did no more than niggle at the doubts he already held about two characters whom he suspected to be involved.

The horse, who was now world famous, went out to grass in the same small flat paddock of Stan Wareing's – 'watched over by Stan's farm-manager, of course' – to spend his summer under the tumbled trees with Andy, that tattered blanket of a donkey. Red Rum was delighted to see Andy again. He bullied his companion whenever he felt like it, chasing him round the field to express what the racing world all recognized – his astounding domination – and yet was delighted to have Andy, as a king has his court-jester, to chat with, and to crop grass with, muzzle close to muzzle, as the summer months slid past.

'He was very stroppy about leaving the donkey that summer,' Ginger remembers, 'particularly stroppy he was. We'd a job separating them.'

But the horse was headed for a repeat of his previous season's programme. The Aintree double and the English and Scottish Grand National double of the 1973–74 season could be improved upon only in one way. This time the horse, aiming at the Grand National once again, was being prepared for an attempt on something which, until Red Rum, had seemed as likely as a man on Mars: the Liverpool Grand National treble.

With another parade in August, three weeks after he came in, at the local Southport Flower Show at which to receive public homage and swell the gate, Red Rum's progress exactly repeated that of the year before.

His first race would again be the Perthshire Challenge Cup Handicap 'Chase at Perth, on the first day of the attractive and social Scottish meeting. This was the same three-mile race which Red Rum had 'won' the year before, beating big Ron Barry on Proud Stone to the line, and then losing in the Stewards' Room to Ron Barry's objection of 'squeezing me at the last and on the run in'.

In 1973 Red Rum had carried 12 st. 4 lb. Now he was lumbered with the maximum of 12 st. 7 lb., a weight which, over the next two seasons, was to drag him down. It is no idle saying in the racing world that 'every pound of over twelve stone counts double'. It was this theme, voiced in sympathy and curses, encouragement and condemnation, which was going to swell over the next two years.

Perth, on the sharp side and right-handed, was not for those reasons exactly Red Rum's cup of tea. But it had suited him reasonably well in 1973. In 1974 he put up, in McCain's words, 'a cracking good performance'.

Only two runners took him on for the £535 race. One was Arthur Stephenson's Southern Lad, carrying two stone less, and ridden by Tommy Stack, who had in earlier days not only frequently ridden, but briefly trained Red Rum, and who would, as things dramatically worked out, be coming back to him again the following year. The third contestant was by no means a useless 'chaser called Dunrobin to whom Red was set to give the maximum range of the handicap.

McCain had seen Southern Lad's previous race that season and been impressed by it. Even he, the eternal optimist, felt it unlikely that his horse, first time out and burlier than in any previous year, would give Southern Lad two stone and a beating.

The public thought otherwise. Betting as they would over the next two years more from their hearts than their heads, they made Red Rum 5–4 favourite to win on a course which was in almost every respect the reverse of Aintree. But the Scots had given the horse a delirious reception at Ayr in the spring. They were determined to support him now. The Stephenson stable, never averse to a gamble, were thus enabled to back Southern Lad at attractive odds: the horse, two years' Red Rum's junior, started at 11–8.

Dunrobin led for a mile with Red Rum close to him until the seventh fence. There the great horse took over, closely followed by Southern Lad. Three fences later Red

Rum made the sort of error which had cost him the Hennessy Gold Cup in November 1973. Four fences from home Southern Lad headed him until, jumping to the right two fences from home, he let Red Rum jump up and join him again. Both horses crossed the last fence together and both sprinted up the run in.

McCain watched anxiously. Peppering the praise which had followed his horse's Liverpool and Ayr National double had been a few barbed criticisms: McCain had asked the horse too much; eight and a half miles over fences in three spring weeks was too severe a trial even for the incredible Red Rum. He would at least lose his zest, the critics warned. His exertions could have 'bottomed' him for ever.

But Red Rum, ridden out strongly by Brian Fletcher, galloped up the run-in with all his famous courage, and was only one and a half lengths behind Southern Lad at the line, Dunrobin finishing a distance behind. Tommy Stack looked admiringly across at his old partner. The crowd buzzed. They had proof positive, it seemed, that not only had the immense strains of the spring not harmed Red Rum one jot; incredibly, the horse looked even better than ever.

The bookmakers with their accustomed caution immediately made Red Rum favourite at the seemingly absurd odds of 7–1 to win his third Grand National half a year, and half a dozen races ahead. Events however would prove them, if not generous, at least sensible: six months later Red Rum was going to start favourite at Liverpool at 7–2.

What was happening was evidence of a public mania about Red Rum which had exploded as he won his second Grand National and which showed no signs of subsiding. There was now no shadow of doubt that Rummy was the most popular racehorse in anyone's lifetime. Whenever he ran, however he ran, he was going to be backed with pounds and pence by men, old women, children, granddads, and tough lads in the services who knew nothing about racing, but who simply loved Red Rum.

As an established star, Red Rum had become public property. He was now beset with the commercial trappings associated with famous names whose presence means money. Business letters had begun to pour into 10, Upper Aughton Road just behind the first tide of congratulatory telegrams. Could W. W. Rouch, 'The Specialists in Horse Photography', make an early date for a session? Could Ginger McCain and Brian Fletcher attend another Anglo-American Sporting Club Boxing Night at the Piccadilly, Manchester, and a Variety Club of Liverpool Dinner at the Adelphi as guests of honour? 'I know full well,' wrote Peter Smith, admirable Secretary of the Jockeys Association, 'that your absence from either function would be a bitter disappointment.'

The Burley-on-the-Hill Jumping Show (which, though run by Joss Hanbury, sporting son of a brave father, would not be Britain's best-known equestrian event) asked if Red Rum and Brian Fletcher could parade during their day in former Rutland. The *Daily Mirror* Punters Club had a bigger plan. They set up a scheme for charity by which 'top quality litho prints' of Red Rum would be offered to their members. When might Kodak come down to Southport to take the photographs?

Worcester Royal Porcelain, producers of the Arkle statue, arranged for the famous Doris Lindner to make her model of the horse. Southport and Formby Boy Scouts brought a party of deprived boys from Glasgow to visit Red Rum. Jannay Films wanted the horse included in a projected TV film for the USA, Schweppes sent copies of their calendar featuring Red Rum (the first time the same horse had appeared two years running in this sought-after publication) and Sol Davies of the Jewish National Fund asked Mr Le Mare if Red Rum 'could come to the Adelphi Hotel and be brought into the dining room.' Mr Davies added, 'Before you think I am quite mad I would tell you we did this some years ago with a pony and it was very successful. I personally think it will hit world headlines, i.e. "RED RUM COMES TO DINNER" . . .'

43. 'All back to square one'

The horse who had become big business next ran in the race he had won in 1973: the three-mile 110 yds. Joan Mackay Handicap 'Chase at Ayr worth £1507 to the winner. He carried his expected 12 st. 7 lb. (up 3 lb. on 1973), and gave the full extent of the handicap to every other runner except Straight Vulgan. He took up the running two fences from home from Meridian II (then Ken Oliver's but who would later become Red Rum's stable companion and ill-fated friend at grass).

This time Brian Fletcher reversed the Perth result with Tommy Stack. Stack on Scout (10 st.), who had won his previous race, sprinted after Red Rum from the last. Both horses quickened and ran on gamely. But even Rummy's 2 st. 7 lb. extra could not hold him back. He won impressively by one and a half lengths, favourite naturally at 5–4. McCain commented, 'That was a dam' good performance with Meridian,' who had finished, carrying 10 st., nine and a half lengths back in third place.

McCain announced that Rummy's next race would be a new three and a half mile 'chase put on by Tony Stratton Smith's Charisma record company at their brand new 'pop' meeting at Kempton Park.

Charisma Records were understandably champing to lure the greatest crowd-puller in equine show-biz down to Kempton Park. Michael Wale, racing manager to the sponsors and a brightly bouncing face on commercial television, urged Ginger McCain: 'Here's hoping Red Rum will come south on that day and therefore entertain thousands of Londoners and make, I'm sure, many converts to National Hunt racing.'

I applauded Wale's sentiments at the time but was convinced that Kempton would not suit Red Rum as a track in any condition and that, wet as it would be, he was most unlikely to act round it at all.

Donald McCain, however, like many proud Northerners, regards southern England as a different country. He had wished, when he took Rummy down for the Hennessy, to show the doubting southerners just how good his great horse was. It had not yet struck Ginger McCain that southerners, whatever else their manifold weaknesses, no longer doubted that there existed in Southport the greatest Liverpool horse of all time and steeplechasing's outstanding hero.

It is worth noting now in view of Red Rum's running and the subsequent criticisms of the 1975–76 season, that those first three victories under McCain's wing in 1972 round Carlisle, Wetherby and Newcastle were won off 10 st. 13 lb., 10 st. 10 lb., and 10 st. 11 lb. The last two weights, what was more, included 5 lb. penalties. Three years on, the horse had risen about two stone in the weights, at the same time as his natural speed round normal park tracks was starting gradually to decline.

But Ginger McCain in 1974 wanted his star to be shown to the Londoners and to win for the first time in the south. And, he argued against my case, the extra half mile must help, he would have half a stone less on his back, and the ground, they'd assured him from Kempton, was never heavy.

'I'll take him down, anyway,' Ginger said. 'I'll parade him. . . .' But I knew that if the horse was on the course, McCain would run him.

When on 19 October the numbers were slid up into the boards for the 2.35, the three and a half miles flag-started

£2309 Charisma Records Handicap 'Chase, there was Red Rum of course at the top. Given 11 st. 13 lb. by the handicapper, his penalty for winning only seven days previously at the other end of Britain raised his weight one pound to the maximum 12 st. A two and a half stone weight difference however still existed, for bottom weight was 9 st. 7 lb. On this minimum were the useful stayers Esban (owned by that forceful singing personality Dorothy Squires) and Fred Rimell's Boom Docker.

For the latter Fred had booked L'Escargot's brilliant Irish jockey Tommy Carberry, who could easily do the 9 st. 7 lb. Fred Rimell's other horse was the fancied Rough House, carrying a mere one pound more. Twelve stone might have looked a light weight to McCain; but Red Rum was still relatively harshly handicapped with some decent staying steeplechasers.

A very mixed assortment of visitors had come to Kempton in the main to study racing's living legend. Few had ever seen the bay horse in the flesh. While they awaited his appearance in the preliminary parade ring they eyed one another curiously. As a number of pop groups performed in the Silver Ring, their supporters in worn, torn jeans and slapping sandals mingled unbelievingly with others wearing matching suits of tweed, ties and even trilby hats.

Ginger McCain had to walk carefully round puddles of water glinting on the grass to saddle Red Rum. The heavy rains had left the 'chase course officially 'yielding'. It would be far too soft for Red Rum. *Sporting Life*, noting that the horse's presence – 'Britain's favourite racehorse' – would bring the crowds 'pouring in', commented equally accurately: 'he faces a tough task today in softer conditions than he relishes.'

The crowd and punters off the course, however, made him clear favourite 9–4, from Rough House at 4's, and that good old chaser Royal Toss at 5's, a winner last time out but still with his penalty carrying the pittance of

10 st. 1 lb. The crowd, expecting another Grand National type triumph, were very soon disappointed. At no stage was Red Rum galloping easily or jumping boldly in the wet ground round the almost continuous bends. After one circuit Brian Fletcher was niggling away to keep the horse in the race at all. He never got closer than fifth place and was falling back when he made a considerable blunder three fences from home, the first in the straight. This knocked him right out of the race and he trailed in last of the eight finishers from the eleven starters.

Rough House beat Esban and Spanish Steps by six lengths and one length, with Boom Docker five lengths away fourth. Then came a great gap to Avondhu fifteen lengths further behind.

The Grand National hero had not reached the last fence as Rough House galloped past the post.

The crowd, grievously let down, murmured uneasily. Ginger McCain and Noel Le Mare's grandson, Michael Burns, a Manchester stock-jobber, strode across to the horse frowning. Brian Fletcher said crossly, 'The horse was never going,' but it was noted that Fletcher was limping badly as he humped his saddle away over the grass. The leg he had injured in a fall at Southwell a week previously was still plainly paining him.

McCain was swiftly surrounded by the courteous correspondents of London's racing press. He squarely accepted all blame. 'I took a bloody liberty running him on this holding ground. Of course, I'm bloody disappointed.' He looked it. He added with only a half-smile, 'He's a better horse than I'm a trainer, that's for sure.'

'Plans?' enquired the press. 'Where'll he go next, Don?'

'Will it be the Hennessy, Ginger?'

'Is he all right, Don?'

'He'll run in the Hennessy,' McCain pronounced, 'if the ground's suitable.'

The bookmakers now suggested that Rough House was a 16–1 chance for the Grand National. And Red Rum?

Still 7–1. 'That's real daft!' Ginger exploded. 'It's 7–1 against *getting* a horse to Aintree, let alone win it!'

In the last nine runnings of the Grand National from 307 horses no less than 195 had failed to complete. The casualty rate had been nearly two out of every three starters.

McCain's criticism was justified. His outburst was due to pressures. Several experts felt that Red Rum looked bored at Kempton. McCain's aim of showing the flag in the south had been singularly confounded. Whatever confidence he still exuded in public, he now entertained several private doubts.

He was also engaged with Billy Ellison on their hardy annual autumnal struggle to clip out the horse. The clipping took over a fortnight, with Red Rum's ears blocked with cotton wool, and a radio blaring to subdue the clippers' roaring.

As November progressed, the rains continued to fall in the south. Leicester, Fontwell, Taunton and Warwick were all water-logged and abandoned.

The rain gods settled the issue. Red Rum thankfully did not even travel south for the Hennessy. When the first day of Newbury looked likely to be abandoned, Ginger McCain, saddling Wolverhampton up at Sedgefield to win for his and Aintree's new owner Mr Bill Davies, announced that Red Rum would definitely not run at Newbury.

Instead McCain aimed his horse for a level-weight clash at Haydock with Fred Winter's Gold Cup class 'chaser, Pendil. His decision was widely criticized. Pendil's stable-companion Crisp had come out nearly a stone and a half superior to Red Rum in the 1973 Grand National. Pendil's form made him superior to the now injured Crisp. To the experts it seemed absurd for Red Rum to take on Pendil in a three-horse race round a mere three miles at Haydock.

There existed however a more personal, human reason for running Red Rum at Haydock. It was one which the public, feeling that they now owned their hero, did not consider. Haydock Park, that go-ahead Lancashire course, was one of the few tracks octogenarian owner Noel Le Mare could now reach without undue fatigue: 'After all,' McCain told me, 'I've got to think about the Guv'nor, haven't I? It is *his* horse. And he isn't getting any younger.'

Apart from Red Rum, only Arthur Stephenson's Tartan Ace, winner of ten 'chases, took on the scintillating Pendil who had been beaten only twice in nineteen steeplechases – and those two defeats had been in the Cheltenham Gold Cup. He had every reason to start 3–1 on favourite for the £1950 Sundew 'Chase, run again on yielding ground. Ridden as usual by Richard Pitman, Pendil made – in commentator Michael Seth-Smith's accustomed phrase – 'every *yard* of the running' and won by a sauntering two and a half lengths from Tartan Ace. Red Rum was made to seem very short of pace against these two, plodding on at his usual speed as the two leaders turned into the straight and came down the last three fences. Pundits who had expected a two horse duel between Pendil, king of the park tracks and Red Rum, emperor of Aintree, were proved expectedly wrong. 'The other two,' Ginger McCain ruefully recalled, 'just sprinted away from us. Yes, I was disappointed. . . .'

He stuck nevertheless to his prepared plan for Red Rum's mid-season break. He would not aim to run him again before February. That would be the start of the final programme leading towards his great objective: their English Grand National hat trick.

Red Rum spent his winter holiday at home. 'We just kept him ticking over, the odd slow canter once or twice a week,' McCain recalls, adding surprisingly, 'he might sometimes have a three-mile canter on the beach.'

But Red Rum had lost his head lad, Jackie Grainger. The power which the horse continued to exert over his human circle now claimed another victim. During 1974 McCain had often been worried by the time Grainger (who drove the horsebox) and Billy Ellison were taking to get Red Rum home after his races and public outings.

'They were a couple of characters, of course,' says McCain charitably two years later, 'but I'd pass the other horse boxes coming away from the races, and ours would still be at the course. Maybe after Ayr they'd not come home till the evening of the day after the race. . . .'

The Grainger-Ellison post-racing carousels had become legendary in the north. The Red Rum song, belted out by them on many a northern racecourse in the dusk, had even reached the ears of a Dutch TV company who solemnly recorded this paean of praise in their excellent documentary about *'Cred Crum'*.

McCain blames himself for not speaking sooner. One evening in November McCain found his head lad and Billy 'scrappin' in the yard. I'd chewed Jackie up a bit,' Ginger reflects, 'because he'd wanted to take two lads and himself to a meeting. I said "we're short-staffed here. You can only take one". He argued. So I said "Right. *I'll* take the box myself and one boy."

'Then Grainger said to me in the yard, in front of all the lads, "If you don't like how I do things you can get my cards stamped up." I went straight to the office and said to Peter Cundy, "Get Jackie's cards stamped up and give them to him." And off I went. Peter came out and gave Grainger his cards and said to him quietly, "You'd better go home now. . . ." '

Two years later, Ginger sighs. 'It's a fault of mine. I do go a bit bald-headed at it, when I do it. But I was too much of a coward to do it before. It was sickening . . . very sickening. You know, I don't think Jackie's worked since he left here, I believe he's done nothing but just been on the dole for two years. To be fair, he'd had his troubles,' says Ginger. 'He'd had a little girl who was very ill. There'd been a telephone call once to the races, a message for Jackie Grainger that his daughter was seriously ill. I gave him my car to get home quickly, but when he got there it was too late.'

The departure of the head lad, usually the lynch-pin of any racing stable, occasioned little comment in the press. Ginger McCain gritted his teeth, as he had so often had to do before, and got down to doing the head lad's job himself. The trainer of the double 'National winner, the TV celebrity, became again the driver of the old horse box all across the north. He did the feeding and all the clipping. . . . 'And then I made Billy Ellison head lad. Right, you're surprised now! But then in the winter of 1974–75 Billy had got a new house, a new wife, even a labrador! He seemed to have settled down. And with Jackie gone I was sure he'd do the job well, with Beryl keeping an eye on the yard. . . .'

In the early winter of 1976 McCain lets out a groan to me in his sitting room which glows with the tangible evidence of the fame Red Rum has brought them: cups, goblets, porcelain models. 'This horse has picked us *all* up. There's no way any of us would have got such a lift without him. But look where they are *now*: Jackie Grainger, Billy Ellison, Brian Fletcher – they're all back to square one.' McCain touched the wood of his table lest the fate which had mown down so many of the Red Rum circle should scythe him away too.

From the sitting-room window the narrowing stable yard, with the old neat lawn gone to make way for that new row of boxes directly resulting from Red Rum's fame, seemed cosy in the grey afternoon. 'And there's the horse – still the same!' exploded McCain, as if exasperated at being unable to control the effect the horse has on people near him. The bay head with the bold eyes and the huge hooped ears was nodding eagerly over his box door. He looked a picture of innocence.

44. 'By God, he surprised us'

The year ended, and with Red Rum absent from the race-track, public interest in him quickly declined. In 1974 he had been voted Racehorse of the Year – 'I think,' says Beryl diffidently, turning over a crisp stack of invitations to functions honouring him, 'that he got a unanimous vote.'

In December Ginger McCain won the Derby Award for the Best National Hunt Trainer of the Year. 'And that was rather nice, you see,' Beryl comments, 'because Mr Le Mare had been the National Hunt Owner of the Year in 1973.'

The elements of fame, signing autographs, posting off hundreds of pictures, have not altered Beryl McCain's astonishing humility. It is always 'Mr Le Mare . . . Mr Wareing. . . .' Sometimes, as trainers' wives' reasonably will, she ventures opinions about the horses. There is no guarantee Ginger will accept it. 'Don't be daft, woman!' he may exclaim. Or, 'That's rubbish! Stick to the point.'

He will, however, as trainers do, refer to Beryl on most points of historical detail. 'Was it November Jackie Grainger went, Beryl?' And 'Ask Beryl, she'll know.'

He also persuades her nearly always to answer the insistent telephone. 'You talk to her. *You* talk.'

By the middle of January 1975 McCain could announce Red Rum's two stepping stones towards his third Grand National. 'He's tremendously well,' he enthused. 'Just ready to start his spring programme. It all depends on the ground,' said McCain, stating one of two strident themes that season, the other being the perennial doubt about the 'National taking place at all. 'Depending on the ground,' McCain affirmed, 'he'll run in the 'National Trial at Haydock on the 5 February, and then the Greenall Whitley there again in March.'

It had been a very wet New Year. Many race meetings were abandoned, and those that took place were run in conditions seldom lighter than yielding, and usually heavy. On top of the anxiety about the Grand National's occurrence (Aintree's new owner, the aggressive property developer Bill Davies, was proving obdurate in his dealings with Levy Board and Jockey Club) doubt about the going now troubled McCain's mind. If the race ever took place, affording Red Rum his chance of a treble, the ground after all the rain seemed likely to prove too heavy for him.

The going at Haydock on 5 February was again yielding. Partly for this reason, but mainly because the horse had not run for nearly two and a half months, Red Rum for once did not start favourite. Put into the betting for the three and a half mile £1646 steeplechase at 4–1, he drifted out to 6's. His friends described him as burly, his critics as fat, and *Chaseform* noted tersely, 'bit backward'.

Noel Le Mare however made the short journey from his comfortable red brick house in Waterloo Road, Birkdale, to watch Red Rum (12 st.) run. Preferred in the betting in a field of seven were Clarification (10 st.) at 11–4 who had won his previous race, with Meridian II (9 st. 7 lb.) and Glen Owen (9 st. 8 lb.) at 11–2. King's Lure (9 st. 5 lb.), Black Tudor (9 st. 8 lb.) and Highland Explorer (9 st. 12 lb.) completed the field.

Another reason why Red Rum was less fancied than usual was Brian Fletcher's luckless season. By the third week in January Fletcher had ridden only five winners in the six months since the season started. The rides he had been offered were so few that their earnings meant that 'I'd not have to pay income tax,' he said grimly from his Back and Sides Farm at Hammerback near West Auckland. Trainers were not ringing him up to ride. As a freelance since he fell out in 1972 with nearby Denys Smith, the Bishop Auckland trainer, Fletcher was as dependent as any struggling actor or actress on offers of work down the telephone. He had served his apprenticeship with Smith and it was ten years since his first winner, Grey Spirit at Ayr.

Scarcely had he split up with Smith and moved into his farm than a young horse fell on top of him, and the half ton smash broke his pelvis. His wife, Barbara, a former nurse, tended him through that disaster. Very slowly he began to ease his way back into racing.

Unfortunately Fletcher has never possessed the charm or quick wits of unemployed actors. He was not outgoing and possessed few friends. He did not put himself forward for rides. He would, as people do when struggling against lack of opportunities, look for an explanation.

'I can only think people believe I don't *want* rides that I'm saving myself for the 'National! That's rubbish. Racing's my bread and butter.'

He believed, too, that his lay-off earlier that season with a broken leg had made trainers forget him. He would not fully admit that the crashing fall he had suffered on Tartuffe for Denys Smith had had serious after-effects. Fletcher had fractured his skull in February 1972 and had been told by specialists (including the Levy Board's official medical officer) of the folly of ever riding again. His troughs of gloom and occasional losses of memory suggested to people meeting him that the Tartuffe fall might have been extremely serious.

It is against the grim background of Fletcher's severe injuries, coupled soon with that of domestic discord and threatened criminal proceedings in the family, that we have to consider the actions of this strange, gap-toothed, boy-faced jockey with the quiff of hair flopping over his brow like a forelock.

In the spring of 1975, it seemed to the racing world a long long time since Brian had been champion northern jockey with seventy-seven winners in 1967–68, the season in which he rode the first of his Grand National treble on Red Alligator.

But, as things turned out at Haydock, Red Rum (12 st.)

astonished and delighted everyone. With Highland Explorer and King's Lure making the running until the last ditch on the far side, but at a steady enough pace, Rummy could always lie handy. He jumped into the lead past Glen Owen three fences from home and quickened away on the run-in to beat him two and a half lengths with Meridian II in third place.

'He was as big as a bull', McCain remembers still astonished. 'I gave him no real chance. And, by God, he surprised us!'

I wondered then, and still wonder, whether Red Rum's first real glow of class that season had not resulted primarily because he was fresh.

McCain does not concur. 'We kept him working during his holiday far harder than the next winter when he went off to Ted Greenway's in '75–76, you know.'

It continued to rain throughout February. The ground at Haydock on Saturday, 1 March was soft, but a keen frost on the Thursday night before had stopped Red Rum's Friday morning thunderous winding-up gallop along Southport sands.

Red Rum with 12 st. 3 lb. did not run like a champion in Haydock's £4576 Greenall Whitley 'Chase. The ground was soft, the distance only three miles, and McCain considered him – by his tough standards – still short of work. Though the horse did not jump with his old bold accuracy and made a considerable hash of the twelfth fence, he recovered his position gradually and was making ground on the leaders High Ken (11 st. 5 lb.) and The Benign Bishop (11 st. 8 lb.) as he swung into the straight. It seemed, going to the third last, as if that impetus might get him at least within striking distance of them and old Spanish Steps (to whom he was conceding no less than 2 st. 3 lb.). But he pitched steeply as he landed down the drop over the third fence from home, lost momentum and was overtaken by April Seventh (11 st. 3 lb.), to finish fourth.

There was a terrific set-to on Haydock's swerving run-in between big Ron Barry on The Benign Bishop and slim Barry Brogan on High Ken. Andy Turnell on April Seventh was third seven lengths away. Red Rum finished fourteen lengths behind the winner.

In retrospect Red Rum clearly had a tough task with these horses at the weights, even had the going and distance suited him. High Ken and April Seventh were going to prove themselves high class 'chasers and Spanish Steps had run a splendid race when second to Rough House in Doncaster's Great Yorkshire 'Chase.

But at the time, many of the great horse's millions of supporters were disappointed. The bookmakers, reckoning that his Grand National chance had not been enhanced, pushed him out half a point from 9–2 to 5–1.

Yet now the real likelihood loomed that there would be no 1975 Grand National at all. The poker game of Aintree which had begun a decade earlier with more finesse but no less steely purpose by Mrs Topham, the Earl of Sefton and the local government authorities was now continued by its new owner, Mr Bill Davies, the Levy Board, the Jockey Club and the local authorities. Public and press were crowding round to try to read the cards. Davies demanded money to put the show on. The great British public demanded the show.

The racing authorities then played an ace: if Bill Davies and Aintree proved impossible, a substitute race would be run at nearby Haydock on the same day.

Ginger McCain declared that this would suit Red Rum just as well, though it patently would not. Piqued by a comment from Brian Fletcher – 'I've never really had a good ride on Red Rum round Haydock' – McCain vented his ire on a persistent caller from a Fleet Street sports desk. 'If the race *isn't* run at Aintree?' he repeated. 'You work and work on a horse's preparation for twelve months and then lose out for something like this! Yes I *am* sick. *And* very sad. It probably isn't worth going on.'

Noel Le Mare, too, was badgered by other worries. Rising eighty-eight he had to return actively to his great family business Norwest Hoist of which he was still president. In 1973 a Manchester property company had built up their 'outsiders' stake in the company to thirty-five per cent, and as Grand National week dubiously opened Noel Le Mare was back in harness, sorting out the board room and control problems of the company he had created over half a century earlier.

45. 'It was only his courage which kept him going'

Heavy ground persisted all over Britain and Red Rum's informed supporters were heartened by only two considerations: the going round Liverpool was never very heavy; and, because this would be the first meeting there of the 1974–75 season, the turf would be fresh.

A third factor then cheered McCain. On the Tuesday of the week in which he declared three runners for the Grand National a cold and drying wind was whistling across Southport. Red Rum would be accompanied by Noel Le Mare's second string, Ballyath, wearing his first colours so that Fletcher could keep the lucky 'second colours' yellow cap on top of Red Rum. The third contender from McCain's yard was intended to be Bill Davies' Wolverhampton who had won three successive races in mid-season. Steve Holland was booked for him and Jimmy Bourke for Ballyath.

In 1974 McCain had approached the Grand National in great awe of L'Escargot – 'a class horse', he had kept saying. But this year, although Red Rum was set to meet the dual Cheltenham Gold Cup winner at 10 lb. worse terms (12 st. to 11 st. 13 lb. in '74; 12 st. to 11 st. 3 lb. in '75), McCain no longer considered L'Escargot a serious threat. 'That old horse,' he laughed, 'we beat him last year. He's twelve years old now. We'll beat him again!' And then he would stop smiling and add, '*If* we get the ground. . . .'

But some observers of the racing scene knew that *this* season as never before, Dan Moore had prepared L'Escargot for nine months towards one single target: the Grand National. Compared with his races in various parts of the world during the previous two seasons, Raymond Guest's class 'chaser had run but four times. His winding-up race in the two-mile Champion Chase at boggy Cheltenham had particularly impressed those in the know.

On the Wednesday before the 'National Red Rum galloped two miles on Southport sands – 'it was dam' hard to pull him up, I can tell you,' McCain enthused. 'He's really super! He'll have an easy day Thursday and then his usual sharp gallop Friday.'

His galloping companion would be Wolverhampton. Bill Davies' horse 'worked brilliantly' (in McCain's words) on their first thunder along the cold wet sands. They went back, normal McCain fashion, to do it again. Then Christine Langhorne, who was on Wolverhampton, felt the horse weaken beneath her and stagger. She shouted out, 'I think he's setfast!' (A sharp painful attack usually in the back and quarter muscles, often resulting from cramming racehorses with strong food.) But it was not. Wolverhampton collapsed onto the sand, stretched out and died.

'He just dropped dead!' Ginger remembers, still grimacing. 'I get the vet, Ted Greenway, and he fixes an autopsy at Liverpool University and it turns out it's a ruptured blood vessel – probably a result of red worms getting into him when he was young. Then I have to get onto the Davies'. I leave messages with his wife. I go over to see him in his office. *He's* preoccupied with the Grand National next day. *I'm* wound up before the Grand National next day. . . .' McCain flushes and shrugs. 'Davies didn't seem to care. Then one of his aides said things to me – ' sparks certainly flew at that sad interview.

Poor Wolverhampton had cost 14 000 guineas and been transferred to McCain from the now retired Tom Corrie's stables before the season's start. Davies, after his long struggle with the Jockey Club and Levy Board, had finally got a grant of £20 000 for the National meeting and reported that gate money at the meeting so far had been 'disastrous'.

There was further cause for depression. Rain had fallen heavily again, and John Williams, manager at Aintree, announced the going on the 'National course was soft.

Brian Fletcher, too, had bad news. His parents split up after a thirty-year marriage and they had been charged with alleged handling of stolen goods. Fletcher had no consolation from the thick clouds in the sky. He knew better than anyone that Red Rum required not only fast ground but sunshine on his back in a race. It now looked thoroughly unlikely that the horse, on whom he had not clapped an eye since Haydock, would get either. Pursuing his accustomed distant relationship with McCain, Fletcher had still never ridden a single gallop on the horse anywhere except on the racecourse. 'They talk about "will *he* do it three times",' Fletcher grumbled to me. 'Think o' the weight on *my* shoulders!' He referred to L'Escargot – 'that Irishman with the French name – they'll have him absolutely right, o' course. . . .'

Perhaps only the bookmakers and the Chancellor of the Exchequer viewed the Grand National with lively anticipation. Chancellor Denis Healey was going to collect about £1¾ million whatever horse won, and the bookies estimated that £20 million – a record 25 per cent increase over 1974 – would be bet with them on that one race.

William Hill announced that they would lose £50 000 if Red Rum brought off his treble, but double that amount should the race be won by L'Escargot, the very heavily backed second favourite. Shrewd observers of L'Escargot's progress and friends of the stable had been punting on him like a good thing. The Dikler (Ron Barry), who had won a Cheltenham Gold Cup, Kempton's King George VI, and Sandown's Whitbread, was the other horse representing top park course class. He, with dashing Glanford Brigg, Clear Cut, and the great public favourite Spanish Steps all started at the sporting price of 20–1.

L'Escargot, Spanish Steps, The Dikler and Beau Bob were all twelve years old – too old in most experts' opinion. Yet all four were going to run outstandingly well.

There was also considerable backing for Money Market, who would start fourth favourite at 14–1, Rough House at 12–1, and Land Lark from the smallest yard with a runner: the Pocock's little stable near Bridgwater, Somerset to which he was never going to return.

To placate the gods, the McCains carried out to a T their routine of the previous victorious years. Beryl plaited Rummy's mane. With exactly the same company they would go to the races again in the same Stan Wareing's car. Red Rum had slept well in his own stable, an inestimable advantage, and there would be fewer runners than in any of the four previous years: thirty-one. Of these twenty-one would fail to complete and two would die in action.

The Red Rum plan was the same as twice before: to 'hunt round' the first circuit until, as Brian Fletcher put it, 'the scrubbers are out, the things with no chance, the fellers tryin' to make the headlines . . . and then to ride the usual sort of race.'

In front of the smallest crowd regulars could recall ('priced out by that Davies' was the common cry), the field finally got off a quarter of an hour late at three-thirty. Junior Partner had to be reshod. Fifteen minutes waiting before any big race is punishing enough: the McCains, Noel Le Mare and the millions of fans who had made their Rummy 7–2 favourite were writhing on the rack.

Zimulator, ridden by the unknown but intrepid Captain Swan, dashed away in front with Junior Partner (Ken White), Money Market (Jeff King), and Glanford Brigg (Martin Blackshaw). The pale-blue hooded L'Escargot who had, with Red Rum and Money Market, looked outstandingly well in the paddock, was well to the fore. L'Escargot was ridden as usual by trainer Dan Moore's son-in-law Tommy Carberry, who had won not only the Cheltenham Gold Cup on Ten Up within the month but also the Irish Grand National that Monday on Brown Lad, both for young Jim Dreaper.

The good amateur Peter Greenall fell on Shaneman at the first and scrambled up to remount. In the scrimmage Rag Trade (Johnny Francome), who was to improve dramatically over the ensuing year, only just got over.

Barely observable by the general public in the wave of horses breaking over the first fence Red Rum was nearly knocked sideways as he landed. 'My God!' swore Ginger McCain, 'He's been brought down!'

Not quite, but Red Rum was lying very far back as the field hurtled away to the second fence where Junior Partner fell with Clear Cut (Tommy Stack), and Glen Owen was nearly brought down.

L'Escargot and The Dikler, in contrast to Red Rum, were soon galloping close up behind the leaders. When Zimulator fell, Feel Free (Taffy Salaman) came to the front closely pursued by Glanford Brigg. The pace for the state of the ground was tremendous. The Dikler followed them over Becher's where Spittin' Image crashed, bringing down April Seventh.

The fence after Becher's, the one at the far end of the track, is often erroneously supposed to be an easy one. Here the fates, who had started to turn against Red Rum, gave his greatest rival first a staggering shock and then an astonishing reprieve. L'Escargot, lying close up fifth, struck this fence a colossal blow, and lurched forwards so precariously on landing that he went half-down with his off-fore stretched right out to prop him up. Carberry's hands shot up his neck to just behind his hood and the jockey's head, two feet lower than the hump of his breeches, was down by L'Escargot's ears. And L'Escargot's ears were less than three feet from the jerking, sodden turf. Even worse, the toes of Tommy Carberry's boots were knocked back right onto the top of his saddle flaps, one foot out of its stirrup iron. He was within a split second of parting company. Had he done so, Red Rum, seven battling minutes later, would have come home an easy winner to be the first triple victor of the race.

Would have. . . . Up came L'Escargot's neck, back sat Carberry and away they went. Some way behind Red Rum followed towards the outer rear of the pack in the position of a rugby wing-forward. He was not going well. The figure that had magically danced across the fast turf of the '74 had vanished. On the soft ground now Red Rum looked a normal horse, moving with resolution but with effort. Brian Fletcher was to report to McCain: 'He was going so badly, I very nearly pulled him up.' And McCain, walking the course after the race beside the railway line, shook his head to see how soft the ground was. 'Their hooves had gone right in – right up to the fetlock joints. It can only have been sheer bloody guts that kept him going. . . .'

At the Canal Turn, L'Escargot jumped seventh with Red Rum still towards the rear, but moving inwards from the outside track he had taken up going to Becher's. There had been many casualties already and the empty horses, three in front and two more close up, were all round Martin Blackshaw on Glanford Brigg – 'blazing the trail,' the BBC's commentator Peter O'Sullevan sung out – as Blackshaw led the survivors back on to the racecourse. Red Rum was crossing the fences with that peculiar economical flexing action of his, almost 'knee-ing' over them. But as he reached the racecourse he was no closer than tenth of the twenty-one runners still remaining. Fletcher suddenly looked around, assessing how many remained behind. Plainly he realized he had to get closer and he now rode Rummy steadily forward, improving through the middle of the field as they came, behind four empty horses, down to the dreaded Chair.

Here, the fifteenth fence, Land Lark seemed to Graham Thorner to die between his knees in mid-air. He was dead certainly soon after he hit the ground.

The loose horses, a fearful menace, hooked right in a pack towards the stables, as what remained of the field swung steadily away. The pace, too, was now somewhat diminished on the next circuit of the battered course. By the first fence second time round, Red Rum had progressed a little. After the Chair and the water he was lying about ninth. But L'Escargot was away in front of him, and seemed to Red Rum's supporters to be galloping with an ominous nonchalance behind Glanford Brigg, High Ken, Beau Bob and Southern Quest. Carberry steadied L'Escargot, but Fletcher continued to drive Red Rum forwards. As the field approached the fence before Becher's Brook Red Rum caught up with L'Escargot on his outside flank. At that instant Tommy Carberry, catching sight of the favourite's colours, turned his head and, so easily was he going, took a long hard look across the flying turf at Red Rum. Carberry observed plainly and comfortably that L'Escargot's main rival and former conqueror was not going half as well as he was. . .

High Ken, given an exhilarating ride by Barry Brogan, had leapt into the lead at the open ditch and was sailing away in front. Then, at the fence before Becher's, he fell. 'High Ken has gone!' shouted Julian Wilson, the BBC's crisp commentator. 'And the ones behind him have just escaped the trouble.' L'Escargot was behind him. But once again the luck rolled right for him. As L'Escargot landed slightly swerving, he struck not the half ton body of High Ken, but the rolling ten stone of the luckless Brogan.

L'Escargot was only slightly impeded. Going down into Becher's it was Glanford Brigg and Southern Quest with Red Rum nearly level with them in Fletcher's normal spot to ease that cliff edge – on the wide outside. The three horses landed safely; The Dikler and L'Escargot followed and went on, but Beau Bob crashed and broke his neck and died.

Then Red Rum showed just in front and briefly going to the fence which four minutes earlier had so nearly cut L'Escargot and Carberry apart. At this fence Red Rum, too, made his one bad mistake of the race. Southern Quest snatched up the lead again and Glanford Brigg too went past our hero. A groan arose from millions yearning into their television sets – Rummy was done for. . . .

After Red Rum galloped The Dikler and L'Escargot, and at that furthest point from the stands, with the field moving distantly left-handed towards the Canal Turn, victory now seemed to lie within the tiring grasp of any one of those five. None seemed predominant. It was now painfully plain that Red Rum was in no way playing with the opposition as he had in 1974. But, we heartened ourselves, he was still there in the front of the hunt. We knew he would stay every yard, and, at that point L'Escargot had temporarily ceased to look as menacing.

Indeed as the field swung for home and into Valentines, Red Rum rose at the fence with Southern Quest and so great was his spring landing out over the 'brook' that he passed the astonishing and now astonished Irish horse in the air. A great cry of joy now fountained up from the stands as the bay head in the white sheepskin noseband emerged for the second time in the race where it belonged: in front.

Cheering for 'Red', bellowing for 'Rummy', we saw Glanford Brigg still close to him and on his inside, Southern

Quest still there and not yet beaten. Then suddenly the sinister blue-hooded head of L'Escargot had crept up close on the inside rail.

It is the nature of racing to elevate and then to cast down. What had been shouts of triumph now changed, wherever the race was being watched, to desperate, growling urgings: 'C'm*on*, Rummy! C'm*on*!' In a few thumping strides what none of Red Rum's fans could admit was slowly dawning: their hero was not cruising; he was struggling.

Glanford Brigg finally dropped back beaten, as Red Rum and L'Escargot came together towards the third last. To the inexpert eye they may have seemed to be racing stride for equal stride. And then you looked at their jockeys. . . . There sat Tommy Carberry still as a mouse with a hold on L'Escargot's head as if he were still cantering leisurely down to the start. His superiority was starkly placarded. And there by Carberry's still side worked busy Brian Fletcher, long-legged, strong-booting, driving Red Rum along and along just to keep up.

We were defeated then. We knew it. There were only seconds now in which Red Rum's miraculous treble could be achieved only if L'Escargot fell or inexplicably, like Devon Loch, collapsed. It seemed to Red Rum's friends long minutes of stoat-and-rabbit torture. For, though Carberry could have accelerated away from his rival at any stride, he did not choose to do so.

Going to the second last, Carberry turned casually towards Brian Fletcher by his side and said something lightly – he doesn't remember what. And poor Brian weighed down with domestic crises, praying the 'National could help him once again, knew then that the 'National and Red Rum could not rescue him. Goaded by L'Escargot's cruel superiority he shouted at Carberry, 'Go *on*! You've won by five minutes!' Partly the shout of one sportsman to another who risks his neck, it was the cry, too, of the victim to the executioner, seeking the sudden end.

But still Carberry coolly waited, so that L'Escargot would have something, would have the great Red Rum as a mere jumping companion, over the last fence. The two horses were so close that the jockeys' knees were almost brushing and their faces, one lean and puckish on the inside, the other, round and schoolboyish, bobbed along within whispering range of one another. Tommy Carberry leisurely looked behind him; no, no danger lurked there either. Brian Fletcher drew his stick and slapped Rummy with it. His right arm whirled. They rose at the last together and Red Rum, such was his final spring, gained in the air and he touched down a foot or two ahead of L'Escargot. In that second our hopes for the last time flared. Then Tommy Carberry gave old L'Escargot a squeeze with his heels and they left Red Rum, hero of Aintree, as if he were standing.

'Here he comes striding clear to win the 'National,' cried Peter O'Sullevan. 'L'Escargot, twelve years old, avenging last year's defeat. . . .'

At the 'elbow', Brian looked back to see if anything was plodding on that might beat the great Red Rum to second place. By the time Brian looked to the front again L'Escargot was pulling up. . . . Getting 11 lb. from Red Rum he had sauntered home to win by fifteen lengths. On the book he had come out 4 lb. superior. In '74 Red Rum had proved, theoretically, 8 lb. superior to him. It was a change round of about a stone. My estimate was that L'Escargot's special preparation accounted for about half of that, and that Red Rum on ground he did not like at all had run only about 7 lb. below his best.

'L'Escargot,' called out O'Sullevan, a cloud of sadness across the lift and beat of his superb professional voice, 'the comfortable winner over the little hero who won it last year . . . *and* the year before. . . .'

Behind the two superstars followed respectfully

Spanish Steps, eight lengths and 25 lb. behind Red Rum, twelve lengths more to Money Market (getting 15 lb.), six lengths to The Dikler (getting 1 lb.) and 10 lengths more to Manicou Bay (getting 21 lb.). Four more finished – Southern Quest, Glanford Brigg, Hally Percy and last of all and out of sound of the shouting, the horse who was going to play the villain's role next year: Rag Trade.

'Red Rum', spoke Peter O'Sullevan, 'has gone down *fighting*, clearly beaten by the weight, the concession of 11 lb. to L'Escargot.'

Four years before Tommy Carberry was born, his father-in-law L'Escargot's trainer Dan Moore had been beaten a head in the 'National riding Royal Danieli by the American-bred Battleship. So America won again. So the Moores were twice revenged by a superb strategy of long-term training.

Raymond Guest, one of the most popular Americans with the Irish and British, was splendidly emotional over L'Escargot. Tears of joy coursed behind his thick glasses. But suddenly and briefly what anybody was saying in the winner's enclosure was drowned by the roar of pride that burst out when Red Rum was led in next to him. 'It wasn't the weight,' Ginger McCain was going to be ingenuously and wearily explaining during the next three months. 'It wasn't the weight. *It was the going*. He was hating the ground nearly every yard of the race,' Ginger McCain declared. 'It was only his courage which kept him going.'

It had been a desperately hard race for Red Rum physically. Psychologically, his struggle over the last half mile on his own victory ground against a rival going outstandingly better would seriously have distressed him.

46. 'A diabolical boob'

It had been a sad Grand National for many, and for thousands a sour one, too. The crowds had stayed away from Bill Davies' Aintree. The stands, never glamorous nor glittering, looked, in their emptiness, even dingier than ever before.

The nation's hero had not contrived to triumph three years running. And even the victory of L'Escargot was not to be savoured over the years: it too ended with a bitter taste. In the glorious elation of welcoming home this winner, Raymond Guest from Powhatan Plantation, Virginia, and Bessemer Securities Inc., New York, owner of two Epsom Derby winners in Larkspur and Sir Ivor and former American Ambassador to Ireland, proudly announced generously to the Moores and gratefully to his old horse, that he had given L'Escargot to his trainer's wife.

The assumption was that the Gold Cup – Grand National National double winner (the first since fabled Golden Miller) would be happily retired. But only five months later he turned out in Ireland at Listowel carrying top weight in the Kerry National and was beaten a head in a close finish. Eyebrows were more than raised. And Mr Raymond Guest, without more ado, forcefully summoned home his great 'chaser to full retirement in America.

Earlier than that unpleasantness, sadness and sourness had cloaked Red Rum's next appearance. To the amazement of racing's experts Ginger McCain, within days of his horse's punishing defeat round four and a half miles of Liverpool, announced that he was sending him up to Scotland for the four-mile Scottish Grand National only fourteen days later. This race he had won in 1974. But then there had been three weeks between the two contests. Even more important Red Rum won the Aintree National in '74 with swaggering ease. This year he had struggled and lost it.

In these circumstances, even without benefit of hindsight, McCain's decision to run at Ayr seems quite unjustifiable. Honestly he now confesses, 'It was a diabolical boob.' Looking back in the autumn of '76 at the Grand National of '75 he seriously considered: '*That* race might have started to *bottom* him.'

But he had allowed himself to become a prisoner of his horse's fame. He respects mankind, is grateful for kind words and hates to disoblige people. For months Lady Yarrow had been working on a huge bronze statue of Rummy and Brian jumping a fence. This, it had long been arranged, would be unveiled on a grassy bank in the paddock at Ayr on Scottish Grand National day. Noel Le Mare and Mrs Doris Solomon were committed to the engagement. Red Rum's biographer had flown up. The occasion would be televised to millions.

Weakly and wrongly Ginger McCain succumbed to the pressures of fame. He sent his horse up to Ayr in the care of Billy Ellison for the last time. And round and round and round that paddock at Ayr walked Red Rum. He walked listlessly. He did not arch his neck nor swing his quarters. But Billy Ellison, aware that the crowds had come to see his 'Red', had the horse out there parading for nearly an hour.

'I don't know,' McCain wags his head. 'He *seemed* sharp and well . . . And there was this statue. . . .' Noel Le Mare, looking a little shaky, came slowly across from the hotel by the paddock. The crowd were restrained, photographers took up their shooting positions, we grouped ourselves and the statue was finally unveiled in a rush to fit it into television schedules.

The race was more briefly dealt with. Red Rum (12 st.) once again made favourite and urged on by a crowd of 13 000, was never travelling easily. At halfway Brian Fletcher really got at him and drove him hard along the back straight in front of the council houses and he made some progress through the field under pressure. When they turned downhill for home it was plain that he had no chance of reaching the leaders. Barona (10 st.), ridden by Paul Kelleway made a great race of it to the line to beat Rubstic (9 st. 8 lb.), Martin Blackshaw showing the same spectacular skill and dash in this 'National as he had at Aintree on Glanford Brigg. The Benign Bishop (11 st. 8 lb.), ridden by Ron Barry, was third and Meridian II (9 st. 9 lb.) and Colin Tinkler were fourth three lengths further away.

Red Rum plodded on without acceleration to finish seventh of the twelve finishers from the seventeen starters. 'He was only beaten about fifteen lengths by Barona – and he was giving two stone, y'know,' urges McCain, recommending even now the reasonable performance of the horse who made him.

But Fletcher, blunt, flushed and angry, said as he got off, 'The horse was *never* going. He *never* gave me the right feel.'

At that instant, I suspect that McCain, smarting already under severe self-criticism, knowing he had made a serious blunder, was so wounded by Fletcher's outburst that he resolved that sooner now rather than later the partnership must end.

McCain's whole yard, certainly by comparison with the glories of the previous two years, had enjoyed only a moderate season. From more than thirty horses in training (a sizeable increase) he had produced but ten winners of £7000. Half of these had been won by Red Rum (2) and Wolverhampton (3).

The former might now at long last have been drained dry of even his unequalled well of endurance and courage; he might have had enough of it. The latter was dead and the subject of two legal actions between McCain and Bill Davies; McCain sueing for unpaid training fees and Davies sueing for the loss of his horse.

Suddenly nothing was rosy any more. A blight fell over all.

There had been previous little love lost between McCain and Fletcher since the two first got together with Red Rum (Fletcher being McCain's third choice after Tommy Stack and Ron Barry) at Ayr on Monday 13 November 1972. I believe that on that sadly sour drive back from Scotland to Southport on Saturday 19 April 1975 McCain decided to part company.

Another, too, was getting close to severing his extraordinary relationship with Red Rum. Billy Ellison had thought it wrong to run his horse. He too travelled back with Red discomforted and discontented. Seeds of disruption were blowing everywhere in the spring air.

47. 'They all go . . .'

Red Rum spent the summer of '75 with Andy the shabby donkey in their usual small flat field. But there had been changes there, too: the old shed in which they used to shelter from the flies had gone; so, too, had the old tree. 'And they didn't ask him to Southport show again,' McCain remembers, still understandably piqued. 'But Doris Lindner came and took photographs for her model of him, and so did David Lovegrove for his.'

In July, just before Red Rum was due to come in from grass to start preparing for his season, and just before Ginger and Beryl McCain were going to Jersey for a short holiday, Billy Ellison, still the head lad, came to Beryl, said he had 'flu or a cold and asked to go home. Beryl gave him some pills and anxiously let him off, hoping to see him next day.

Shy Beryl McCain confesses to some friction with tough Billy the boxer throughout the summer. 'Billy had this young girlfriend – he'd split up with his wife – who would keep coming round the yard. I'd told him, "You couldn't have girls in factories. Stables are a place of work just like that." ' Beryl McCain also makes the point – 'There's the security side of it, too, when strangers come into racing yards.'

Beryl and Billy did not get on. Their life styles were utterly opposed. She refers to him now as Ellison. Ginger, in spite of all, can still laugh about it. But a trainer's wife, always handy for complaints, is the victim of most staff grumbles. 'Ellison was always pressuring me about holidays and things,' Beryl says. 'He thought I'd pass them on to Ginger.' She seldom did.

After Billy had been absent with his cold for a few days, Beryl McCain went round to see when he would be coming back. She thought she heard the sounds of hammering and decorating in the house he was sharing with his girlfriend. She knocked, waited, and after some delay, Billy Ellison appeared at the door and, just in case any light comedy were now needed in this extraordinary story, heavily cloaked in a blanket. Beryl gave evidence to the subsequent Industrial Tribunal that Billy was shaved and in a T-shirt and trousers. Billy declared he was in pyjamas. She suggested that if Billy were fit enough to decorate his house, he might be fit enough to return to work. After a brief exchange, duly recorded in different versions before the tribunal (to which Ellison swiftly reported the matter) Ellison offered a week's notice. Beryl was alarmed about telling Ginger that his head lad, Red's special lad, was going. 'I hummed and ahhed, but when I told Ginger he just said, "Right! Send his cards round." '

Ellison's cards went round. 'But, half an hour later,' McCain now recalls, unable to suppress a grin, 'that Billy was round on a bicycle going up and down the street outside the stables shouting, "Don't go sick here! You'll get a week's notice!" '

It was not however to continue on such a merry note. If Billy Ellison had believed that McCain would relent, he was wrong. Ellison's notice was accepted. The proceedings for 'wrongful dismissal' which Ellison brought before the Industrial Tribunal were not pleasant, but eventually Billy's complaint was dismissed.

Meanwhile Red Rum was returning to his box and required a lad. Christine Langhorne believed she should and would get him. She had been in the yard a long time. Her father, a former head lad in another stable, lived in the same street as the McCains, frequently dropped in for chats and owned a half-share in a horse in the yard.

Christine's father had pronounced ideas on how racehorses should be trained, as the author had discovered on earlier occasions, and was neither slow nor brief in airing them. Partly for this reason, but mainly because McCain was convinced that no girl would be strong enough to ride Red in his work down Southport sands, he decided to give the horse to Billy Beardwood.

Christine Langhorne was bitterly upset. She came to McCain. 'Will you take two weeks' notice?' she asked almost in tears.

'I will,' declared McCain, never a man to react favourably to threats.

He says resignedly now, 'And she never came back, and since then we're not speaking with the family at all, though we all live so close. It's very sad.'

Ten days before the split with Billy Ellison, Beryl McCain had sacked a junior stable girl. Derek Critchley, who had had quite a few rides in public, had also left during the summer. The old staff at Upper Aughton Road were disappearing like the daffodils. All was changing.

In July for the first time McCain spoke publicly about a possible change of jockey, too. He told a reporter: 'Red Rum was beaten in his last three runs and may be getting a little stale. I may even consider putting up another jockey. Brian Fletcher rode him superbly at Aintree. But it may be that a fresh jockey could renew his zest.'

Meanwhile McCain went back to doing the head lad's job yet again while eighteen-year-old Billy Beardwood, nicknamed 'Billy Two', took over Britain's best loved horse. Beardwood had done Prehistoric (then belonging to Noel Le Mare's son) the previous season and had been in the stables nearly two years. Beryl McCain reported, to the relief of all women, children and most men anxious about Rummy's welfare, that 'Billy's real soft with his horses'.

He was, however, as Ginger put it, 'bang in the hot seat.' Letters were already coming in from well-wishers agitating that Red would pine for Billy Ellison. 'Billy Beardwood', declares McCain, 'is a top-class lad and a good work-rider. But the boy was on a hiding to nothing.' And then, sadly thinking of all the people in Red Rum's life, McCain adds, 'They all go. . . . They all go . . . and the horse stays for ever. . . .'

Billy Beardwood was born nearby in Liverpool on 2 August 1956, but in a family which had nothing to do with racing. He was not only much younger, but gentler than Billy the first. He is more of a thinker, enjoys working out weights for handicaps (his racing interest started from having the odd small bet) and he likes the idea – if he were ever to become a trainer – of planning out horses' programmes.

'I was sittin' on that bath there in the yard and the Guv'nor came up and said, "You can do the horse for me. We'll see how you get on." And that's how it's been,' says Billy still marvelling. 'I didn't believe it really. It took a lot of time to sink in. . . .' He adds modestly, 'But there were a lot of girls in the yard then, and they'd not have been strong enough to ride him out.'

McCain had the same plans as usual for Red Rum. 'Carlisle first.' He gnaws his lip. 'It's always an anxious time.

the first race, wonderin' is the "snap" still there. . . . And this time particularly, after those hard races at the end of the previous season. . . .'

It was also a particularly anxious Saturday, that 27 September, for young Billy. 'The first time I took him to Carlisle I were that nervous I were all fingers and thumbs. I'd me new suit on, and he pulled me down the ramp of the horse box, and I fell over and I was all covered in mud right from here [touching his hair] down to me shoes. The horse got loose. He could have run off anywhere. But he was just stood there – when I picked myself up – grazin'. . . .'

McCain believed Red Rum was fit and well. 'He's been working keenly,' he announced before the race with his accustomed optimism. 'And he's very well in himself. If all goes well, we'll run in the Jean Mackay again at Ayr – ' one of the two races the horse had won the previous season.

Set to carry 12 st. 7 lb. on ground which was, as Billy Beardwood had discovered, distinctly muddy, Red Rum finished third, beaten two and a half lengths by the favourite Meridian II (10 st. 6 lb.) and Mr. Wrekin (10 st.). The pace was very steady – nearly half a minute slower than average – but, though Red Rum joined the early leaders at the twelfth fence and was in front four from home, he came under tremendous pressure from Brian Fletcher before the second last fence. In spite of that he was overtaken and dropped back.

Privately McCain did now suspect that the 'snap' had gone. He had decided in August that in mid season he would give Red Rum for the first time a total holiday away from it all at Southport. He had arranged to send the horse in December to his vet, Ted Greenway's Cheshire place. He was thus signalling loud and clear to other horsemen that he feared that dreaded boredom was closing in.

However, there were the usual self-encouraging 'perk-ups' before Red Rum's Ayr race on Saturday 11 October.

The ground at Carlisle had after all been yielding. He'd given over two stone to Meridian II. It had been Red's first race. At Ayr the ground was firm; all would be better. Red Rum loved the track after all, didn't he, having won this race twice already and the Scottish Grand National round it. But *did* he like it? Would he not more likely recall his last sad, weary visit there in the spring, the day of his statue?

Red Rum, however, was widely tipped and started favourite at 6–4.

The race was run at a pace so sizzling that Duffle Coat (11 st.) broke the course record which Red Rum had himself set up in 1973. Red Rum then carried 12 st. 4 lb. Now under 12 st. 7 lb. he was never in the hunt, dropped his legs in the water, received plenty of stick earlier than usual from Fletcher and came home fourth beaten twelve and a half lengths by Duffle Coat who clocked 5 mins. 58.9 secs. Meridian II (10 st. 6 lb.) was second two and a half lengths ahead of Red Rum, and Merry Bent (10 st.) third a length in front.

'Never going well at any stage,' grunted Brian Fletcher, as he got off. Fletcher looked more than disappointed. Anger glowered in his red face.

'RUM SHOW BAFFLED TRAINER MCCAIN,' The *Sporting Life* headlined their commentary. 'I'm mystified,' said Ginger McCain with real anxiety. 'I'll have to get him home before I decide what we're going to do.'

48. 'Sure, we'll be lucky even to get to the post'

It was McCain's first announcement of indecision. He says, 'People began to *query* the horse. And I *did* think he'd have won it. But when a horse is going on eleven, you're looking for him to spring a leak – for the tension to go out of the spring. Maybe because of that, I'd not wanted to be so hard on him.'

He was blaming himself now not for over-racing, but for under-training the great champion.

But all around Britain people were beginning the talk which would mount over the next six months: that the great Red Rum had 'gone', that he'd had it. Some said, even directly to McCain and not always anonymously, that he had ruined the heroic animal. It was not, they pointed out, as if the handicapper alone was stopping him. With only 3 lb. less he'd run a very different race at Ayr two years earlier.

The General Manager of Equivitale Ltd wrote consolingly with a complimentary six weeks' supply of SPECT-RUM-4 – 'which I am sure you will find will bring back his sparkle.' And a friend of Brian Fletcher 'and devoted fan of the wonderful Red Rum' wrote from Milton Keynes with some astrological advice. 'On each occasion when he has run up to form or better the Rum has occupied a favourable position. At Ayr it did not. My advice would be to run him at Newcastle and Newbury for the best results.'

In the manner of a dramatist keeping his plot spinning Red Rum confounded his critics within four days at Haydock; and did so furthermore by not completing the course.

McCain had come in for plenty more criticism for running the horse again so soon. But in the £792 Peacock 'Chase there on 15 October on good ground and set to give 29 lb. to Royal Frolic (John Burke) who would win that season's Cheltenham Gold Cup, Rummy came like a rocket round the last bend, closing on the leaders like a tiger after flying deer.

McCain was following the race round the inside of the track in vet Ted Greenway's car. 'The horse has got a bit under one or two fences. I don't think I'd been entirely happy with his jumping with Brian. But that was Brian – he always left him alone. If I'd had a big yard with a second jockey in it, maybe I'd have suggested we made a change *that* way.

'Anyway I see him catching the leaders, look away for an instant and Ted shouts "He's *down*!" "Hell, how *can* he be?" I shout. Then, looking round I see him sliding all across the course so that he took the rail out on the other side!'

Red Rum had slipped up on the flat. He scrambled up, jumped the last three fences without Brian Fletcher and was caught unscathed.

Fred Rimell, Royal Frolic's trainer, said to McCain with his usual open sportsmanship, 'Bad luck. You'd surely have won it.'

Fletcher reported, 'Showed all his old sparkle. I'd just given him a crack. He was pickin' up the leaders fast. Then he lost his feet on that bend. I was *sure* he'd have won.'

But Ted Greenway had said something else in the paddock before the race. He had looked at Red Rum's quarters and asked Ginger, 'Is he quite all right?' Ginger studied the horse walking round. Perhaps there *was* something stiff in his quarters as he walked away. 'But you can make any horse lame, can't you,' he said afterwards, 'if you look at 'em long enough.'

Here, of course, sprang up another seed of doubt. And worse was immediately to come. McCain was keeping

Red Rum under very severe pressure, for when he went to Newcastle on 30 October it would be the horse's fourth three-mile 'chase in just over four weeks. This was not, as some critics now pointed out, the expected preparation for a Grand National horse aiming at a date at the far end of the season. But Red Rum had to find fast ground and McCain has always maintained his system of that mid-season break. So away the horse travels across northern England from the west coast to the east coast to run in the £680 John Eustace Smith Trophy. The ground is firm. And so, too, would prove McCain's resolve.

It is not much of a five horse race. 'Top weight again,' Ginger reflects; 'favourite again, of course. And I go down to the silver ring to watch it from the last fence.'

Collingwood (9 st. 11 lb.) made the running until just before the third last when Even Swell (10 st. 4 lb.) passed him. Collingwood blundered and lost his jockey. Meridian II fell back quickly after the thirteenth fence, where Tartan Tutor improved rapidly and went after Even Swell. Red Rum was making a series of mistakes and had only travelled one and a half miles before he was being driven along by Brian Fletcher in the tough and badgering manner he had so frequently endured in those dour years before the autumn of '72. Now three and a half years later, after the golden years, it seemed that the bad times were back. And these days he was carrying two stone more.

McCain, standing by the last fence at Newcastle and shouting, 'Get *on* with it!' in October 1975, did not see it that way, as his famous horse and the humble Tartan Tutor came to the last together.

'I couldn't believe it! Brian is sitting *absolutely bloody still*! Okay, he's never going to beat the winner. But I thought he'd give him just one slap. But no! He just *sat* there. I came back and I was bloody choked.'

Young Billy Beardwood leading the horse away suffered some abuse. 'Those times when he was getting beat the lads'd say to me, "He's not half missin' old Billy." They didn't half pick holes in me.'

Even Swell beat Tartan Tutor by an easy seven lengths and yet set up a course record for the three-mile 'chase. Tartan Tutor beat the great Red Rum a short-head for the second prize of £180.

Fulminating, Ginger waited until Brian Fletcher had changed and come out of the Weighing-Room again. Fletcher told him bluntly, 'The horse isn't the same.'

McCain raged, 'At least you should've been second.'

'I'm not knocking him about,' snapped Brian, 'for a few hundred quid.'

'God! It's not the bloody money. I'm not having him made *non-competitive*. That's the bloody point. You haven't got him *involved* in the race!'

Fletcher looked up at the tall and furious McCain. 'Why don't you retire him?' he asked and went away.

McCain nearly exploded. When he had time to cool off he told those round him with heavy sarcasm, 'I'm not happy with the jockey's opinion.' He resolved to seek Noel Le Mare's agreement to an immediate change in jockey. A formula for the change presented itself on his way to Le Mare, a phrase which would let Brian down more lightly and which sounded less permanent: he would 'ask for a second opinion'.

Fletcher had said to the press at Newcastle, 'I think the horse has "gone".' His belief was shared by a number of observers that day. One, the *Sporting Life*'s northern correspondent Joe Rowntree declared himself convinced. Under the headline TIME FOR RED RUM TO RETIRE Rowntree reported:

'Red Rum is but a shadow of his old self and perhaps it is time he was turned out to enjoy the honourable retirement he so richly deserves.

'That is my opinion after seeing the dual Grand National hero struggle home third of four in the John Eustace Smith Trophy Handicap Chase at Newcastle yesterday.

'And the ten-year old managed to take minor honours only because of the penultimate fence fall of one of the five runners.

'An even-money favourite and giving 26 lb. and more away to his rivals, Red Rum never appeared to be going really well at any stage and it is really sad to see a horse who has won the hearts of so many people struggling under huge weights for such minor prizes.

'After all, Red Rum has netted more than £72 000, yet yesterday he could earn only £80 for finishing third against horses he could have picked up and carried only twelve months or so ago.

'Brian Fletcher reported afterwards that Red Rum was never really giving him the old feeling, and that has been the jockey's comment on several occasions lately.'

The opinion of Joe Rowntree was not one which Ginger McCain would greatly value. It was, however, to be echoed by squawking flocks of the public whose letters, urging Rummy's retirement, now descended on 10, Upper Aughton Road. Mingled with the abusive – 'Butcher McCain' – were those from old women and young girls begging Mr McCain to let 'dear old Rummy have a holiday'.

But Ginger McCain intended to get that second opinion first. Noel Le Mare had said simply to him, 'You're in charge. Do what's best.' For five days McCain braced himself to ring Fletcher and sack him. 'I rang several times and when there was no answer I was that relieved. . . .' Then he told him and the news broke.

'Racing's greatest partnership,' declared the *Evening Standard* on 5 November, 'split up today.'

McCain had already been in touch with Ron Barry, a man whom he liked as well as admired. He announced that, so far from retiring the horse or even resting him, Red Rum would be running a fortnight later in Newbury's Hennessy Gold Cup and that Barry would ride.

Ron Barry, twice champion jockey from 1971 to 1973 and holder of the record number of 125 winners in a season, had only that August parted from his long-time stable, Gordon Richards' at Greystoke, near Penrith. A few harsh words had been uttered then and an inference made that bold Barry at the tottering age of thirty-two might be getting past it. 'Big Ron' made a joke of it when he happily agreed to ride Red Rum at Newbury. 'With two old "has-beens" like us together,' he burbled in his barely comprehensible Limerick brogue, 'sure, we'll be lucky even to get to the post!'

McCain resolutely denied then that his horse had deteriorated and, a year later, confirmed this view: 'I don't think the horse *did* run a bad race that season.' However, he had to justify the most dramatic jump jockey-sacking since World War II. His reasons were, firstly, that Brian Fletcher had declared too often that he had lost faith in Red Rum; and secondly that horse and jockey had got used to one another – 'like an old married couple,' he said to me, 'that's been to bed together that often there's no more excitement in it.'

Very few of Red Rum's teeming, puzzled and now generally indignant public were aware of the personality clash between trainer and jockey. To them Red Rum and Brian Fletcher constituted one element, like fire, and represented one British emotion now sorely lacking, pride.

The public's outrage at the sacking of Brian Fletcher exploded in letters to the press and to the McCains at home. It was a distinctly nasty period for every single person still connected with the horse.

Possessed of most of the facts, using my former experience but out of touch with Red Rum's daily attitude, I found myself assailed with requests for my opinion. It was that the horse had lost some speed and some interest; that he had grown bored; that the Scottish 'National piled on top of his defeat by L'Escargot had knocked the stuffing and heart out of him; and that his hard races in almost a year of defeats could well be associated in his mind with the unlucky jockey. I concluded that a change of jockey 'for a second opinion' could do no harm. 'But,' I begged

Ginger on behalf of Rummy's millions of fans, 'if Ron Barry tells you after the Hennessy that the horse has "gone", will you stop him?'

'I will,' declared McCain. 'Immediately.'

49. 'Because he's a real professional'

It would be a fair test, for there could be no excuse about the going at Newbury. It was firm. With Ron Barry in his place on Red Rum's back, Brian Fletcher had the distasteful sight for the first time in three years of watching his old companion go round. Fred Rimell had given Fletcher the ride on Iceman. Another life-belt for his torpedoed morale was tossed to him by Midlands trainer Alan Jarvis. 'Brian rode a brilliant race for him to win for me on Kilmore Boy at Warwick. I'd be delighted for him to ride him or Amigris in the 'National,' then adding another witness of public doubt: – 'If *there is* a 'National, of course.'

Aintree was in its customary state of flux, confusion, counter-statements and big-deal bluffing.

As the Hennessy turned out, Brian Fletcher did not see much of his old comrade in the race, because while Iceman was always in the rear, the Grand National hero ran a distinctly improved race. Ron Barry had him well up in the fighting line. He was never further back than sixth of the thirteen runners and sometimes a close fourth. Although the pace mostly set by Collingwood (9 st. 8 lb.) was very fast, Red Rum this time was able to keep in touch.

Although he was no longer carrying the maximum, his 11 st. 9 lb. still turned out to be top weight. It was five pounds more than he had carried when being beaten a short head by Red Candle two years earlier. He was still well there jumping the cross-fence with the drop at the east end of the track. Then the leaders Collingwood, Cuckolder (10 st. 3 lb.), Credo's Daughter (10 st. 9 lb.), and Noble Neptune (10 st. 9 lb.) accelerated round the last bend into the straight in a spurt which Red Rum could not immediately match. But as the battle for the lead developed going to the last fence between the rapidly improving April Seventh and Collingwood. I saw from down on the track Red Rum in the brilliant sunlight steadily closing on the leaders again. He finished sixth, running on more strongly than ever like a motor nicely warmed. He was seeking another mile after the three and a quarter miles in which to show these dainty short-runners what real steeplechasing was about. He was beaten only fourteen and a half lengths by April Seventh (11 st. 2 lb.) who had won the Whitbread in April and to whom Red Rum was giving half a stone.

'Big Ron' confirmed watchers' views about Red Rum: ' 'Goin' on better than anything at the finish.'

Ginger McCain said, 'Frankly, I'm delighted. The horse *has* probably lost a bit of his speed [Ron Barry nodded at this] but his jumping couldn't be faulted today, could it?' It had indubitably been a performance totally contrasting with the blundering, fiddling, reluctant struggle round Newcastle. Perhaps the change of jockey had worked.

The bookmakers certainly made Red Rum clear favourite for the 'National at 12–1, but could Ron Barry ride him there? He was committed to his old favourite The Dikler who, plagued with muscular troubles, had not yet appeared, but was being prepared by Fulke Walwyn with Aintree as his prime target.

In any event, McCain and Le Mare now had their 'second opinion'. The horse was not 'finished'. He would set off, as originally intended, for his mid-season holiday at Ted Greenway's. Or so McCain declared, adding that Red's next two preliminary races before the Grand National would both be at Haydock in the early spring. Red Rum's manifold supporters breathed relieved sighs.

'After the Hennessy,' Ginger recalls. 'I felt a fair bit happier.'

And then, to everyone's astonishment, within three days of returning from the south and three and a quarter miles round Newbury, there was Red Rum turning out in the three mile Sundew 'Chase at Haydock again on 26 November. Ginger McCain explained, 'He ate up after last Saturday and was so well, and the race looked like cuttin' up, and the Guv'nor's eighty-eight and does like to see his horse run close at home....'

McCain's sudden switch of plan provoked outbreaks of indignation. A racing man at Haydock was reported as having burst out, 'And after this, I s'pose you'll be sending the poor old blanker all the way back to run down at Sandown at the weekend!'

Ginger was now inured to criticism. He takes counsel from and respects only a handful of trainers and jockeys whom he regards as top of their professions. The rest of the knockers he ignores without even a pink furrow of rage on his brow.

He said gently to me, 'I reckon the horse has a fair bit more time than the old man. And if I can give the Guv'nor pleasure....' His voice trailed away.

The race cut up to four runners. Last year Fred Winter had sent Pendil. This time it was his Bula, winner of two Champion Hurdles and third in the Gold Cup, having his first race of the season. He scared away all opposition except Royal Relief and Kilvulgan (to both of whom he gave 5 lb.) and Red Rum whom he met at level weights. Brian Fletcher rode the first winner that day at Haydock. But, though Ron Barry was down at Ascot, it was not Fletcher who got the ride again, but Rummy's old jockey and one-time trainer: Tommy Stack. It was to be the sharp-featured, sharp-minded teetotaller Stacky who was going to stick with Red Rum all season.

For once Red Rum was untipped and unfancied: in the field of four he started 6–1 others. Bula was 11–10 on favourite, and Royal Relief 5–2. They finished like that. Bula, rather portly, was held up and sprinted away from Royal Relief on the run in. Red Rum took over the lead from Kilvulgan at the fourth, led all the way to the thirteenth when Royal Relief and then Bula overtook him, and galloped on steadily to be beaten eight lengths and two lengths.

Two days later he at last left for his Cheshire holiday. There had been some talk of his being hunted – one of the best restoratives for any jaded horse – but even Ted Greenway's able staff soon found Rummy far too much of a handful for that. 'They'd no idea he could blackguard about as he does!' said Ginger delightedly. 'They're just keeping him canterin' about. They've some lovely rides there through the trees and little jumps to hop over.'

Back in Upper Aughton Road a new head lad had arrived to assume the tasks formerly undertaken by Jackie Grainger, Billy Ellison and, twice, by Ginger McCain. 'Taffy' Wiliams, born on 30 August 1936 of farming parents in North Wales, was the newest member of Rummy's inner circle.

Taffy had seen McCain's advertisement in the *Sporting Life*. From travelling head lad in a large stable (Frank Carr, with over 50 horses) to head lad in a smaller one (McCain had about 25) is the natural progression of a stableman's life.

'I used to like the travelling at Frank Carr's. But I'm purely an armchair jockey now. You learn twice as much on the telly.' He only goes racing to the 'National, 'or if old Red's in at Haydock nearby.

'For a head lad this is a *beautiful* little yard. It's compact. You soon get round. And I can *hear* everything that happens. My bedroom's overlooking the yard – I look directly into "the maestro's" box. The night before the 'National I nearly slept in it. I get terribly geed-up.'

Taffy Williams bustles about the little yard, barking out orders like a Welsh terrier. 'C'mon, c'mon, last out again!' he cries, but no one seems particularly alarmed. He is small, bright-eyed and wears a smart flat cap and long brown stableman's coat.

Taffy considers Red Rum. 'Most probably that break at Ted Greenway's did him the *world* of good. Even *we,*' says Williams, who has endured the rigours of Southport sands only since November 1975, 'do get bored with the beach after a bit.'

'Mind with his feet, the beach does *suit* that horse.' He absolutely despises soft ground. If he were mine, I'd simply play around with him, and take him to the little 'gaffs'. Oh, there were tears in my eyes over the 'National.'

With Red Rum forty-five miles away in Cheshire Ginger McCain 'hated losing touch. But I left it all to Ted Greenway, who rode an awful lot of point-to-point winners, and his son Robin was leading point-to-point rider.'

McCain however, and understandably, could not resist going over. 'I watched him work. He was hacking about and popping over little jumps. And people kept coming from all over the place just to see the horse. Ted said they drank him out of house and home!'

Red Rum returned in the New Year and McCain admits 'the old horse took a fair few days to settle in again. He was a bit down at first.' It is possible to deduce that, as with a man just back from holiday, routine work did not immediately appeal. 'But then, because he's a real professional, he settled down to it all again.'

But that left little more than three weeks before 11 February in which to prepare the horse for Haydock's three and a half mile 'National Trial, the last race he had won, a whole year ago. Then he had reappeared looking tubby, but yet had run with verve and Brian Fletcher. This time, partly because frost on the sands had held up his last few days' work, he looked even more portly. He carried, for him, a mere 11 st. 7 lb, though it still remained the highest weight to run. The ground was good and though his loving fans would not dream of forsaking him, the professional punters did. He started a weak-priced 7–1, less fancied than Rubstic and Lord Browndodd (both 10 st. 1 lb. and joint favourites) and Ken Hogg's astonishing Forest King (10 st. 7 lb.) who, trained on the fells and eccentrically fed, had already won seven steeplechases that season.

'My horse was *very* burly,' McCain reflects. 'He wasn't fit. He'd come back to me just about fourteen days too late. *And* he'd been held up. He virtually blew up – 'cept that he's too old a pro really to blow up.' He meant that, like an experienced athlete, Red would not burst himself to exhaustion, as a young colt can.

The race, with ten runners, was run at a sensible pace. Three horses including Feel Free (Brian Fletcher again observing his friend) pulled up. Rag Trade (10 st. 6 lb.) was well placed and galloping strongly when he fell at the sixteenth fence on the far side. Red Rum, driven busily along by Tommy Stack almost from the outset, made impressive headway along the back straight and was well in touch when he made a serious blunder at the fence opposite the stands. This was the fifteenth, the fence before Rag Trade fell. The mistake knocked the breath out of him, stopped his run and lost him his place. He continued steadily without again improving and finished sixth and last.

He came in thirty-three lengths behind Forest King with Tommy Stack sitting quietly. The public and many racing experts expressed their disappointment. But Stacky, not given to wild day-dreams, was 'really pinned down' by McCain who wanted his considered verdict. Stack surprisingly said, 'He's going to take a bit of beating in the 'National.'

Ladbrokes now made Red Rum and Money Market joint favourites at 10–1. The winner Forest King, declared only a possible 'National runner by Ken Hogg, was quoted at 20–1. Rubstic who had finished second, beaten six lengths after having had a somewhat unlucky run, was cut from 25's to 20–1.

Fred Rimell, listing his five probable runners for the Grand National, significantly named Rag Trade last after his other four. But he could have been awaiting any ill-effects of his gigantic horse's fall....

A poll of racing's trained observers after the 'National Trial at Haydock on 11 February would have produced an immense majority convinced that dear old Red Rum was now but a dimming, even a guttering light. Studying the comments in newspapers after the race, I find no correspondent who held out any real hope for Rummy's golden future. All, however, dug his grave with a sad decorum. Though the press may mightily rejoice when uppity personalities finally slip on fate's banana-skin, Red Rum's long strong struggle against the odds was a very different story. This was the sort of hero no one wished to see put down. I was personally disappointed because my theory that he had been bored, that a holiday away would perk him up and that he ran better (as in this race last year) when fresh, big and well, seemed all to have been confounded. I *hoped* he might win another 'National, but I did not believe that he could.

I viewed Rummy's next appearance just under a month later at Haydock with gloom. True, the ground on 6 March was firm, but he had 11 st. 13 lb., giving 1 st. 4 lb. to Fred Rimell's fancied Royal Frolic, and the £5796 Greenall Whitley was only three miles. It was furthermore thirteen months and a long succession of beatings since he had last won.

In the event, Red Rum once again greatly surprised the racing world, heartened his supporters, and caused the bookmakers to cut his Grand National price to 10–1.

Ginger McCain went down to the water jump to watch. 'I was *very* pleased. He was making up a *lot* of ground and though he'd been jumping his fences a bit slovenly, he never made a bad mistake. What pleased me was that he was really *running*. He was relishing every minute and really hitting his stride – ' Ginger flings his arm forwards. 'A lot of people, mind, weren't all that impressed. But I knew he'd got very fat inside.'

So, in a race run at a cracking pace – Royal Frolic beat the course record – Red Rum (though lacking that accelerating surge as the leaders whipped round the far left bend), plugged on tenaciously to be beaten only a head and a neck out of third place by Glanford Brigg (11 st. 9 lb.) and Notification (11 st. 2 lb.). Barona (10 st. 3 lb.) just over four lengths ahead of Red Rum at the finish, was outpaced early but stayed on strongly down the straight to finish second, beaten a swaggering ten lengths by Royal Frolic.

Even without knowing that Royal Frolic was about to win 'chasing's level-weight classic, the Cheltenham Gold Cup, this was a first-class performance by Red Rum against good horses over a distance at least three-quarters of a mile too short. McCain reckoned that without another race in the ensuing four weeks he could get his horse fully fit for the Grand National.

50. 'I know my duties to the public, my lord'

'In my own mind,' says Ginger McCain in the following autumn, 'I was happy enough before the 1976 'National. I thought the horse was possibly as well as we'd *ever* had him. As you know, knowledgeable people had been having a cut at us. . . . But I thought that anything that beat us would win – I fancied The Dikler and Barona. I thought that winning the Welsh Grand National would have seen off Rag Trade.'

Cyril Stein, head of Ladbrokes, a man highly respected in his own profession and hailed as the saviour of the Grand National, had given McCain permission to work Red Rum a few times on the course. Neither Mrs Topham nor Mr Davies had ever done this. On Aintree frantic activity crackled to get the derelict place ready in the three brief months left after Ladbrokes had at last concluded a deal with Bill Davies' successor in the actual ownership of Aintree.

The great machine which gives the Ladbroke Group gambling profits exceeding £12 million a year and which promotes all the aspects of punting's lure, swung into well-oiled, thrusting action. Cynics observed that the 'rescue' of the 'National gave bookmakers not just something to bet on, but one of Britain's two most heavily supported races. Up to £20 million was likely to be wagered on the race, Ladbrokes expecting to handle £2 million of this themselves and Corals £1¾ million. Over £1 million would be riding on Rummy's back alone. . . .

Cynics also pointed out that drinkers did not thank brewers for charitably providing public houses in which to sell their beer. But these were ungrateful thoughts. The bald truth was that, where Jockey Club and Levy Board had failed, the money, zeal and organization of Ladbrokes had saved the Grand National from demise. And if the rescue was also a Public Relations exercise on the grandest scale, who could blame the bookmakers for that?

Little publicized, the *News of the World* put up no less than £40 000 of the prize-money.

McCain was delighted when the 'National weights came out. Red Rum had 4 lb. less than 1975 with 11 st. 10 lb. – 'a winning weight', he said. Colebridge and Soothsayer, Gold Cup horses, had been given more. Neither ran. McCain, too, thought that The Dikler at thirteen years old had been given enough with 11 st. 7 lb. to stop him. So too with Glanford Brigg, beaten 200 yards by Red Rum in '75 and now three pounds worse off. 'Red Rum will win the 'National!' declared Ginger. 'It's as simple as that!'

Fred Rimell thought Rag Trade with 10 st. 12 lb. had a little more than he had hoped for. Tom Jones, whose Jolly's Clump had briefly been favourite, was delighted with his weight: he would carry 10 st. 3 lb.

The generality of tipsters, however, recommended Barona, a view with which the author concurred, lest he tempted fate by hinting that his hero might yet, at his second attempt, bring off the treble. Of the thirty-two runners for the *News of the World* Grand National 'Chase Barona started favourite at 7's, followed by Red Rum at 10's, and Jolly's Clump at 12's with Tregarron and Money Market. Rag Trade was briskly backed from 20–1 down to 14's.

Of the ten newspaper tipsters selected by the *Sporting Life* on the morning of the race only Robin Goodfellow of the *Daily Mail* selected Rag Trade. Five picked Barona, two Jolly's Clump and only the *Sporting Life*'s own 'Form' man, David Cox, voted for Red Rum.

The horse was 'fancied' not by the experts, but by literally millions of fans not only in Britain but across the world. Their small bets, their urging hearts, and few calculating heads, made Red Rum seem to have a chance. In the morning papers he had been favourite almost everywhere.

That morning Fred Winter was in his accustomed place at the top of the trainer's table; forty-one winners and £14 000 ahead of Fred Rimell. One of five other trainers in the list could overtake him by winning the 'National. He had very little hope himself with the newly-arrived, small and fussy Golden Rapper.

The McCains had two obstacles to overcome immediately before the race. Superstitious as ever about the way they went to the course and the company they kept, they were dismayed to hear that Janet, the young friend of the Wareings' daughter, who had made up the eightsome for the last three years, had been involved in a road accident. Riding her bicycle, she had been hit by an articulated lorry a few days earlier.

But the loyalty which Red Rum engenders overcame pain and injury. Heavily bruised, wounds stitched and her arm in a sling, young Janet made her way up from Taunton to get to the Wareings on Friday. 'Our usual eight in the car,' in Beryl's words, 'was made up.'

The McCains broke tradition by having, Ginger remembers, 'A super party the night *before* the 'National – we'd never done that before.' He had worked Red Rum on the Friday with Silent Comfort, 'A horse he could canter over, to make him feel good. I thought then he would run a blinder!'

Just before the race when tension was at its most taut, McCain was delayed saddling Red Rum. He was also running Meridian II whom he had bought for local landscape gardener Brian Aughton out of Ken Oliver's yard for £6000. The horse was going to run second for them in the Midlands Grand National.

McCain saddled Meridian II first and was then kept waiting and waiting 'for an amateur to get finished in one of those saddling boxes. I'd got into that much of a state I couldn't *believe* he could take another minute longer. Then the steward came fussing round, and gave me a sharp sixpennyworth for being late, and we saddled in a hurry and rushed into the parade ring.'

McCain was reported for tardiness and, after the race, was summoned before the Earl of Derby. 'Lord Derby said, "I want to draw your attention, Mr McCain, to the special responsibilities you have to the public when you train a horse like Red Rum." '

McCain took a deep breath, but maintained his grip on the handle. 'I know my duties to the public, my lord,' responded Ginger gravely and dashed away to saddle Prehistoric for the George Wigg 'Chase.

For McCain himself the Grand National could become a public pillory. Where more retiring, less ebullient trainers would have throughout the disappointing season nodded with the press and murmured the possibility that the great horse's star was now descending, Ginger would have none of that. He was on record again and again declaring that the horse was as good as ever. He had sacked the horse's jockey. He had pronounced that the horse had a genuine favourite's chance. McCain had not merely stuck his neck out; he had wobbled it about waiting for fate's axe. For, if the world's beloved Rummy did not win or very nearly win (and there were statistically thirty chances to one against that happening) then the public would bay for McCain's blood. Not only would he have failed – trainers do that continually; but his judgement would appear ludicrous; and worst of all, he would be vilified for ruining the most popular jumper Britain had known since Arkle.

51. '*The* Aintree horse'

It was a warm beautiful April day. The grass was a bright spring green against the newly painted white rails and the blueness of the sky was shown off by white puff-ball clouds. Compared with the dreariness of the '75 'National under the grim Davies regime, all seemed sweetness and light. An enormous crowd of 42 000, the largest for years, alerted by vigorous advertising and drawn out by the weather, once again jammed the stands. The mass confounded those grey critics of a year before who had grizzled, 'Who wants the nasty old 'National anyway?'

After Red Rum had led the parade down the course, the horses' lads, some walking, most running to get good positions, came down the green finishing straight, the old horses' final battlefield. The horses cantered down past them and on past the start, crossed the Melling Road, which this year was deeply covered in yellow straw, and pulled up to look at the first fence.

Back at the start Tommy Stack, reigning champion jockey, adjusted his leathers after he had got the feel of the horse. The horses were down early and, although there was no repeat of the '75 delay, they kept walking around for nearly four minutes. Red Rum looked magnificent, reflecting the months of care and muscle-building, thought and good food crammed into him by trainer and staff over the long eight months which had all been pyramiding towards this minute. It was nine years of racing since he was first here, to dead-heat in that £133 selling plate for insignificant two year olds. This was his ninety-fifth race. . . .

Waiting, the tension showed on his neck. Dark sweat stained the skin which, in the sunlight, had the glow of a ripe 'conker'. Tommy Stack kept him walking round quietly at the side of Paul Kelleway, having his ninth 'National ride on the favourite Barona, and Jeff King on Spanish Steps (who had been twice fourth, then third, in three Grand Nationals). The Dikler (Ron Barry) moved across Red Rum, making him look small, though beautifully conformed.

They lined up with Red Rum in the middle and were gone in a flash. So quickly did the field thunder away towards the first that, as they crossed the straw-covered Melling Road in a retreating wave of quarters, flying tails and bobbing white breeches, Red Rum was at least three-quarters of the way back towards the rear of the field. Tommy Stack was kicking him on to keep in touch. The ground, officially returned as 'firm', was plainly very fast.

If the horse's zest and courage were only still there, he must run very well indeed.

Money Market, reportedly the subject of a single £4000 each-way wager in the last minutes before the start, galloped away in front, as if sharply aware of his responsibilities.

Tregarron (young Colin Tinkler) and Nereo, ridden by his storybook owner, the hawk-nosed, huge-jawed, broken-boned Duke of Alburquerque, soon went up to Money Market. Rag Trade, as L'Escargot had been in '75, was at this point far ahead of Red Rum. As they crossed the third fence (an open ditch) Rag Trade was just behind the first half dozen. Red Rum had only half a dozen behind him.

Spittin' Image with Andy Turnell perched above him, short-leathered like a sparrow, Nereo, Money Market, The Dikler and Rag Trade landed out over Becher's and had turned left-handed, as Red Rum on the very wide outside came to the great drop fence. He jumped it so well that he improved rapidly on the outside of the field. He was not too far behind the thick frame of his old partner Brian Fletcher who had the ride this year not on the public's darling, but on the unconsidered hobdayed mare Eyecatcher, owned and trained in Oxfordshire by sporting amateur rider John Bosley.

At the Canal Turn The Dikler, one of McCain's two 'dangers', was lying fourth behind Spittin' Image and Money Market, but the other danger Barona was well back. Red Rum, as the flood of runners spread out and contracted, moved between eighth and twelfth positions; just about right at this stage. Spanish Steps had improved quietly on the inside running down to Valentine's, but the dark-visaged Spanish Duke in his red and blue sweater was thrusting along in fourth place. Huge Rag Trade was galloping steadily in seventh place and then, a couple of horses behind him, we picked up Red Rum again moving far more jauntily than he had the previous year and with almost the dancing grace of the year of '74 when he had played hare to rival tortoises.

Money Market and Nereo joined Spittin' Image after the Melling Road as they came back onto the racecourse for the first time. Rag Trade was close behind Spanish Steps who was sticking to the inside rails and behind Spanish Steps galloped Red Rum, still well enough placed.

Ahead loomed two plain fences, then the daunting Chair, the water, the thronged and shouting stands and then two and a quarter miles more round the great fences. So far, so good, breathed Red Rum's million fans. Going well, placed right, so *far*, we murmured, eyes locked onto that big white sheepskin noseband bobbing as the bright bay head nodded on each stride.

Racing loves human heroes, too, and a roar went up from the crowd as they saw the hunched Duke of Alburquerque (who admitted to fifty-seven years of very sporting life) suddenly dash to the front on Nereo. He had hardly done so, with Meridian moving up on his outside, when down the Duke crashed, lurching and heavily, at the thirteenth fence. The Spanish grandee was hurled spinning into the forelegs of Meridian so fast that he brought the horse down, and lay very still as the field thundered around him like a speck of jetsam.

At the Chair, Rag Trade was still fifth with Red Rum lying about tenth close to Ceol-na-Mara (Jeremy Glover) with Barona behind him.

Going away on the second circuit the leaders showed as Spanish Steps, Money Market and the diminuitive Golden Rapper (John Francome) who had been purchased at the eleventh hour by Fred Winter as a prize for the winner of a commercial competition. The little chestnut had been well to the fore for over two and a half miles and now danced away down the right-hand side of the track. Behind them, Red Rum, aware by old knowledge now that at this point he always improved, began without any urging from Tommy Stack to advance through the field. He galloped more strongly, he jumped far more boldly than he had done so far down those five fences looming up like serried ramparts in the straight run to Becher's.

And as he approached Becher's Brook for the second time that year, he was going so well, he was galloping so strongly within himself that Stack, as Fletcher had done twenty-four months before, could actually take a pull on him to steady him. It was as if a Grand Prix driver quietly eased his foot off the accelerator. And Stacky looked calmly right and left assessing the opposition.

The impossible dream was suddenly within grasp. As they came to Becher's, the BBC's Julian Wilson called out 'still spread *right* across the course . . . The Dikler very prominent . . . towards the outside Red Rum and Barona. . . .'

At Becher's litle Golden Rapper led, jumped and crashed. Spittin' Image went on again from Churchtown Boy who, with Prolan, had been right in the vanguard as they raced away from home. Rummy soared over Becher's, plunged deeply – and his nose dipped right down, almost touching the turf. Eyecatcher was third as they turned left-handed to jump the twenty-third fence – and Red Rum was just behind on the outside: his pitch and peck at Becher's had scarcely checked him.

As they jumped the Canal Turn an élite group of eight survivors was clear of the trailing remainder. Then, as they turned towards us, Ginger McCain let out a deep grunt of joy. He had perceived how easily Red Rum was travelling. 'It's *no* contest!' shouted Ginger suddenly carried away in bliss. 'No contest at all.' He was confident he had won his third Grand National.

At Valentine's we all saw that one horse stood out as he galloped. All around in the group of Churchtown Boy, (weakening) Spittin' Image, Eyecatcher, The Dikler, Sandwilan, Coel-na-Mara, and Spanish Steps only one was going superbly well: Red Rum. Around him jockeys were pushing and driving on, heads and shoulders thrusting like rowers against the tide and huge waves. Then behind Red Rum and sitting almost as still on the enormous back of Rag Trade I glimpsed the tall, bent figure of John Burke.

'Kick on, Stacky! Kick *on*!' I bellowed among the hub-bub. There were five fences more. We knew Rum stayed every yard of the four and a half miles. 'Kick *on*! Go *on*!' We exhorted. Get clear, we meant, shake 'em off *now*, we urged. But so far Tommy Stack had not moved. Even so, Red Rum was cruising so easily that at the next fence he jumped to front and the man just behind and inside him was Brian Fletcher on the mare Eyecatcher. Brian did not need to turn his head. He had worn Red Rum's colours for three glorious years. He saw how well his old partner was travelling. Yet, in the superb way in which Fletcher excelled round Aintree, he was getting a performance out of the Oxfordshire mare which far transcended anything she had shown so far. The thought zig-zagged like lightning through the minds of all of us concerned with Rummy – 'Fletcher will do him!' In this most dramatic of all races, what was more likely then that the jocked-off, struggling, hard-up jockey should, in the last three quarters of a mile, amazingly avenge himself and overwhelm the public's hero.

We looked at Stack and we looked at Fletcher side by side, as last year we had watched Fletcher on Rummy kicking and driving while Carberry on L'Escargot played with him. Now Fletcher was sitting down and booting in the green colours and Tommy was sitting easy, like a king, not quite as imperiously as Carberry had a year before, but going supremely well. The Dikler was slowly weakening behind, Coel-na-Mara was under pressure, and Burke began to drive Rag Trade closer. We would win it. Rummy would win it. He was the only horse still going easily. 'Come *on*, Tommy!' we screamed uselessly in the soaring blare of voices rooting Red Rum home.

There must have been shouts for others, but it was 'Red!

Red! RED! *C'mon* Rummy, *c'mon* screaming all round the stands.

The third last came and Red Rum jumped it easily, level with Eyecatcher, clear of The Dikler and Coel-na-Mara and with Rag Trade still several lengths back. At that fence I was convinced that Red Rum would win. Only two more fences to survive, still full of running, Eyecatcher under pressure, Rag Trade being ridden along – win it he must, he would. . . .

Over the Melling Road for the last time and the order was still the same and so was the state of the struggle. But Rag Trade was fifth – 'breathing down their necks!' O'Sullevan exclaimed – and the big horse suddenly started closing. He had come out from behind Red Rum and Eyecatcher and was moving with huge strides towards their outer flank, as a hound may turn two hares. It was an amazing Grand National spectacle to have half a dozen horses racing to the second last fence within touch of one another, as close as an orderly charge by a troop of cavalry at a battle's end. Each of the six clung to a squeak of a chance still, should something befall the others. Fletcher and Stack had been side by side all the way from Valentine's. They still never spoke a word.

Eyecatcher, with the benefit of the inside bend, was just in front as she and Rummy rose at the second last, but Stack got the better jump out of Red Rum. He touched down first. Now and at last Stack began to drive the Aintree hero towards the last fence, for outside him, lollopping in brave 'Teazy-Weazy' Raymond's ice-blue and wine colours the huge Rag Trade was moving closer.

For the third incredible year running Red Rum, with a staggeringly long leap, landed first over the final fence of the Grand National. Tommy Stack thought afterwards the length of this leap might have checked him on landing. But his trajectory took him well clear of the mare. Fletcher saw Le Mare's old colours and his old yellow cap now on top of Tommy Stack's neat taut frame and he says he thought then, 'The old horse has done it. Good luck to him.' He declared later, that, in spite of all the bitterness of their parting, he wished that Red Rum would win a third Grand National, if he, struggling at the end of his jockey's life, could not win a fourth.

Then on the bright green turf between the last fence and the white rails of the 'elbow', all changed. Rummy was not accelerating away. Under 11 st. 10 lb. he was staying on, but Rag Trade with nearly one stone less on his back for four and a quarter miles was joining him very wide on the stands side, was passing him, was clear of him, was cutting across Rummy's old head to make for the white rails after the 'elbow', to have them to guide him on and on up the long run-in.

We were done. We were suddenly beaten. It was over.

And then, as Tommy Stack drove Red Rum on with all his renowned vigour, the scene once again changed. 'Red Rum', shouted Peter O'Sullevan to millions round the world, 'Red Rum is *fighting back*!' From four lengths clear by the elbow and with the race apparently well won, Rag Trade's lead was being, stride by stride, slowly bitten back. Rag Trade looked exhausted. He rolled. John Burke's whip was whirling. Red Rum's bay neck was stuck out horizontally like a ramrod and he was closing perfectly evenly, closing with desperate resolution, closing that gap of green....

There were tears in Ginger McCain's eyes as he watched; there were very few dry eyes in the stands. For what we were watching was the superlative Grand National horse of all time, fighting back in the last panting, pounding, sweating seconds, to keep what he must have felt he had won again after the last fence, his own throne at Aintree.

Closer and closer he galloped. The screams and bellowings from the gigantic crowd reverberated like the battle cries of manic hordes. 'Ah yes,' said twenty-three-year-old John Burke afterwards with a wry smile, 'Red Rum was going well. I knew he was coming at me when I heard the crowd roaring, really *roaring* for him! And I didn't dare look behind.'

The winning post came too soon for Rummy. He was a short and shrinking two lengths behind Rag Trade on the line. Eight lengths back came Eyecatcher and Brian Fletcher (receiving 1 st. 3 lb.), then Barona a further three lengths coming in fourth under 10 st. 6 lb. Then Coel-na-Mara, The Dikler, Sandwilan, Spittin' Image, Spanish Steps and Black Tudor. Sixteen of the thirty-two starters finished – a blessedly abnormal proportion. And the time was 1/10th of a second faster than standard.

Red Rum had made up two lengths out of the four lengths he was behind at the elbow. He crossed the line strong as a lion. How much further would he have needed to catch the weary Rag Trade; another fifty yards, another furlong? If, after Valentine's or at least from the Melling Road, Tommy Stack had driven Rummy hard for home, would he not have won? But Stack had not ridden him round Aintree. He had had a few disappointing rides on him that season. Though he knew how well he was going from the second Becher's onwards, the thought must have locked in Tommy's cool, skilled and experienced mind: 'To kick on hard three-quarters of a mile from home in a 'National under top weight must be madness with any horse.'

Red Rum, however, is not any horse. 'Ifs' win no races and many brilliant victories are ridden by spectators in grandstands. And yet, seeing that race run and rerun on the BBC's videotape my conviction grows that, given it all again, champion jockey Tommy Stack would have gone hell for leather for home from somewhere between Valentine's and the Melling Road. That done, and other things remaining unaltered, I believe Rummy would have won his third Grand National.

Nothing detracts from his triumph. He had set up an unequalled Aintree record even by coming second. McCain's constant faith and his repeated public affirmation of it had been gloriously vindicated. As Rummy came in, Ginger's face glowed as he strode towards him. It was one enormous grin of sheer delight and brimming-over pride.

Billy Ellison, too, over from the new stables in Ireland where he was temporarily working, ran across behind Rag Trade towards his old horse, his boxer's face alight with happiness, too, and his damaged eyes wet with excitement.

And the immense roar, as of a tidal wave, when Red Rum came in to be unsaddled, would have stirred the past heroes and heroines of Aintree in their Elysian fields, causing their heads to rise in recognition of the greatest of them all, still down there, doing his damnedest to the end.

'He's a *marvellous* ride round there,' said Tommy Stack to David Coleman. 'He's like a cat, because twice goin' to Becher's, horses fell in front o' me, and he's like a ballet-dancer – he just side-steps 'em. I thought,' said Stack, 'that comin' across the racecourse I was goin' better than anythin' on the inside o' me. And I looked on me right-hand side and there were two going better, I thought. I jumped the second last and I thought I'd a real good chance. And fractionally, after the last, I thought I was goin' to win. . . .'

Tommy Stack, back in the days of the late Mr Bobby Renton, had met Red Rum as a three year old, eight long years ago. 'No,' said he, grinning, 'I never thought then that he'd develop into an Aintree horse – *The* Aintree horse.'

52. 'Red Rum slept here'

There had been no possibility of running that year in the Scottish National. It fell only a week after Liverpool. So Red Rum went down south instead to end his season at Sandown. He would contest the £12 487 Whitbread Gold Cup, first of steeplechasing's sponsored races. The ground was firm, the distance three miles, five and a half furlongs which was, if not long enough for our hero, at least not one and a half miles too short. He had 11 st. 10 lb., still top weight of the runners, but shared this time with the previous winner April Seventh. Tommy Stack rode Red Rum again, and Colin Tinkler rode Meridian II for cheerful Brian Aughton.

It was the first time Noel Le Mare had ever been racing in the south. 'They looked after the Guv'nor marvellously,' says Ginger, 'letting him bring his car right up to where the Queen Mother goes, and so on right up in that lift.'

And in the paddock, McCain dashing across from Meridian to Red Rum to have a final word with Tommy Stack, slices through the Royal party. 'And,' says Aughton still chafing Ginger for disrespect, 'you as near as nothin' knocked the Queen Mother over. Typical of you – only thinkin' about that horse. Never lookin' where you're goin'.'

For a horse after a hard race three weeks earlier, Rummy looked superb. 'An absolute picture,' in John Oaksey's expert and balanced words, 'of health and enthusiasm. If he could win I think the stands would be knocked down by the cheering. There he is, the great, *immortal* Red Rum!' The public made their darling favourite. And he ran very well to finish fifth, after blundering at the open ditch, second time round, which comes third of those seven spectacularly close together fences along the railway stretch.

The champion hunter chaser Otter Way (10 st. 10 lb.) of unknown maternal line won from Collingwood (9 st. 9 lb.), Black Tudor (10 st.) and The Dikler, thirteen years old, who was making his final appearance of a wonderful career. April Seventh finished half a length behind Red Rum in sixth place. The winner set up a course record and, receiving a stone from Red Rum, beat him sixteen and a half lengths.

Red Rum had raced ten times between late September and late April, and had not won. Yet he had so nearly triumphed in the Grand National at Liverpool which, with the typical uniqueness of the Red Rum saga, is the only place which now brings out his very best. The fates have never made it easy for him: during the prime of his 'chasing career the old autumn meeting round Aintree ceased to exist.

Red Rum requires at least four miles. Yet, in the calendar there are no four-mile 'chases before mid-winter when the ground is too heavy for Red Rum and he is having his mid-season break.

He is restricted to an early season campaign on firm ground when, if he is well-placed and the lure of distant prizes resisted, he may win small races and have his morale uplifted. After that, under his accustomed programme, he has only the Grand National at which to aim. *Only* the Grand National? His aim throughout the last half of his career has been nothing else.

Would he be better trained elsewhere? I remain positive that, trained on ordinary gallops, without benefit of soft sand and cold sea, his dreaded pedalosteitis would have returned.

Could he then have been better placed in his races? I believe so. I consider, and have said so frankly to Ginger McCain, that running Red Rum in the 1975 Scottish Grand National and in both the 1974 and 1976 Kempton races were three serious errors of judgement. I understand and commend McCain's interest in putting wonderful old Noel

Le Mare first. But those three races were wrong. Inflicted on a horse less redoubtable and less shrewd, they might in combination have done him serious harm.

In other respects the season 1975–76 had been a very disappointing one for Ginger McCain. He had won only eight races worth £2700. He was involved in two-way litigation with Bill Davies. He had parted from his head lad, from Rummy's lad, from several other staff, and from Red Rum's jockey, Fletcher of Aintree. McCain has suffered savage criticisms and anonymous cursings. He is aware that people in racing, nearly all of whom admire and like him personally, think of him as 'a one-horse' trainer. It pains him that he has so very few local owners in his yard.

Around the horse which, as Ginger McCain so freely proclaims, 'has lifted us all up,' an abnormal number of casualties have occurred. The superstitious have suggested that the extraordinary horse might be putting a spell on his immediate circle. Indeed in the summer of '76 when Meridian II, instead of Andy the donkey, was turned out with Red Rum in a new field by the Tarleton by-pass, Brian Aughton's good 'chaser without warning dropped dead in the night. The field's owner Albert Wake, an associate of McCain's in the motor trade, saw the dead body, believed to his terror that it could be Red Rum's and beseeched Ginger instantly to take the great horse home – 'I can't sleep at nights now, Don, in case Red Rum might die, too.'

Meridian died not from witchcraft but of a ruptured artery of the bowels. Probably (as had been the case with Wolverhampton the day before the '75 National) it was the result of infestation by red-worm when young. But both circumstances were passing strange and Red Rum's proximity too close for comfort.

Red Rum was therefore brought in three weeks early to encounter his customary shoal of letters begging his attendance at various horsey functions. He performed for three days at Southport Show.

One of the next invitations he could accept was the Cheltenham and District Race Club's gala day on 5 September on the racecourse, in aid of that worthy charity, the Riding for the Disabled Association. He would require a jockey to ride him in the Parade of Champions.

The unhappy Brian Fletcher had been failed by doctors as unfit to continue race-riding. Steeplechasing had finally finished with him at the age of twenty-nine. His domestic situation was reportedly also in a state of flux, and he was looking for work.

On the 12 August, soon after Fletcher had announced to the press that he would never be able to ride in a race again, Ginger McCain wrote him the following letter:

'Dear Brian,

'Myself and Beryl would like to wish you all good luck in your retirement and wish you every success in whatever venture you decide upon.

'Red Rum has been invited to take part in the Parade of Champions at Cheltenham on Sunday 5 September and they would like, if possible, for him to be ridden. We wondered whether you would like to partner him for this parade. If so, drop us a line.

'Once again, wishing you Good Health and Every Success,

Yours sincerely,

Donald McCain.'

McCain received no reply, and on 21 August he wrote to Cheltenham telling them so and asking them to contact Tommy Stack, who gladly consented to ride the horse.

Therefore when the Horse of the Year Show invited Red Rum to appear at Wembley to climax their parade of personalities in October, McCain, in accepting, asked that the show director should deal directly with Brian Fletcher, if they wanted the ex-jockey to ride the horse.

Several other unusual honours had been bestowed upon Red Rum. The great Arkle's owner, Anne, Duchess of

Westminster, asked through the medium of her Cheshire neighbour Lord Leverhulme, then Senior Steward of the Jockey Club, whether she might pay a call with him to visit Red Rum. She wrote charmingly afterwards, apologizing for staying so long, and saying that she could not remember any two hours passing so quickly.

Bee's, the horticulturists, sought and obtained from Noel Le Mare permission to name a new rose 'Red Rum'. Two record companies, Polydor and Jet issued records about the legendary horse: Polydor's made by a group with a thumping Western background; Jet's spoken in reverent tones by one Len Marten.

Brian Aughton, owner and market-gardener, offered for sale 'piles of muck, *Red Rum's own manure* – and people were sendin' in all over for it. Couldn't possibly sell enough!'

Red Rum's fan-mail at last overwhelmed Beryl McCain and an agent, as for a great human star, had to be appointed. The Provincial Press Agency of Norwood Road, Southport now handle the famous horse's account and requests for photographs.

And at Aintree, unique among racehorses still alive and on the active list, a special race on the day before the Grand National is being named after him. Comparisons between the superlative Arkle and the heroic Red Rum have been made earlier in this book. Suffice now simply to say that no horse in Britain has ever matched Red Rum's colossal *public* popularity.

For his appearance at the Horse of the Year Show, Red Rum went down to stay in the splendid new stables at Kempton Park on Sunday 3 October with Billy Beardwood and McCain's new travelling head lad Harry Wright. 'Harry and I were in the Army together. He had a little transport business in Liverpool – till the dock strike sunk him.'

The famous horse and his entourage were magnificently looked after at Kempton – there is to be a plaque on his box there, '*Red Rum slept here,*' – and for three evenings in succession he was chauffered across to Wembley to receive his public's homage.

He was in sparkling form, because he had already received what he now regularly needs: acclamation and an easy victory. On 25 September he had gone to Carlisle, one of his favourite haunts, tough and not too far from home. McCain states bluntly, 'He does need a very stiff track now.' There he met two humble opponents for the three mile Windermere 'chase. The ground, too, was just what he now physically needs: firm, but no longer jarring – his old bones have had hammering enough as he enters his tenth year of racing. Ginger had been in a state before the race. 'I'm bound to be looking now at the old horse all the time and wondering every race whether, at his age, he's started to spring that leak. . . .' McCain frowns and adds, 'For now, of course, there can't be all that number of races left in him. . . .'

But Red Rum was going so well, after half-whipping round at the start (portent of reluctance, some of the crowd briefly feared) that Tommy Stack had to stand up and take a really strong pull on the reins to steady him. 'Instantly,' McCain reported, 'the old beggar just sailed away.'

This is what the horse adores. To those critics of Billy Ellison's desperately hard-pulling position on board Rummy on the scudding beach I would always say, 'But that's what this old battler *loves* – to feel like the man who's made it in the world, to be boss, to be running away, in control of his destiny.'

Thus when Tommy Stack tried to take a strong pull at him at Carlisle, the old horse seized his bit like a leopard grabs a rat. He bent his neck over the reins like a taut bow above a twanging bow-string, and away he bowled, leaping and springing, and laughing at life. He cantered past the winning-post twenty lengths clear on a tight rein. The crowd cheered. 'Ah, yes!' said Ginger, 'he does love his crowds.' Walking away, he nearly jerked light Billy Beardwood to the ground as he swaggered off, cock of the roost among people who loved him.

In these high spirits he arrived nine days later at Wembley. Just outside the illuminated and packed arena in London's suburb there is a sort of waiting limbo, confused and darker where, as beyond the grave, so people say, souls assemble, dally and await their call. Red Rum found it perplexing. Beryl McCain and Carol Wareing had come down to help with him. They watched Harry Wright manoeuvre the horse box as close as possible to the collecting ring.

They drop the ramp. Out of the ring whirls Britain's most famous whip, Mrs Cynthia Haydon, spry as a Corinthian buck behind her dashing hackneys. 'Mind out!' cries Mrs Haydon. 'Don't make a noise with that box! Don't disturb my horses!'

As she comes back, cigarette-holder jauntily jutting, Beryl McCain gently remonstrates with her: 'This is Red Rum, you know....'

'My God!' cries Mrs Haydon, eyes popping. 'Red Rum,' she breathes, top exponent of another equine discipline, regarding an international hero with real awe. 'In that case, *we* mustn't disturb *him*....'

Brian Fletcher came and said barely a word to the lads and nothing at first to Beryl McCain, but got up on the horse who has made such a pilgrim's progress through the world of British racing. Red Rum has passed, as Bunyan's pilgrim did, the slough of Despond and Giant Despair. He has become, in his crammed life-time, a legend and a hero to millions. As a magnificent survivor who has achieved greatness in the face of seemingly overwhelming odds, he is, at this low, grey point in the history of these islands, a blazing example to us all.

Inside the area now were the Four State Trumpeters from the Blues and Royals wearing the ceremonial dress of the Queen's Life Guard. There followed in the police horse of the year, a Welsh pony stallion, a great shire horse foster-mother, Black Beauty from the London Weekend Television series, and Britain's Gold Medal Pentathlon Team victoriously returned from the 1976 Olympic Games in Montreal.

Now in that uncertain limbo outside the glow and warmth and lights in the arena, Red Rum waited to be summoned in. Ahead of him the more normal equine personalities had passed through the divide into the ring, were illuminated and introduced at length. His time was coming. He would come, in pride of place, at the end. His great ears were cocked. His huge eyes stared, peering ahead for the next adventure, as they gaze up into the changing skies over Birkdale.

He drew close to the curtains and hesitated. Then he sprang through them into the celestial beam of the sole spotlight. The announcer needed no words to introduce him.

'Red Rum,' he simply said, and the cheers reverberated like thunder around the bowl of heaven.

53. 'We'll learn one day, I suppose'

The choice of our hero's next race was considerably influenced by the kindnesses shown to him by the Kempton management. On 16 October '76 Charisma Records were again sponsoring a £4000 three and a half mile handicap 'chase round Kempton's sharp circuit. Red Rum, after his previous winnerless season, was given the tempting racing weight of 11 st. 7 lb., though this would be the highest weight accepting.

There was no excuse this year that the ground at Kempton was too soft for Red Rum. The going was good for Sports Aid Foundation Day. Red Rum's presence and the bright sun dazzling across the brilliantly green watered turf, together with less obvious attractions like competitions for the Best Turned-Out Bookmaker ensured a large, happy crowd. But racing's professionals gave Red Rum little chance of winning the Charisma. . . . None of the experts tipped him. Most had sensibly reached the conclusion that our hero was the great Aintree horse, full stop. Other advisors pointed out that Kempton, almost continuously on the turn, and admirably suited to non-stayers, would not suit Red Rum. It did not.

Although he performed better than on his previous appearance in this race, Red Rum could never go the pace. Tommy Stack bluntly reported afterwards, 'He just couldn't handle the bends. Always changing legs. Never on an even keel.' Red Rum beat three of the eight finishers, coming in fifth, twenty lengths behind Andy Pandy. He showed no reluctance to race, but rather a casual flippancy in both his galloping and jumping such as a professional footballer might when only kicking about in some trivial practice for a future great event. His public had backed him with small change, but not the professionals, and he started at 13–2.

Ginger McCain with his frank honesty damned himself for running the horse again at unsuitable Kempton. Wagging his head, he remarked ruefully, 'Well, we'll learn one day, I suppose,' and came away to have a drink.

Red Rum's next race three weeks later was a bonus: Cheltenham's November meeting had been transferred from that fractured track to Haydock, and so was handy for Red Rum. Three of *Sporting Life*'s tabled tipsters now selected him, but 'Augur' disagreed with 'Man on the Spot', writing 'The task will prove beyond him.' Forecast favourite, Red Rum drifted in the market out to fourth favourite of seven runners at 5–1.

He cantered down to the post with his ears ominously laid back and examined the first fence opposite the stand side by side with Rag Trade. The 1976 Grand National winner stands 17 hands 2 ins. and towered over the dual victor of 1973 and '74 by exactly a hand. In Tommy Stack's absence at Doncaster, Ron Barry rode him at 12 st. 7 lb. in what was still called the Cheltenham Chase. As at Carlisle and Kempton he ran about a stone better than he had in his autumn races of 1975. It seemed possible now that the horse, though rising 12, was still astonishingly improving. We dare to hope. On Guy Fawkes Day 1976, giving weight all round in a good three mile £1500 'chase he finished third – and only a photographed short-head third – to Even Swell (10 st. 2 lb.) and Kilvulgan (11 st. 5 lb.). He finished only just over seven lengths behind the winner, having been kept well up among the action.

'Big Ron' would not tolerate any of the casualness of Kempton. When Red Rum treated one of Haydock's early fences with insouciance, Ron concentrated his mind upon the obstacles by switching Rummy from the inner to the outer and back again several times. The fences thus constituted more of a challenge to the old pro. He was not lackadaisical. Ron Barry had deliberately upset his plodding rhythm as a skilled child might do with an idle pony. The horse jumped superbly.

'Ron gave him a cracking ride,' Ginger McCain commented. He was planning to make Red Rum's next race the Hennessy. His strategic programme was already fixed: 'Then his winter holiday, two races back here at Haydock as usual. Then Liverpool.' As we were all admiringly to acknowledge five months later, McCain had constructed a wonderful campaign.

It would not be Red Rum's story however, if everything ran smoothly. The steady climb on to those early sunlit uplands immediately tripped into a glacier. A disastrous race at Newcastle and the worst winter of training weather that McCain recalls lay ahead. Stress too was going to threaten, for one grim day and night, Ginger and Beryl McCain's marriage.

54. 'The old boy's had it'

'Newcastle was bloody awful. There's no two ways about it,' Ginger McCain wags his head. 'We were all very, very disappointed. To tell you the truth there was a time after Newcastle that I did think, well, that the horse *could* be finished. . . .'

It was Red Rum's one hundredth race. The press, attuned to public interest, drummed up the occasion. The horse who had only once been brought down and once slipped up on the flat was going for his century on 20 November 1976. That alone was news, but when the runners were published Red Rum's millions of supporters realized that he would probably now do one of those story-book things and win. The three mile Salamanca Chase had cut up to the sort of easy three horse race like the one at Carlisle.

There was important racing that day at Ascot with two Black and White Whisky races. There was excellent racing at Warwick with three good sponsored races. But racing people everywhere wanted to watch the 1.30 at Newcastle. The ground was on the soft side of good. 'Sticky,' said Tommy Stack. 'Dead,' said McCain, 'without that spring he must have.' But with only two opponents. . . . One of them Yanworth had travelled up from the Cotswolds, the other Lingus was down from Hawick. Most of the tipsters at last went for Red Rum. . . . And he let them and his public and his stable right down with a sickening bang. He mooched home, last of the three, beaten a dreadful twenty-eight lengths.

The groans went up all over. He had galloped so reluctantly and jumped so gloomily that sceptics believed he might have been 'got at' by villains, and his critics, forgetting last season's lessons, again cried, 'The old boy's had it. He must be retired.'

Ginger said immediately, 'We'll forget about the Hennessy now,' and told me afterwards, 'I was a bit windy about his whole future to be quite honest.' It was left to cool and brainy Tommy Stack to point out the probable cause. 'He's never run well at Newcastle, Ginger, even tho' he's won there.' Five months later McCain picked up this thread. 'Of course that's it! It was after that bad race at Newcastle that Fletcher and I split. And four years ago at Newcastle in his first season with me, Stacky gave him that hard race. He'd said to me "Make sure you give him a real long break now, for I've been real hard on him". Then he came out again nine days later at Haydock and won so easily Stacky couldn't believe it. But I reckon that's right,' said McCain puzzling back over the years. 'He might always be remembering that hard race at Newcastle in October 1972. . . .'

Following the 1972 pattern Red Rum went quickly on to Haydock. And there in Ginger McCain's words, 'he ran a blinder!' This was in no handicap. He was meeting champion hurdler and near Gold Cup winner Bula at level weights. Winter's star, that season had nearly won the Mackeson Gold Cup at Haydock giving Cancello a stone. Summerville, who now made up the third member of the field, had finished third in the Mackeson, beaten Broncho II at Worcester and won at Wincanton. The great old Aintree stayer was being pitted against two high class park 'chasers. They must prove far too fast for a specialist requiring four and a half miles.

In 1975 Red Rum had run in this Sundew Chase and been easily beaten by Bula. The experts gave our hero no chance whatsoever against his two fast and classy rivals and he started the long outsider of three at 12–1.

Ron Barry drove him into an early lead and he was never out of the hunt until they reached the last fence. The three horses were all in the air over the last fence 'then the other two had too much toe,' says Ginger, 'and they sprinted away. Ron was very full of him, and we were absolutely delighted. Ron said to me in that way of his, "Don't forget he doesn't go too bad for me, will you, if that Stacky should try to cry off the ride at Liverpool!" '

The disaster of Newcastle had been expurged in ten days, and Red Rum went off to his customary winter holiday with Ted Greenway in Cheshire.

But in the stables in Upper Aughton Road things were less happy and more tense; so far in all the season there had only been one winner in the yard since Rummy's victory at Carlisle back in September. And there was going to be no other winner until April.

With the star away in Cheshire, 'The One Good Horse' for which Ginger had been yearning all those lean years was no longer around to lift morale. Despondency slunk about the place. Ginger McCain began, as all winnerless trainers will, to go through a gnawing period of the self-doubt which follows frustration.

Nor was there good news from Stonehouse Farm, Little Budworth. Ted Greenway reported that the weather was hampering what should have been Red Rum's happy winter break. Lashing rain day after day prevented him from being turned out to relax in a paddock. Heavy going on the land blocked those sprightly cross-country rambles which had so rejuvenated him the year before. Ted Greenway and Ginger were sharply disappointed. The winter's rest was leaking unhelpfully away. 'Through no-one's fault – Ted and George White there were giving him the best care in the world – but just through that shocking weather, the horse didn't come back to us looking as he had the previous year. He wasn't sparkling, and his coat had gone.'

The weather continued to oppose Red Rum on Southport sands. For the first time since McCain had started humbly training on the beach twenty-five years earlier the sand was waterlogged week after soaking week.

'For nearly three bloody months,' Ginger swore, 'I couldn't even prepare a gallop, the beach was that waterlogged. I could only canter steadily. Seemed like all bloody winter. I even sent him out to canter the very edge of the tide, a mile and half out, right along on the very edge of the sea where the fishing lines were. I couldn't get out to him myself. I had to leave it all to the lads.'

McCain, though very doubtful now about Red Rum's fitness, stuck to his programme. The horse reappeared at Haydock nine weeks after his Sundew race. He ran in a new-styled race, the three and a half mile £2,460 Malcolm Fudge National Trial Stakes.

Red Rum, still two months from his goal, was fat. Little was expected of him by the pundits. 'He was not,' Ginger McCain assessed afterward, 'sixty per cent ready. Even so, I was that bit disappointed in him.' Red Rum finished a long way last of the six runners and over forty lengths behind the fancied Grand National hope Andy Pandy. He lost ground quickly after a mistake on the far side, 'so Tommy,' said McCain, 'wasn't hard on him.'

He was giving 3 lb. to Forest King and 18 lb. to Sir Garnet. Andy Pandy carried 4 lb. less to a hard fought victory and received enthusiastic notices. Rain had drenched the ground into soft going and the races were run in a sharp wind, conditions which have never appealed to Red Rum. His critics took little note of these and once more berated his trainer.

At this period the domestic pressures on the McCains grew almost unbearable. Biting doubts that he could get the horse fit in time badgered McCain. Nor were his other horses winning. One evening, his anxieties exploded in a wild rage. Someone had mentioned to McCain the chance of training in Singapore. Dining out he quarrelled with Beryl. 'I'm off,' he said, 'you have the horse, the house, the kids. I'm going.' He jumped out of the car and strode off into the night.

Six weeks later both Ginger and Beryl were laughing about the scene. 'Wasn't funny then though, was it?' says Beryl. 'No,' says Ginger, 'but when you went past me in the car and went like that with your hand. . . .' 'I didn't,' exclaims Beryl, laughing, 'I called out "Goin' home to Mummy?" in a silly voice!'

So he had. 'Found him on his mother's couch,' says Beryl fondly. The outbreak had cleared the air.

Ginger grew less tense and paid little attention to racing critics' views of the Malcolm Fudge race. He sensibly hearkened to Tommy Stack. 'He's an astute person you've got to listen to. He told me the horse was so far from being ready he actually gurgled during the race.' Stack would confirm this to me after the 'National, when paying full tribute to McCain's expertly timed training of Red Rum. 'And Ginger had left something to work on,' Stack ended admiringly, 'even in his next race at Haydock a month later. The horse gurgled just a bit then, too, but much less than in February.'

This race, the Greenall Whitley, pleased all Red Rum's supporters and even softened the barbs of most of his detractors. It was his fifth successive year in the 'chase, now accepted as the famous horse's regular pre-National wind-up. Sir Garnet who had finished forty-two lengths ahead of him in February now met him on 2 lbs better terms.

The first three in the £9,800 race led by General Moselle were not engaged in the 'National, but most of the post-race press coverage concentrated on the twelve year old who had already twice won the world's greatest steeplechase. From all sides flowed praise for Rummy's performance.

Tommy Stack kept him right up in the front line so that he would be actively embattled. His jumping shed its slipshod shuffles. 'Some fences he really pinged,' said Stack, delightedly. He led for half a mile in the middle of the race and was galloping there with a real chance until the field turned into the straight. His remarkable improvement with Sir Garnet, only eight and a half lengths ahead compared with over forty lengths a month earlier, gave McCain his first real encouragement. 'They were fancying Sir Garnet for the 'National, so by God, I had to fancy the old horse, hadn't I?'

To enliven Rummy's preparation, Ginger McCain took him three times to work on Aintree racecouse. He sent two galloping companions, working Red Rum between them. 'He's full of himself and fresh and very gassy each time we go there. Of course, he knows where he is exactly! He's very intelligent.' McCain sent him twice over one and a half miles before the Greenall Whitley, 'using the mile gallop inside the hurdle track, then once more afterwards over a mile.'

In the week before the 'National McCain was round with eighty-nine-year-old Noel le Mare. He walked round the snug drawing room in Waterloo Road looking up at all the pictures of Red Rum from previous years and victories. 'He looked so fit, so light in those pictures, I suddenly thought, "He can't be ready now. He's so *big* this year. He's so thickened. The race will come at *least* a week too soon."' When he went back to the stables the sight of Red Rum only confirmed his doubts. 'The horse is heavier all round this year.'

On the day before the 'National the McCains' good friend and supporter Stan Wareing made his annual pilgrimage to see his hero's final gallop. Wareing eyed Red Rum expertly. 'Ginger,' he said, 'he looks bigger and stronger than I've *ever* seen him in these last five years!'

Journalist and ex-amateur jockey John Oaksey came down to ride work on Valley of Rocks. Oaksey, physically and morally courageous, appeared that morning in *Horse and Hound* tipping Red Rum hot and strong. IT'S RED RUM FOR A THIRD VICTORY trumpeted his headline. He had written his piece five days earlier. Oaksey's expert confidence rang out like a clarion in a mob of other's ifs and buts. On the beach stable-girl Kate Wilson rode the second galloping companion. Night Adventure, and 'Billy Two' was on his 'Red'.

McCain fretted. Reporters and photographers, small Lowry-like encumbered figures, trotted about the beach's vast expanse. 'Now don't head Red Rum,' McCain repeated to Oaksey and Kate. 'He *must* finish in front of this gallop.' It was sound training psychology. McCain warned the other two riders, 'These two can go a bit. They've got speed.'

To McCain's alarm he saw Rummy's two work horses thunder away, both riders pulling hard to steady them. 'Oh God,' groaned Ginger. Then his face lightened, brightened and broke into its famous grin. Red Rum 'hit his stride', caught the others like an eagle and swept ahead with Billy Beardwood jack-knifed in the horse's now famous 'stopping position'. 'They went just over four and a half furlongs. And the other two were niggling and pushing to try and *keep* with him!' McCain adds, typically, 'I thought first that the other two were *sick*, he was going that much better!'

'Then,' recalls Ginger warmly, 'as Red walked back through the sea with the press people running after him, I could see he was that well! He was full of himself. He was lit up and dancing. His legs just flowed. And he walked out clear.'

55. 'Marvellous, just bloody marvellous'

The annual rhythm of Grand National morning was repeated. Beryl McCain came out to plait Rummy's mane, and Bob Marshall, the brilliant blacksmith who has so improved the horse's delicate feet, quietly plated him. The McCains as usual went over first to the Wareings. 'We had a scoop or two of champagne!'

What most impressed both Ginger and Beryl about Red Rum before the 1977 Grand National was his peculiar calmness. 'He was,' says Beryl, 'completely and utterly relaxed this year.'

Ginger adds, 'Other years you can see he's nervous – that old lower lip going flap, flap, flap. This time not at all. He was,' Ginger fumbled for the phrase, 'at ease.' It was going to prove the most tremendous portent. 'He was contented with his world,' Beryl says, 'contented with his lot.'

It was the same when he arrived at Aintree. Even when the sunshine which he requires bloomed goldenly and enveloped him in its warmth, he hardly sweated on his burnished coat. With Tommy Stack riding in the race before, there was a long wait before he came out to join Rummy. McCain asked Billy to walk the horse around on the grass.

Stack looked pale and his intelligent face was drawn in sharp, anxious lines. He was not riding the bookmakers' favourite – Andy Pandy at 11–2 was that. But to Stack's care was entrusted the favourite horse of tens of millions of people all round the world.

The rain, which on Thursday had soaked the turf and fallen like lead on the spirits of Rummy's friends, had stopped. By Friday the going was plainly faster. On Saturday the man who cares for the weather cared for Red Rum. He sent the drying wind. But none of the eight crack tipsters listed by *Sporting Life* had selected Red Rum. As Rummy paced out on to the course a burst of cheering greeted the announcement that Billy Beardwood had won the prize for the best turned-out horse. Red Rum instantly responded to his public's acclaim, and proudly took up his accustomed position at the head of the parade.

The race, delayed by some protestors, finally burst forward in a flood. They were nine nervous minutes late away.

It was soon clear to all tense watchers that Rummy's bobbing white nose-band was far closer to the front than usual. In the run to Becher's, Stack had selected a fortunate course down the middle. Grief and disaster exploded on either side of him, more horses truly falling than being unluckily capsized by others. After only three fences more than one quarter of the forty-two starters had already crashed to the ground. The scene resembled the horrors of Balaclava. But, as the field streamed towards Becher's, spread all across the track, Stack could be seen sitting comfortably in 10th place. He was already within touch of the thundering vanguard.

'*The* Aintree horse' was jumping in his skilfully economic way, occasionally putting in as many as three short strides before a fence to ensure, like a pony in a hunter trial, that he got absolutely right for it. Tommy Stack closely observed his signals: 'If he was going to be right, he just galloped on at the fence with his ears back. But each time he felt he might meet it wrong, he cocked his ears – three strides out even – and I felt him,' Tommy weaves his shoulders like the school rugby player he was, 'I felt him beneath me shifting his shoulders, altering his angle and putting his stride just right. He is quite different from any other horse. . . . He doesn't stand off and sail over and waste energy and risk himself. He'll get to the *exact* spot before a big ditch and over he'll pop.' Stack said with bright-eyed wonderment to McCain: 'Those big fences just feel small on him. He just flips through the top. What's more,' said Stack even more amazed, 'he looks *ahead* of the fence to see what's going on the other side!'

Nothing was more needed as Red Rum, far nearer the van than in any previous year, approached the colossal Chair. Boom Docker, who had been leading with the sort of extravagant leaps of which Rummy disapproves, was clear. But in second place Sage Merlin crashed, rolled and lay hidden on the far side. His jockey Ian Watkinson scrambled up as Red Rum was galloping at the fence. Watkinson ducked right for the rails and Rummy instantaneously switched himself half-left, jumped the enormous obstacle on a slight incline towards the inner and dodged the fallen horse with the power and grace of Rudolf Nureyev.

He was amazingly lying seventh as he set out for his second sweep round his kingdom. Boom Docker, leading Andy Pandy, suddenly refused, and Rimell's horse, evidently cantering in the hands of John Burke (last year's victor), sailed on towards Becher's alone. As he approached the fence Andy Pandy's attention seemed to wander. Astonished by the plunging drop, he over-jumped, crumpled, staggered, then went down. Burke raging at losing another victory flung down his arms. And Red Rum, gliding smoothly past, was now in front.

Stack said afterwards, 'I was going as well as Andy Pandy.' Rimell's big horse looked to us to be only cantering, but his long energetic stride sharply contrasted with the old professional's leisurely flick of his legs.

'It was landing over Becher's,' said Stack, 'that I began to hear this *extraordinary* roar. Everyone at every fence began to shout "Come on Red Rum! C'm on Red! Rummy c'm on! *Red Rum! RED RUM!*" It was quite fantastic!'

Eight fences more to go for the legend. Leading the remnants now of his pursuers. But the horses of the fallen were everywhere charging about. Tommy Stack bellows back to Jeff King on What A Buck, 'C'm on, we've got to dodge these!' and then an astonishing event occurs. As Stack for the first time kicks Rummy firmly on, the horse shoots forward like the five furlong sprinter he was ten tough years and one hundred and five races ago. The loose horses were smoothly overtaken. The ridden pursuers were devastatingly outpaced. Red Rum, unhampered, swerved nonchalantly round the Canal Turn to head for home and glory.

People at every fence would relate how, as commentaries and radios reported the hero's progress, spontaneous cheering erupted and continued louder and louder into a continuous roar all round the course. His caution and Stack's calm were not affected. He was carefully, wisely, popping homewards towards the colossal clamour of the grandstands. He had, as his busy stride and flickering ears showed, an important job on hand.

Then there appeared behind him Chantilly-based Yorkshireman Martin Blackshaw, who had so adroitly snapped up the ride on Churchtown Boy, easy winner of the Topham Trophy here forty-eight hours earlier. Churchtown Boy moved closer, ready to pounce. It seemed for one doubting furlong as if the L'Escargot conquest of 1975 was about to be re-enacted. 'Certainly,' claimed a disconsolate Blackshaw afterwards, 'I thought I could eat Red Rum any time I chose.'

For Stack the main dangers appeared to be the glancing loose horses, as unpredictable as sticks on a river's current. This superb jockey has repeatedly said with the modesty of the truly great, that Rummy did it all. But Stack's avoidance of these uncontrollable hazards around him was the work of a cool quick expert. There was no question this year of Stacky sitting quietly waiting to make his run. He drove Red Rum along all the way. And still Churchtown Boy moved smoothly closer.

Then in one ecstatic instant the battle was won. At the third last fence Churchtown Boy blundered, grunted, lost momentum and lost the race. Rummy skipped over the last two and then the roaring to which each stride had brought him closer boomed to such a crescendo that Stack dreaded that his horse might stop. 'It was like going into a funnel – a narrowing funnel,' he kept repeating, moving his arms together like a press. 'People everywhere seemed to be leaping up and rushing in. I thought we'd stop.'

But Red Rum never wavered.

A final astonishing thing happened. It is well said that no horse can sprint twice in a race. Red Rum had sprinted clear of the loose ruck of horses a mile away after Becher's. Then he had settled down again for a long slog home. Now, unbelievably, as Stack urged him, he sprinted again up the long run-in, accelerating away from the weary Churchtown Boy like a class horse leaving a plater. And did the tumult worry him? He gloried in it. These were his people screaming him home. He spurted for the post like a bright bay arrow.

'Couldn't pull him up,' said Stack marvelling. 'He'd have gone on galloping – oh, at least as far as Becher's once again....'

In 1976 Red Rum had given the brave mare Eyecatcher 17 lb. and beaten her eight lengths. In 1977 he gave her 21 lb. and beat her thirty-one lengths, an improvement at the age of 12 of nearly 2 stone. His victory, run at 28.42, mph, had broken the prize money record over jumps with £114,370.

Weights and measures. The treble after five years was at last accomplished. A horse had been witnessed unlike any other in anyone's lifetime, in anyone's memory.

And suddenly everyone was crying.

Cool little Tommy Stack cried. Great Ginger McCain

came bursting through the crowd shouting, 'Bloody marvellous, just bloody marvellous!' And tears rolled down his face. Old peers in tweeds cried. Trendy lads in jeans cried. A wet-eyed bookie burst into the pressroom blubbing out, 'We've lost a quarter of a million quid and we don't care!'

The horse, of course, was quite the coolest person on the track. 'He didn't blow at all,' McCain relates amazed. 'Save where the saddle was,' says Stack, 'he wasn't even sweating,' and the jockey, once again bewildered, shakes his head.

Red Rum led BBC TV's evening newscast, relegating the doings of Presidents to the also-rans. The front pages of the Sunday papers were reset to carry shouting accounts of his triumph. Monday's nationals, right across the spectrum, front-paged him all again. And a gentleman from Oswestry wrote to *The Times*: 'Sir, if Caligula could, Callaghan should; for certainly Red Rum has given us a better run for our money and a surer return than any Chancellor in history.'

The final astonishing act of celebration took place at ten o'clock in the evening. Once again, it could only have happened to Red Rum. His horsebox, easing through the crowds, swept up outside The Bold Hotel in Southport's smartest Edwardian street. The revolving doors had been removed. Down came the box's ramp, and up the steps into the hotel's jammed, jostling lobby walked the horse. The press was such that Rummy, still wearing his blue riband of victory, had to squeeze delicately through the foyer. On the left in the restaurant people leapt whooping upon the tables. Out of the bar on the right, applause roared and another crowd rushed forward. He walked on calmly, on past the other crammed bar ahead to the swing doors into the ballroom. A strip of red carpet had been unrolled for him across its glossy surface.

Tommy Stack was watching, eyes agog. Beryl McCain watched anxiously. Both saw one hoof for an instant come off the carpet. It tested the floor, found it slippery, and stepped back carefully on to his special red strip. He progressed to the ballroom's end and turned and posed himself for his photographers. The lights flashed. The crowd shouted. They milled all round him, pressing against him. He never shifted. Someone stood upon a table above the throng and declaimed a long paean of praise in his honour. The horse turned towards him and listened attentively.

And the modest Tommy Stack, who had declared at Aintree that there could never be another horse like Red Rum, suddenly realized, staring at our hero in the clamorous ballroom on Grand National Night, that this was really more than just a horse. 'He is,' said Tommy Stack simply, 'a different *being*.'

56. 'A Different Being'

But the greatest Liverpool horse of all time was not yet done. Red Rum would be thirteen if he ran in his sixth Grand National and, up until the very morning of the race, he was being prepared to do so.

'He was that well,' says Ginger McCain, 'we'd no thought of retiring him. We were even thinking if he kept well and Mr Le Mare was well too, of running the following year as well!'

He ran five times in his last season of racing. The patter was as before, with three early races before his midwinter break. In all he carried 12st 2lb or more, was described by *Chaseform* as 'looking well and jumping well', and he ran well too: two seconds and a fourth, before his customary winter holiday.

But this year he did himself too well. He had grown very portly before his two comeback races at Haydock. He was tailed off in the first, in February, and then, in March, got well behind after blundering badly. 'But that was Tommy Stack's first ride since he had badly fractured his pelvis,' explained Ginger McCain. 'He was bound to be a bit rusty. The horse really middled that last open ditch on the far side. You could count Tommy's toes pushing through his boots! But Tommy was very enthusiastic about the horse.'

During the last weeks before the National, Ginger thought that Red Rum was slightly lame in his off-hind.

'Looked like a touch of string-halt. I kept in the sea and we called in Ted Greenway. Couldn't find anything then. But we thought something must have happened to him either at Haydock or just after. I worked him a couple of miles on the course at Haydock. Fine. Then on

Friday before the National, I worked him five or six furlongs on Aintree racecourse. He was that well he was running away with Billy Beardsley – Billy had to aim him at the stable wall to stop him! But as he walked away from us he was definitely a touch lame. The only other person out there that morning to notice was Peter O'Sullevan.

'Then back at the stables the horse pulled out lame. We had his foot nerve-blocked. That proved it was definitely in his foot: it was a stress fracture, a hairline fracture.

'Ron Barry said "Forget it. When he warms up in the race, he'll be OK." But we couldn't. When he paraded he jumped and kicked and I wondered whether we should have run. But he was intermittently lame afterwards for five or six weeks. Well, if he'd run and won, we'd have gone on. We'd talked about it. He was all the guv'nor had left – Mr Le Mare lived till he was ninety-two and died on the Isle of Man. He was alert as always, just physically more frail.

'A big Japanese American restaurateur called "Rocky" Aoki came into my lounge one day and offered us $1 million for the horse as a personality. His firm was Benihana of Tokyo, with offices in Florida and New York. He said "I open a new restaurant every week!" And he estimated the horse could earn him $1 million in eighteen months! We said "No", of course.'

Until the spring of 1986 McCain used him as his hack: 'He was a bloody old idiot at times! Then sometimes he'd come in sweating, a bit distressed. We found that an artery had contracted in that off-hind leg. He was getting a blockage. So I didn't ride him after that. He was led out, of course, but not ridden. He was led out first lot to keep up the rhythm of his life. We'd put him back to third lot after his lameness, after the off-hind trouble. He didn't like that at all. He missed going out on his engagements. He started going back. He was unhappy. Then his leg got right – he still had eight grammes of warfarin daily – and we put him back in his old routine again – led out first lot, as it should be. And he had a couple of engagements every month booked up to a year ahead. He lived for those engagements. He needed them. You know, when he started going back on us that time in 1986, I thought for the first time there'd be a time we would lose him forever.'

It had been another close run thing in Red Rum's remarkable life. But, as with senior gentlemen of high resolve, he made another comeback, avoiding death as he used to swerve around disaster at Aintree. He resumed his full round of public engagements, about twenty-five a year, all over Britain, from opening betting shops to parading at country shows. All were performed on behalf of Red Rum Ltd. In the spring of 1989 he was, reported Ginger McCain, 'absolutely grand. He'd have been a big part of my life gone, a part of all our lives, if we'd lost him in 1986.'

Then came another sharp change to Red Rum's lifestyle. Like a millionaire who has made a fortune and seized fame in the city, he then retired to a pleasant country estate. Ginger and Beryl McCain had always yearned for the country. Their neat Southport house between Ginger's second-hand car business and the cramped stable yard, overlooked by a row of urban back window, was not the place they had dreamed about. Stuck away on slippery streets on the wrong side of the railway tracks, facing a row of little shops, grimy and noisy with traffic and trains, it had been the unlikeliest springboard for Rummy's gigantic triumphs.

In December 1990 Ginger McCain moved his home and stables to a sizeable red brick farm house on the Marquess of Cholmondeley's beautiful estate at Malpas in Cheshire. Red Rum was back in the country air again, as he had been with Tim Molony near Melton Mowbray, and with Bobby Renton, Tommy Stack and Anthony

Gillam in Ripon. He and thirty-five other horses in training plus three brood mares enjoyed green rolling hills and the fresh winds blowing in from the Welsh hills. From his field there's a glimpse of the lake and Cholmondeley castle chapel. Here Red Rum spent the last five years of his life. In the line of boxes in the stable yard behind the farmhouse he had pride of place: his box was at the end. From it he could loftily regard his inferior companions going in and out to work. All his life he preserved his lively sense of self-regard.

In the winter of 1991–92 he fell ill again, but struggled back from a few strides of the Elysian Fields, not yet ready for his last turnout to grass. He had recovered, but when I called on him in November 1992 he looked elderly and testy. In human terms he was pushing ninety. I made the customary offering of Polo mints, his abiding passion, and his big eyes brightened. Then those eyes, which had so safely led him five times around the Liverpool fences, gave me his old look of interested, affectionate superiority. He probably shared his trainer's scorn for the modern, softer fences of today. 'Nowadays you can brush through them,' McCain said scornfully. 'Ordinary three-mile chasers can come up to Liverpool and get round. In Red's years you couldn't do that. The premium was on *jumping*. That's what the National used to be about. What it *ought* to be about.'

In 1994, Red Rum was officially retired from all public engagements and, for the first time, he was unable to lead the parade before the 1995 Grand National. His myriad fans missed him terribly. But, as always, Ginger put 'the old boy's' interests first. But the horse was not yet done. Within a few weeks he had perked up sufficiently to make his last appearance. Typically this was at the scene of his greatest triumphs, at Aintree, during the new May meeting. By one of those astonishing coincidences that had made up the links of his life, the date was his birthday, 3rd May. The racecourse deftly named all six races after highlights in his career, starting with the Red Rum 30th Birthday Chase and ending with the Local Hero Novices Hurdle.

The international hero then spent the last summer of his life in the green fields of Cheshire. Then within six months of that final Aintree appearance, the news burst out on the front page of all the leading newspapers. Red Rum had died. From the front page headline and coloured photograph in *The Times* to a ten page tribute in the *Daily Mirror* to 'Britain's best loved racehorse' and an 'exclusive, four page tribute in *The Sun* – 'Death of a Champion', the news of Red Rum's death shot around the world. The two racing papers carried special sections. In red and gold *The Sporting Life*'s only front page headline boomed out 'Death of Red Rum'. Inside its leader described 'a fairy tale come true' ... 'The greatest of them all' ... 'The people's horse'. The *Racing Post* carried a special twelve page supplement entitled 'Tribute to a Legend' with pictures of the ten men whose lives were touched by the horse 'who became the greatest to grace the hallowed Aintree turf.'

The end had been simply conducted, with the same kind of thoughtfulness that had enriched all Rummy's twenty-three years with the McCains. On Wednesday October 18th 1995, Ginger had found him in a distressed state. 'He couldn't get up,' he said. 'He was basically dying'.

His vet John Burgess was immediately called. He reported 'I found him obviously very weak and showing signs of circulatory failure. In consultation with Mr McCain it was decided immediately to put him to sleep in his own box'.

'Only three weeks before he died', said Ginger McCain afterwards, 'he was out in his field when the Cheshire Hounds came by. And the old boy stood there rigid, head up, ears cocked, you know, loving it all.' Ginger added, 'I felt his life was coming to an end when he went over on a visit to Ireland and stayed on the same stud, Rossenara, where he'd been born. And at Martyn McEnery's, he stood in the next box to the one he'd stood in as a yearling. I felt then that he'd come full circle.'

Long before he died, Ginger and John Burgess had discussed the best way to end Red Rum's life when the time came. They had decided firmly on the bullet – 'so much quicker' – and not a lethal injection. 'Sometimes brave racehorses fight against that,' Ginger explained. After his death Ginger went back to see his old friend. 'He was lying against a wall of straw, ears still cocked, as if he was sleeping. He had just slipped gently down.'

By prior arrangement with the racecourse's managing director Charles Barnett, Red Rum was buried by the winning post under a simple plaque. Aintree's head groundsman was in charge of the arrangements. He'd been with Bobby Renton, Ginger explained. 'He rang me and said "We've done it all with dignity. He's laid to rest the right way, facing towards the finish".'

'We already have Philip Blacker's marvellous statue of him at Aintree,' said Barnett, 'but we will be erecting a permanent memorial where he lies buried'. Barnett touched the heart of the matter when he declared 'he was particularly important to Aintree in its dark days and has ever since been an inspiration to many'.

A tide of tribute immediately started to pour in like the waves surging on his old Southport sands. From Lester Piggott (who rode him in 1967) 'he was a racing institution'. The reigning champion trainer, David Nicholson, declared him 'the epitome of what National Hunt racing is all about' and Tommy Stack, who won Rummy's third National in 1997 and rode him in his final race on 4th March 1978 at Haydock, said 'He was one of the best advertisements racing has had for a very long time'.

Ginger McCain, who had lost the true old friend who

made his name, continued keenly and correctly to emphasise 'Red's' other victories, particularly his win in the Scottish Grand National (a win which deeply impressed Brian Fletcher, too) and his narrow defeat in the Hennessy Cognac Gold Cup at Newbury in November 1973. Red Rum's talents were not confined to Aintree.

There was much more to this remarkable horse than his performances. He became the nation's hero by virtue of his history and character and his courageous determination to survive against all odds. Like the occasional great person he made his own extraordinary luck. Through hardship and by valour he made it from the bottom rung to the top. There was inside him some strange spirit. Like that other great horse of our time, Arkle, he used to stand, ears cocked, eyes huge, gazing up at the heavens. What did he see or hear up there? He was, as Tommy Stack declared with simple awe, 'a different being'. How fortunate we were to know him and to be uplifted by his example.

Red Rum's career record

Red Rum bg 1965 Quorum-Mared (Magic Red)

Pos	Name	Dist	Course	Date	Jockey	SP
1967						
(Flat)						
1dh	Thursby (S) Pte	5f	Liverpool	Ap 7	P Cook	5-1
0	Tickton Juvenile Stks	5f	Beverley	Ap 29	J Sime	10-1
0	Vane Arms Ptd	6f	Teeside	June 19	E Larkin	10-7
3	Angerton Stks	6f	Newcastle	June 30	G Cadwaladr	33-1
1	Pinley Nursery	7f	Warwick	Aug 28	D W Morris	6-1
0	Bishopthorpe Nursery	7f	York	Sept 7	G Sexton	100-8
3	Minor Nursery	1m	Pontefract	Sept 30	L Piggott	6-1
4	Nanpantan Nursery	1m	Leicester	Sept 25	D W Morris	10-1
1968						
(Flat)						
1	Waterdale (S) H'cap	7f	Doncaster	Mar 27	G Lewis	11-4f
2	Earl of Sefton Stks	1m	Liverpool	Mar 30	L Piggot	11-4f
1968/69						
2	Junior Novices Hdle (Div II)	2m 200yds	Cheltenham	Sept 18	J Gifford	8-1
4	Hainton Hdle	2m	Market Rasen	Oct 19	A Turnell	5-2
3	Merit Hdle	2m	Nottingham	Nov 18	J Cook	100-8
3	Plant Novices Hdle (Div II)	2m 150yds	Doncaster	Nov 22	T S Murphy	5-2f
0	Harewood Hdle	2m	Wetherby	Mar 8	J Doyle	10-1
2	Lancashire Hdle	2m 100yds	Liverpool	Mar 27	P Broderick	100-8
1	Bilton Hdle	2m	Wetherby	Apr 7	P Broderick	15-8f
1	Bradmore H'cap Hdle	2m	Nottingham	Apr 15	P Broderick	5-1
1	Teeside Celebration H'cap Hdle	2m 176yds	Teeside	Apr 25	P Broderick	5-2
0	Orchardstown H'cap Hdle	2m	Ayr	May 20	P Broderick	6-1
1969/70						
0	Andoversford H'cap Hdle	2m 200yds	Cheltenham	Sept 18	T Stack	100-6
0	Town Field H'cap Hdle	2m 150yds	Doncaster	Oct 24	J Doyle	100-8
0	Tadcaster H'cap Hdle	2m	Wetherby	Nov 8	J Doyle	9-1
0	Dormer Drill H'cap Hdle	2m 150yds	Doncaster	Nov 22	P Broderick	
2	Dick Whittington H'cap Hdle	2m	Catterick		T Stack	6-1
3	Tockwith H'cap Hdle	2m 4f	Wetherby	Jan 20	T Stack	6-1jf
0	January H'cap Hdle (Div II)	2m 4f	Doncaster	Jan 23	T Stack	11-2
0	Bishopsthorpe H'cap Hdle	2m 4f	Wetherby	Feb 7	R Edwards	6-1
0	Long Dog H'cap Hdle	2m 5f	Teeside	Mar 13	B Brogan	11-2
0	George Duller H'cap Hdle	3m	Cheltenham	Mar 18	R Edwards	25-1
0	Ronald Royds H'cap Hdle	2m 4f	Cheltenham	Apr 11	T Stack	6-1
2	Perth Drag Hunt H'cap Hdle	3m	Perth	Apr 21	T Stack	6-1
F	Church Fenton H'cap Hdle	2m	Wetherby	May 6		10-1
0	Milsington H'cap Hdle	3m	Ayr	May 18	T Stack	5-1

1970-71

3	Vittoria Novs Ch	2m 120yds	Newcastle	Oct 28	T Stack	7-1
1	Town Moor Novs Ch	2m 150yds	Doncaster	Nov 6	T Stack	100-7
3	Borough Ch	2m	Cheltenham	Nov 13	T Stack	9-2
3	WD & HO Wills Premier Ch (Qualifier)	2m 4f	Wetherby	Nov 20	T Stack	100-8
1	Hope Inn Ch	2m 250yds	Sedgefield	Dec 5	T Stack	4-5f
3	Rowland Meyrick H Ch	3m	Wetherby	Dec 26	M Gifford	10-1
1	Girvan H Ch	2m 4f	Ayr	Feb 5	T Stack	4-1
4	Compton Ch	3m	Newbury	Feb 13	T Stack	7-2f
3	Facey Romford H Ch	3m	Teeside	Feb 26	T Stack	4-1
4	Mildmay of Flete Challenge Cup	2m 4f	Cheltenham	Mar 18	T Stack	16-1
3	Crossley H Ch	2m 4f	Wetherby	Apr 12	T Stack	7-2
0	Rigton H Ch	3m	Wetherby	May 5	T Stack	7-2
3	Spittalfield H Ch	2m 4f	Perth	May 30	T Stack	5-2

1971/72

4	Colonel R Thompson Memorial Trophy	3m	Southwell	Oct 12	T Stack	16-1
0	Anthony Marshall Trophy Ch	3m	Kelso	Oct 23	T Stack	12-1
2	John Eustace Smith Trophy Ch	3m	Newcastle	Nov 6	T Stack	16-1
0	Sundew H Ch	3m	Haydock	Dec 1	T Stack	10-1
1	Charles Vickery Memorial Cup	3m 300yds	Catterick	Dec 11	T Stack	9-2
3	Denby H Ch	3m 300yds	Catterick	Dec 22	T Stack	15-2
1	Zetland H Ch	3m 300yds	Catterick	Jan 1	T Stack	7-2
0	Busby H Ch	3m 300yds	Catterick	Mar 6	T Stack	4-5f
3	Trent H Ch	2m 6f	Nottingham	Mar 21	M Gifford	5-1
3	Wetherby H Ch	3m 100yds	Wetherby	Apr 3	T Stack	9-1
0	Scottish Grand National	4m 120yds	Ayr	Apr 15	M Blackshaw	33-1
4	Champagne H Ch	3m	Market Rasen	Apr 29	T Stack	7-4f

1972/73

1	Windermere H Ch	3m	Carlisle	Sept 30	T Stack	6-1
1	Gordon Foster H Ch	3m 100yds	Wetherby	Oct 11	R Barry	3-1
1	Salamanca H Ch	3m	Newcastle	Oct 25	T Stack	9-4
1	Southport H Ch	3m	Haydock	Nov 3	T Stack	2-1f
1	Mauchline H Ch	3m 3f 150yds	Ayr	Nov 13	B Fletcher	11-8f
3	Cumberland Grand National Trial	3m	Carlisle	Jan 31	B Fletcher	7-2
2	Haydock Park National Trial	3m 4f	Haydock	Feb 7	B Fletcher	5-1
4	Greenall Whitley H Ch	3m	Haydock	Mar 3	B Fletcher	5-1f

1 GRAND NATIONAL H CH 4m 856yds Liverpool Mar 31 B Fletcher 10st 5lb
2 Crisp (R Pitman), 12st
3 L'Escargot (T Carberry), 12st
4 Spanish Steps (P Blacker), 11st 13lb
Dist: 3/4l, 25l, 12l. SPs 9-1jf, 9-1jf, 11-1, 16-1. 38 ran.

1973/74

2	Perthshire Challenge Cup H Ch	3m	Perth	Sept 26	B Fletcher	4-1
1	Windermere H Ch	3m	Carlisle	Sept 29	B Fletcher	8-13f
1	Joan Mackay H Ch	3m 110yds	Ayr	Oct 13	B Fletcher	10-11f
1	John Eustace Smith Trophy	3m	Newcastle	Oct 31	B Fletcher	13-8f
2	Doncaster Pattern Ch	3m 2f	Doncaster	Nov 10	B Fletcher	5-2
2	Hennessy Cognac Gold Cup	3m 2f 120yds	Newbury	Nov 24	B Fletcher	8-1
1	Brettanby H Ch	3m 300yds	Catterick	Feb 20	B Fletcher	3-1
U	Greenall Whitley Ch	3m	Haydock	Mar 2	B Fletcher	5-1

1 GRAND NATIONAL H CH 4m 856yds Liverpool Mar 30 B Fletcher 12st
2 L'Escargot (T Carberry), 11st 13lb
3 Charles Dickens (A Turnell) 10st
4 Spanish Steps (W Smith), 11st 9lb
Dist: 7l, sh, 8l. SP 11-1, 17-2, 50-1, 15-1. 42 ran.

1	Scottish Grand National	4m 120yds	Ayr	Apr 20	B Fletcher	11-8f

1974/75

2	Perthshire Chall Cup	3m	Perth	Sept 25	B Fletcher	5-4f
1	Joan Mackay H Ch	3m 110yds	Ayr	Oct 12	B Fletcher	5-4f
0	Charisma Records H Ch	3m 4f	Kempton	Oct 19	B Fletcher	9-4f
3	Sundew Ch	3m	Haydock	Nov 27	B Fletcher	3-1
1	Haydock Park National Trial	3m 4f	Haydock	Feb 5	B Fletcher	6-1
4	Greenall Whitley H Ch	3m	Haydock	Mar 1	B Fletcher	13-8f

2 GRAND NATIONAL H CH 4m 856yds Liverpool Apr 5 B Fletcher 12st
1 L'Escargot (T Carberry), 11st 3lb
3 Spanish Steps (W Smith), 10st 3lb
4 Money Market (J King) 10st 13lb
Dist: 15l, 8l, 12l. SP 13-2, 7-2f, 20-1, 14-1. 31 ran.

0	Scottish Grand National	4m 120yds	Ayr	Apr 19	B Fletcher	3-1f

1975/76

3	Windermere H Ch	3m	Carlisle	Sept 27	B Fletcher	7-2
4	Joan Mackay H Ch	3m 110yds	Ayr	Oct 11	B Fletcher	6-4f
SU	Peacock H Ch	3m	Haydock	Oct 15	B Fletcher	2-1f
3	John Eustace Smith Trophy	3m	Newcastle	Oct 30	B Fletcher	Evens f

0	Hennessy Cognac Gold Cup	3m 2f	Newbury	Nov 22	R Barry	8-1
3	Sundew Ch	3m	Haydock	Nov 26	T Stack	6-1
0	Haydock Park National Trial	3m 4f	Haydock	Feb 11	T Stack	7-1
0	Greenall Whitley H Ch	3m	Haydock	Mar 6	T Stack	6-1

2 GRAND NATIONAL H CH 4m 4f Liverpool Apr 3 T Stack 11st 10lb
1 Rag Trade (J Burke) 10st 12lb
3 Eyecatcher (B Fletcher) 10st 7lb
4 Barona (P Kelleway) 10st 6lb
Dist: 2l, 8l, 3l. SP 14-1, 10-1, 28-1, 7-1f. 32 ran.

0	Whitbread Gold Cup	3m 5f 118yds	Sandown	Apr 24	T Stack	5-1f

1976/77

1	Windermere H Ch	3m	Carlisle	Sept 25	T Stack	2-5f
0	Charisma records H Ch	3m 4f	Kempton	Oct 16	T Stack	13-2
3	Cheltenham H Ch	3m	Haydock	Nov 5	R Barry	5-1
	Salamanca H Ch	3m	Newcastle	Nov 20	T Stack	11-8f
3	Sundew Ch	3m	Haydock	Dec 1	R Barry	12-1
0	Malcolm Fudge National Trial	3m 4f	Haydock	Feb 9	T Stack	9-1
0	Greenall Whitley H Ch	3m	Haydock	March 4	T Stack	16-1

1 GRAND NATIONAL H Ch 4m 4f Liverpool Apr 2 T Stack 11st 8lb
2 Churchtown Boy (M Blackshaw) 10st
3 Eyecatcher (C Read) 10st 1lb
4 The Pilgarlic (R Evans) 10st 4lb
Dist: 25l, 6l, 8l. SP 9-1, 20-1, 18-1, 40-1. 42 ran.

0	Scottish Grand National	4m 120yds	Ayr	Apr 16	T Stack	100-30f

1977/78

2	Windermere H Ch	3m	Carlisle	Sept 17	R Barry	2-1f
2	Gordon Foster H Ch	3m 100yds	Wetherby	Oct 12	R Barry	4-5f
4	WL and Hector Christie Memorial Trophy	3m 300yds	Catterick	Oct 29	R Barry	13-2
4	Malcolm Fudge National Trial	3m 4f	Haydock	Feb 8	R Barry	25-1
0	Greenall Whitley H Ch	3m	Haydock	Mar 4	T Stack	33-1

Flat: Ran 10, won 2.5, placed 4
Jumps: Ran 100, won 24, placed 45

Ivor Herbert is the author of over twenty books, including *Arkle: The classic story of a champion* ('Ivor Herbert's definitive book *Arkle* is an absolute must for any lover of a good steeplechaser' – John Oaksey), also published by Aurum, and *Vincent O'Brien's Great Horses*. He was a successful National Hunt trainer, who won the 1957 Cheltenham Gold Cup with Linwell, and then for twenty years was Racing Editor of the *Mail on Sunday* since the paper's birth. He has written three major TV documentaries on racing subjects and also heads Equus Productions, making promotional videos for the Jockey Club and others.

Also by Ivor Herbert

BOOKS
Riding through My Life with HRH The Princess Royal
The Winter Kings (Lottery to Desert Orchid)
Red Rum
Come Riding
Winter's Tale: Study of a Stable
The Winter Kings
The Queen Mother's Horses
Six at the Top
Spot a Winner
Vincent O'Brien's Great Horses
Reflections on Racing (with Mercy Rimell)
Longacre
Herbert's Travels
Over Our Dead Bodies!
Scarlet Fever
Point-to-Point
The Diamond Diggers
The Way to the Top
Eastern Window
The Filly
Revolting Behaviour

CINEMA
The Great St Trinians' Train Robbery

THEATRE
The Night of the Blue Diamonds

TELEVISION
Odds Against?
Hyperion: The Millionaire Horse
Stewards' Inquiry
The Queen's Horses
Classic Touch: The Life and Times of Vincent O'Brien
Derby 200